Consuming Interests

SELECTED AND EDITED BY
Donald H. Whitfield

CONTRIBUTORS
James A. Barham
Kristine Bergman
Allie Hirsch
Patrick Hurley
Mary Klein
Judith McCue
Dylan Nelson
Mary Williams

Cover illustration: Lisa Haney
Cover graphic design: Gregory Borowski
Interior design: Judy Sickle, Forward Design

About the cover: Artist Lisa Haney, whose sharp-witted illustrations have
appeared in the *Wall Street Journal* and other national publications, has created
a phantasmagorical take on the complex interrelations of the economic world,
centered around Adam Smith's "unseen hand" (can you find it?) and under the
bemused eyes of some of the authors in *Consuming Interests* including Smith,
Keynes, Marx, Hume, Veblen, and Marshall. For better or for worse, a bull and
a bear are also at large in Lisa Haney's marketplace!

Consuming Interests: Great Ideas in Economics was made possible with generous
financial support from Robert and Mary Galvin, Alex and Anne Pollock,
Sheldon and Barbara Stein, the Chicago Mercantile Exchange, and the
Wintrust Financial Corporation.

Consuming Interests: Great Ideas in Economics

THE GREAT BOOKS FOUNDATION

A nonprofit educational organization

Published and distributed by

THE GREAT BOOKS FOUNDATION
A nonprofit educational organization

35 E. Wacker Drive, Suite 400
Chicago, IL 60601
www.greatbooks.org

Shared Inquiry™ is a trademark of the Great Books Foundation. The contents of this publication
include proprietary trademarks and original materials and may be used or quoted only with
permission and appropriate credit to the Foundation.

First printing
9 8 7 6 5 4 3 2 1

The Library of Congress cataloging-in-publication data has been applied for.

The Great Books Foundation is an independent, nonprofit educational organization that provides opportunities for people of all ages to become more reflective, critical thinkers and readers through Shared Inquiry™ discussion of written works and ideas of enduring value.

The Great Books Foundation was established in 1947 to promote liberal education for the general public. In 1962, the Foundation extended its mission to children with the introduction of Junior Great Books.® Since its inception, the Foundation has helped thousands of people throughout the United States and in other countries begin their own discussion groups in schools, libraries, and community centers. Today, Foundation instructors conduct hundreds of workshops each year, in which educators and parents learn to lead Shared Inquiry discussion.

The Great Books Foundation's workshops in Shared Inquiry help people get the most from discussion. Participants learn how to read actively, pose fruitful questions, and listen and respond to others effectively in discussion. All participants also practice leading a discussion and have an opportunity to reflect on the process with others. For more information about Great Books materials or workshops, call the Great Books Foundation at 800-222-5870 or visit our website at www.greatbooks.org.

CONTENTS

Preface   ix

About Shared Inquiry   xi

How to Use This Book   xiii

Ethics and the Economic Interpretation   1
Frank H. Knight

Of Money   19
David Hume

Of Restraints upon the Importation from Foreign Countries   29
Adam Smith

Selected Essays   49
Thomas Robert Malthus
   An Essay on the Principle of Population   50
   High Price of Provisions   54

Of the Demand or Market for Products   63
Jean-Baptiste Say

On Machinery   73
David Ricardo

That Which Is Seen, and That Which Is Not Seen   83
Frédéric Bastiat

Principles of Political Economy (selection)   109
John Stuart Mill

The Fetishism of Commodities and the Secret Thereof   151
Karl Marx

Why Lombard Street Is Often Very Dull,
and Sometimes Extremely Excited   163
Walter Bagehot

Contents

**Application of the Laws of Demand and Supply
to the Special Problem of Wages**   179
Fleeming Jenkin

The Substance of Economics   191
Alfred Marshall

Industrial Exemption and Conservatism   205
Thorstein Veblen

Transactions   221
John R. Commons

The Civilization of Capitalism   235
Joseph A. Schumpeter

The General Theory of Employment (selection)   247
John Maynard Keynes

The Road to Serfdom (selection)   257
Friedrich Hayek

Political Aspects of Full Employment   271
Michał Kalecki

The Social Responsibility of Business   281
Milton Friedman

Perspectives on Theory   291
Hyman P. Minsky

Bibliography   309

Acknowledgments   311

The following collection of twenty writings on economics spans the last two and a half centuries. It traces the evolution of the economic interpretation of society from its beginnings as a branch of moral and political philosophy, through the emergence of economics as a distinct field of study in the nineteenth century, to its position in the twentieth century and beyond as a fundamental component of public policy. While by no means providing a thorough history of economic thinking, the selections in *Consuming Interests* touch on many of the most influential ideas that have been advanced since the eighteenth century to create a body of knowledge about how the material goods of society are produced, exchanged, and distributed in order to satisfy human wants. Many of the selections deal with the implications of various economic interpretations of society, and in doing so, touch on matters usually addressed by political science, philosophy, history, anthropology, and psychology. In this regard, *Consuming Interests* is firmly within the realm of Great Books programs that invite readers to reflect on and discuss ideas of perennial significance across the disciplines that are fundamental to an understanding of the Western intellectual tradition.

The twenty selections in *Consuming Interests* were chosen for their ability to prompt lively discussions of the issues they raise, rather than to educate readers about the kinds of technical matters that would be covered in an economics course centered on a textbook. None of the selections requires specialized knowledge in economics, though some readers may find it helpful to seek out more thorough presentations of some of the terms and concepts introduced. For this purpose, a bibliography is included.

Each selection is preceded by a brief introduction that will orient readers to the author and to the intellectual and historical context in which he was working. The questions for discussion that follow each selection were carefully written to provide points of entry into the ideas advanced by the authors and also to suggest broader topics for discussion that relate the selections to contemporary issues.

The selections in *Consuming Interests* are ordered chronologically according to the birth years of the authors. The exception to this arrangement is the first selection, "Ethics and the Economic Interpretation," by Frank H. Knight. This essay is placed first because the editor believes that it raises fundamental questions about the position of economics among the various fields of knowledge. In doing so, it sets the tone for the entire anthology, which is intended to prompt readers to examine the strengths and limitations of the economic interpretation of human society.

Shared Inquiry™ is the effort to achieve a more thorough understanding of a text by discussing questions, responses, and insights with others. For both the leader and the participants, careful listening is essential. The leader guides the discussion by asking questions about specific ideas and problems of meaning in the text, but does not seek to impose his or her own interpretation on the group.

During a Shared Inquiry discussion, group members consider a number of possible ideas and weigh the evidence for each. Ideas that are entertained and then refined or abandoned are not thought of as mistakes, but as valuable parts of the thinking process. Group members gain experience in communicating complex ideas and in supporting, testing, and expanding their thoughts. Everyone in the group contributes to the discussion, and while participants may disagree with one another, they treat one another's ideas respectfully.

This process helps develop an understanding of important texts and ideas, rather than merely cataloging knowledge about them. These guidelines keep conversation focused on the text and assure all the participants a voice.

1. **Read the selection carefully before participating in the discussion.** This ensures that all participants are equally prepared to talk about the ideas in the work and helps prevent talk that would distract the group from its purpose.

2. **Discuss the ideas in the selection, and try to understand them fully before exploring issues that go beyond the selection.** Reflecting on the ideas in the text and the evidence to support them makes the exploration of related issues more productive.

3. **Support your ideas with evidence from the text.** This keeps the discussion focused on understanding the selection and enables the group to weigh textual support for different answers and to choose intelligently among them.

4. **Listen to other participants and respond to them directly.** Shared Inquiry is about the give and take of ideas, the willingness to listen to others and talk with them respectfully. Directing your comments and questions to other

group members, not always to the leader, will make the discussion livelier and more dynamic.

5. **Expect the leader to only ask questions.** Effective leaders help participants develop their own ideas, with everyone gaining a new understanding in the process. When participants hang back and wait for the leader to suggest answers, discussion tends to falter.

The first set of questions following each selection is *interpretive*—these questions call for the task of close reading. What is the specific language of the text meant to convey? Are there several interpretations, and can we justify our interpretation by appealing to the text itself? What key passages in the text help unlock its meaning? What passages are confusing and seem to defy understanding? In successful learning situations, close reading evolves into a rich give-and-take between participants who are able to cite specific passages in order to make a point. Thus the text does not get lost in the conversation between discussion participants, but is viewed as the principal voice in the dialogue.

The second set of questions ("For Further Reflection") is *evaluative*. These questions invite participants to weigh the significance or validity of the work in a larger context, and they are best addressed after interpretive discussion has taken place.

Be aware that the temptation to skip interpretive questions and jump straight into evaluative judgments can short-circuit meaningful conversation. Watch out for untethered, rambling testimonials and personal anecdotes or unrestrained monologues. These can distract a group from genuine textual encounter and interpretation.

When grounded in a prior discussion of the text, on the other hand, evaluative questions can push participants to a deeper level of engagement. These questions demand the resources of wider observation, experience, and reading. In the best discussions, evaluative questions can lead to extended dialogue that helps develop thoughtful articulation of ideas and beliefs.

FRANK H. KNIGHT

Frank H. Knight (1885–1972) helped found the Chicago school of economics. Born on a farm in rural Illinois, he never completed high school but eventually enrolled in a series of small colleges in Tennessee. Knight studied a wide range of subjects and acquired the breadth of learning reflected in his later work, before finally earning both a bachelor's degree in natural sciences and a master's in German from the University of Tennessee. He went on to Cornell University with the intention of studying philosophy but soon transferred to the economics department, where he earned his PhD in 1916.

After teaching briefly at Cornell and the University of Chicago, Knight taught for several years at the University of Iowa, where he did much of his most important theoretical work. In the late 1920s he returned to the University of Chicago where he spent the rest of his academic career. There, he helped to develop one of the first economics departments in the country and was influential in defining the curriculum of graduate studies in economics. Much of Knight's influence on twentieth-century economics flowed not only from his writings but also from his teaching at Chicago, where among his students were James Buchanan, Milton Friedman, and George Stigler—all future Nobel laureates.

Knight's most important contribution to economic analysis, elaborated in his 1921 work *Risk, Uncertainty, and Profit*, was his distinction between risk and uncertainty. The term "risk," as Knight defines it, refers to situations with unknown outcomes that are nevertheless governed by known probability distributions. He reserved the term "uncertainty" for situations whose outcomes are not governed by known probability distributions. Knight maintained that uncertainty is an aspect of entrepreneurship, and indeed of the human condition in general, that cannot be eliminated. This uncertainty both justifies the profits of the few successful new enterprises and explains the failure of most of them.

For Knight, the study of economics offers a particularly important perspective from which to understand the range of human activities, but by no means an exclusive perspective. He always retained a lively interest in philosophical problems and their relation to his chosen field, as in the following selection in which he explores the basis of human action and the status of economics as a science.

Ethics and the Economic Interpretation

Certain aspects of the doctrine of the "economic interpretation" form a natural and convenient avenue of approach to a consideration of the relations between economics and ethics and throw light on the scope and method of both these divisions of knowledge. It is this more general problem which is the object of attack in the present paper, which is not primarily an attempt to make a contribution to the technical discussion of the famous theory named in the title. This theory is useful for present purposes because it suggests the fundamental question as to whether there is really a place in the scheme of thought for an independent ethics or whether ethics should be displaced by a sort of higher economics.

Economics and ethics naturally come into rather intimate relations with each other since both recognizedly deal with the problem of value. Two of these lines of relation are especially interesting in their bearing upon the vexed problem of scope and method in economics. In the first place, the separation between theory and practice, or between science and art, offers special difficulties in this field, for reasons which it would carry us away from our central theme to elaborate here. The unfortunate but familiar result of this fact is that economists have spent much of their energy in disputations as to whether the science is properly concerned with facts and cause-and-effect relations, or with "welfare." In other provinces of science such controversies would seem absurd.

There is another and deeper source of confusion in the conception of the method of economics which also involves the relation between economics and ethics and which will lead directly into the problem of this paper. It relates to the ultimate data of economics, regarded as a pure science, dedicated to the search for truth and purified of all prejudices as to the goodness or badness of its principles and results. In this respect also economics has been far behind the natural sciences. Insufficient attention has been given to the separation between constants and variables; needless controversy and wasted effort have resulted from overlooking the fact that constants from one point of view may be variables from another, particularly that factors which are sensibly constant over short periods of time must be treated as variables when longer periods are under discussion.

Of the various sorts of data dealt with in economics no group is more fundamental or more universally and unquestioningly recognized as such than human wants. Yet one main purpose of the present discussion is to raise serious question as to the sense in which these wants can be treated as data, or whether even they are properly scientific data at all. We propose to suggest that these wants which are the common starting point of economic reasoning are from a more critical point of view the most obstinately unknown of all the unknowns in the whole system of variables with which economic science deals. The answer to this question of whether and in what sense wants are data will be found to involve a clarification of the nature of economics as a science, of the nature of ethics, and of the relations between the two. If human wants are data in the ultimate sense for scientific purposes, it will appear that there is no place for ethical theory in the sense in which ethicists have conceived that subject, but that its place must be taken by economics. It will be interesting to observe that in view of a logically correct distinction between ethics and economics, the great majority of economists not only, but in addition no small proportion of thinkers calling themselves ethicists, have not really believed in ethics in any other sense than that of a more or less "glorified" economics.

To state the fundamental issue briefly at the outset, are the motives with which economics has to do—which is to say human motives in general—"wants," "desires" of a character which can adequately be treated as *facts* in the scientific sense, or are they "values," or "oughts," of an essentially different character not amenable to scientific description or logical manipulation? For if it is the intrinsic nature of a thing to grow and change, it cannot serve as a scientific datum. A science must have a "static" subject matter; it must talk about things which will "stay put"; otherwise its statements will not remain true after they are made and there will be no point to making them. Economics has always treated desires or motives as facts, of a character susceptible to statement in propositions, and sufficiently stable during the period of the activity which they prompt to be treated as causes of that activity in a scientific sense. It has thus viewed life as a process of satisfying desires. If this is true then life is a matter of economics; only if it is untrue, or a very inadequate view of the truth, only if the "creation of value" is distinctly more than the satisfaction of desire, is there room for ethics in a sense logically separable from economics.

In a more or less obscure and indirect way, the treatment of wants as data from which and with which to reason has already been challenged more than once. More or less conscious misgivings on this point underlie the early protests made by economists of the historical variety against the classical deductive economics, and the same is true in a more self-conscious way of the criticism brought by the modern *historismus*, the "institutional economics" of Veblen, Hamilton, and J. M. Clark. Thus especially Clark, whose position most resembles that herein taken, observes that the wants which impel economic activity and which it is directed toward satisfying are the products of the economic process itself: "In a single business establishment one department furnishes the desires which the other departments are to satisfy." Hitherto the chief emphasis has been placed on the factual instability of wants and their liability to be changed as well as satisfied by business activity. This is usually coupled with a deprecating attitude, a tendency to regard the growth of wants as unfortunate and the manufacture of new ones as an evil; what have not advertising and salesmanship to answer for at the hands of Veblen, for example! From the standpoint of hedonism, which is to say of the economic philosophy of life, this conclusion is undoubtedly correct. If the Good is Satisfaction, there are no qualitative differences, no "higher" and "lower" as between wants, and that is better which is smaller and most easily appeased.

It is not on any sentimental or idealistic ground, but as a plain question of the facts as to how the ordinary man conceives his own wants and interprets them in conduct that we shall argue against this view of the matter. Wants, it is suggested, not only are unstable, changeable in response to all sorts of influences, but it is their essential nature to change and grow; it is an inherent inner necessity in them. The chief thing which the common-sense individual actually wants is not satisfactions for the wants which he has, but more, and better wants. The things which he strives to get in the most immediate sense are far more what he thinks he ought to want than what his untutored preferences prompt. This feeling for what one *should* want, in contrast with actual desire, is stronger in the unthinking than in those sophisticated by education. It is the latter who argues himself into the "tolerant" (economic) attitude of *de gustibus non disputandum*; the man in the street is more likely to view the individual whose tastes are "wrong" as a scurvy fellow who ought to be despised if not beaten up or shot.

A sounder culture leads away from this view, to be sure, but it leads to a form of tolerance very different from the notion that one taste or judgment is as good as another, that the fact of preference is ultimately all there is to the question of wants. The consideration of wants by the person who is comparing them for the guidance of his conduct and hence, of course, for the scientific student thus inevitably gravitates into a *criticism of standards*, which seems to be a very different thing from the comparison of given magnitudes. The individual who is acting deliberately is not merely and perhaps not mainly trying to satisfy given desires; there is always really present and operative, though in the background of consciousness, the idea of and *desire for* a *new want* to be striven for when the present objective is out of the way. Wants and the activity which they motivate constantly look forward to new and "higher," more evolved and enlightened wants and these function as ends and motives of action beyond the objective to which desire is momentarily directed. The "object" in the narrow sense of the present want is provisional; it is as much a means to a new want as end to the old one, and all intelligently conscious activity is directed forward, onward, upward, indefinitely. Life is not fundamentally a striving for ends, for satisfactions, but rather for bases for further striving; desire is more fundamental to conduct than is achievement, or perhaps better, the true achievement is the refinement and elevation of the plane of desire, the cultivation of taste. And let us reiterate that all this is true *to the person acting*, not simply to the outsider, philosophizing after the event.

In order to substantiate and support the doctrine thus sketched we turn to consider briefly the opposite view, which is that of the "economic interpretation." Historically this doctrine is associated with the so-called "scientific" socialism, but we are here interested in it not in connection with any propaganda or policy, but simply as a theory of conduct, as one answer to the question of the relation between economics and ethics. Our first task is to find out what the doctrine really means.

The somewhat various statements of the theory reduce in general to the proposition that the course of history is "determined" by "economic" or "materialistic" considerations. All these terms raise questions of interpretation, but the issue may be stated briefly. In the first place, the course of history is a matter of human behavior, and we shall as already indicated consider the problem in its broader aspect as a general theory of motivation. As to the word "determined," it is taken for granted that conduct is determined by motives; the statement is really a truism. The issue then relates to the fundamental character of motives; are they properly to be described as materialistic or economic, in their nature? Between these two terms it is better to use "economic"; a "materialistic" motive would seem to be a contradiction in terms; a "motive" is meaningless unless thought of as a phenomenon of consciousness. The opposite view would merely throw us back upon a denial that conduct is determined by motives at all. Without attempting a philosophical discussion of this question we shall take the common-sense position.

Are human motives, then, ultimately or predominantly economic? If the expression "economic motive" is to have any definite and intelligible meaning, it must be possible to distinguish between economic motives and other motives. The expression is, of course, widely used in learned and scientific discussion as well as in everyday speech, with the feeling that such a differentiation exists, but examination fails to show any definite basis for it or to disclose the possibility of any demarcation which is not arbitrary and unscientific. In a rough way, the contrast between economic and other wants corresponds to that between lower and higher or necessary and superfluous. The economic motives are supposed to be more "fundamental"; they arise out of necessities, or at least needs, or at the very least out of the more universal, stable, and materially grounded desires of men. The socialistic popularizers of the theory under discussion have leaned toward the narrower and more definite and logical conception of downright necessities.

The view of the man in the street, as shown by students beginning the study of economics, and also common in textbook definitions of the science, is that the economic side of life is summed up in "making a living." But what is a living? If by a living we mean life as it is actually lived, everything is included, recreation, culture, and even religion; there is no basis for a distinction between the economic and anything else, and the term has no meaning. At the other extreme would be the idea of what is really necessary, the physiological requisites for the maintenance of life. Even this turns out on examination to be hopelessly ambiguous. Does "life" mean the life of the individual only, or that of the group or race? If the latter, does it include the increase of numbers, or only their maintenance at the existing level, or some other level? Does what is "necessary" refer to conditions under which life *will* be preserved or numbers maintained or increased, or only those under which it *could* be done? And under what assumptions as to the taste and standards, and the scientific and technological equipment of the people? Even if we think of a population rigidly controlled as to their reproductive function (which is scarcely conceivable), the birth rate necessary to maintain numbers at a constant level would depend upon the death rate and hence would vary *widely* with the scale of living itself. We doubt whether the conception of necessity can even theoretically be defined in sufficiently objective terms to make it available for scientific purposes.

Between these two extremes of what people actually get and what they rigorously require in order to live, the only alternative is some conventional notion of what is "socially necessary," or of a "decent minimum." It is obvious that such a conception of a "living" is still more indefinite than the others, and the way seems to be closed to any objectively grounded differentiation between the making of a living and any other kind or portion of human activity.

Another common-sense notion of the meaning of economic activity is that it includes everything which involves the making and spending of money or the creation and use of things having a money value. It will presently be argued that this is substantially correct for practical purposes as far as it goes, though it directly or indirectly covers virtually the whole life activity of a modern man and has to be limited to certain aspects of that activity. It is interesting to ask how much of our ordinary economic activity (economic in the sense indicated) is concerned with things which can reasonably be argued to be "useful" not to say necessary—if by useful we mean that it contributes to health and efficiency, or even to happiness. If we begin with food, the most material and necessary of our requirements, it is obvious that but a fraction of a modest expenditure for board in an American town would come under this head. And proceeding in order to our other "material" needs, clothing, shelter, furniture, etc., it is apparent that the farther we go the smaller the fraction becomes. And it is not a large fraction of a fairly comfortable income which goes for all these items, if the purely ornamental, recreative, and social aspects are excluded.

Moreover, when we scrutinize the actual motives of actual conduct it is clear that the consciously felt wants of men are not directed toward nourishment, protection from the elements, etc., the physiological meaning of the things for which money is spent. They desire food, clothing, shelter, etc., *of the conventional kinds and amounts.* It is an ethnological commonplace that men of one social group will starve and freeze before they will adopt the ordinary diet and garb of other groups. Only under the direst necessity do we think in terms of ultimate physical needs as ends; the compulsion to face life on this level is equivalent to abject misery. A large proportion of civilized mankind would certainly commit suicide rather than accept life on such terms, the prospect for improvement being excluded. This interpretation of motives, which is the nearest approach to a definite meaning that can be given to the economic interpretation, is almost totally false. It is simply contrary to fact that men act in order to live. The opposite is much nearer the truth, that they live in order to act; they care to preserve their lives in the biological sense in order to achieve the *kind* of life they consider worthwhile. Some writer (not an economist or psychologist!) has observed that the love of life, so far from being the most powerful of human motives, is perhaps the weakest; in any case it is difficult to name any other motive or sentiment for which men do not habitually throw away their lives.

When we turn from the preservation of individual life to that of the race as a motive, a similar situation is met with. Men will give up their lives for the group, but not for its *mere life*; it is for a better or at least a worthy life that such sacrifices are made. The life of the individual is logically prior to that of the group, as our physiological needs are logically prior to the higher ones, but again that is not the actual order of preference. Probably few civilized men would refuse to die for their fellows if it were clear that the sacrifice were necessary and that it would be effective.

But when materialistic interpreters speak of the perpetuity of the group as a motive they are likely to have in mind not this result in the abstract, but rather sex-feeling, the means by which continuity and increase are secured in the animal world. Here again they are squarely wrong; social existence and well-being in the abstract are more potent than sex attraction in any crude interpretation. With sex experience as with food, it is not the thing as such which dominates the civilized individual. His sex requirement is as different from that of animals as a banquet with all fashionable accompaniments is from the meal of a hungry carnivore which has made a kill, or a buzzard whose olfactory sense has guided him to a mellow piece of carrion. It is again a question of fact, and the fact patently is that when the biological form of the motive conflicts with the cultural, aesthetic, or moral part of it—as more or less it about always does—it is the former which gives way. Sex debauchery is, of course, common enough, but this also rather obviously involves about as much cultural sophistication as does romantic or conjugal love, though of a different kind.

On every count this biological interpretation of human conduct falls down; no hunger and sex theory of human motives will stand examination. It will not be denied that human interests have evolved out of animal desires, and are ultimately continuous with them; and an understanding of animal behavior can throw light on human problems, but only if interpreted with the utmost caution. Man has risen clear above, or if this seems to beg any philosophical questions he has at least gotten clear away from the plane where life is the end of activity; he has in fact essentially reversed this relation. It is not life that he strives for, but the good life, or at the ultimate minimum a decent life, which is a conventional, cultural concept, and for this he will throw away life itself; he will have that or nothing. He has similar physical requirements with the animals, but has become so "particular" as to their mode of gratification that the form dominates the substance. A life in which bare existence is the end is *intolerable* to him. When his artificial, cultural values are in ultimate conflict with physical needs he rather typically chooses the latter, sacrificing quantity of life to quality, and it is hard to see how he could be prevented from doing so. We can scarcely imagine a slave society placed under physical compulsion so effective that men would permanently live in it. If they were given the least sight or knowledge of their masters and their masters' way of life, no provision however bountiful for all physical wants would prevent some irrational individual from setting up a cry for "liberty or death" and leading his willing fellows to the achievement of one or the other. It is a familiar historical fact that it is not the violently oppressed populations which rebel, but those whose milder bondage leaves them fairly prosperous. The assumption of the materialistic, or economic, or biological interpretation of conduct is that when men must choose between some "real need" and a sentimental consideration they will take the former. The truth is that when the issue is drawn they typically do the reverse. For any practical social purpose, beauty, play, conventionality, and the gratification of all sorts of "vanities" are more "necessary" than food and shelter.

Some attention must now be given to another method of interpreting conduct, closely related to the biological and like it aimed at supplying an objective measure of well-being. This is the theory that man has inherited certain *instincts* which must achieve a substantial measure of successful expression in action or the individual will develop maladjustment, balked disposition, and unhappiness. We cannot go at length into the failure of this theory either to explain actual behavior or to yield ideal requirements, and fortunately it is unnecessary to do so as the doctrine is now properly passing out of favor. The significance to be claimed for the theory is that of supplementing the biological interpretation. Certain acts not now useful in the biological sense are assumed to have been so in the past under different conditions, and the organism has become so adjusted to them that its normal functioning depends upon their continued performance.

If instincts are to be scientifically useful, it must surely be possible to get some idea of their number and identity. But there has always been substantially unanimous disagreement on this point. Logically the choice seems to lie between a meaningless single instinct to do things-in-general and the equally meaningless hypothesis of a separate instinct for every possible act. Between these two views is a free field for arbitrary classification. Such fairly concrete lists as have been given consist chiefly of enumerations of the possible alternatives of action in possible types of conduct situations, and largely reduce to pairs of opposites. For a single illustration, an animal in danger may fight or run. Hence our theorists come forward with an "instinct" for each of these types of reaction. This of course tells us nothing of what we want to know, which is, *which one* of the possible reactions will take place. It is not enlightening to be told that conduct consists in choosing between possible alternatives.

A mere classification of feelings or cravings has some interest, however void of scientific utility it may be, but the psychologist can hardly claim to have "discovered" the emotions. In this connection it is interesting to consider the extent to which motives do fall into pairs of opposites. There are numerous such couples or polarizations which cut deeper into human nature than do the proposed instincts. Our reasons for wanting things come down in astonishingly large measure to the desire to be like other people, and the desire to be different; we wish to do things because we can, or because we cannot; we crave companionship, of the right kind, but the requirement of privacy, even solitude, is equally imperative; we like the familiar, also the novel, security but likewise adventure, and so on. Acquisitiveness, the instinct which should be most saleable to the

9

economist, is perhaps but the opposite of our alleged gregariousness, one being essentially the desire to exclude others from certain interests and the other the desire to share them. All these, like selfishness and unselfishness, have some meaning, but are hardly suitable bases for a scientific classification. It is significant that McDougall, the father of the modern instinct theory, regarded the feeling element as the only stable part of the instinct, both stimulus and reaction being subject to indefinite shift and change. The unsuitability of such a view as a foundation for the superstructure built upon it in the way of scientific laws of *behavior* hardly calls for comment.

From the instinct theory we turn naturally to the ancient doctrine of psychology and ethics to which it is a handmaiden, that the end of activity is a "harmonious adjustment" of the organism, a smooth and unobstructed functioning of the digestive, neuro-muscular, and glandular systems (and perhaps the reproductive also, and any special structures concerned with tending the young or other social activities) and for consciousness the feeling of satisfaction or comfort that goes with this condition. Freudianism and abnormal psychology have seemed to confirm this view, and Thorndyke also though rather guardedly speaks of behavior as controlled by "satisfiers" and "annoyers." Perhaps a sufficient comment on the hedonistic theory would be to run through again the main categories of economic wants, food, clothing, shelter, amusement, etc., and simply ask the candid question as to what fraction of the ordinary man's expenditure for any of them makes him "feel better" or is expected to do so. The higher one is in the economic scale, the more successful in doing what all are trying to do, the larger is the proportion of his consumption which tends to make him less, and not more, "comfortable."

The authors of great imaginative literature—always indefinitely better psychologists than the psychologists so-called—have never fallen into any such palpable delusion as the belief that men either strive for happiness or expect to be made happy by their striving. The same has been true of philosophers and religious thinkers of all time, and even economists have recognized the futility of attempting to satisfy wants. It is obvious that wants multiply in at least as great a ratio as the heads of the famous hydra. Greeks as well as Hindus, and Epicureans as well as Stoics and Cynics perceived at the dawn of modern culture that it is indefinitely more "satisfactory" and "economical" to repress desire than to attempt to satisfy it. Nor do men who know what they do want—and who have not sapped their vitality by unnatural living or too much of a certain kind of thinking—want their wants satisfied. This argument of economists and other pragmatists that men work and think to get themselves out of trouble is at least half an inversion of the facts. The things we work for are "annoyers" as often as "satisfiers"; we spend as much ingenuity in getting into trouble as in getting out, and in any case enough to keep in effectively. It is our nature to "travel afar to seek disquietitude," and "'tis distance lends enchantment to the view." It cannot be maintained that civilization itself makes men "happier" than they are in savagery. The purpose of education is certainly not to make anyone happy; its aim is rather to raise problems than solve them; the association of sadness and wisdom is proverbial, and the most famous of wise men observed that "in much wisdom is grief, and he that increaseth knowledge increaseth sorrow." Thus the pursuit of the "higher things" and the crasser indulgences are alike failures if the test is happiness.

But the test is not happiness. And by this we do not mean that it ought not to be, but the simple fact that that is not what men want. It is a stock and conclusive objection to utopias that men simply will not live in a world where everything runs smoothly and life is free from care. We all recall William James's relief at getting away from Chautauqua. A man who has nothing to worry about immediately busies himself in creating something, gets into some absorbing game, falls in love, prepares to conquer some enemy, or hunts lions or the North Pole or what not. We recall also the case of Faust, that the Devil himself could not invent escapades and adventures fast enough to give his soul one moment's peace. So he died, seeking and striving, and the Angel pronounced him thereby "saved": "Wer immer strebend sich bemüht, den können wir erlösen."[1] The pleasure philosophy is a false theory of life; there abide pain, grief, and boredom: these three, and the greatest of these is boredom. The Hindus thought this question of happiness through to the end long ago, and reached the inevitable conclusion—nirvana—just life enough to enjoy being dead.

The idea of a distinction between economic wants and other wants must be abandoned. There is no definable objective, whether subsistence, gratification of fundamental impulses, or pleasure, that will serve to separate any of our activities from the body of conduct as a whole. Nor, we aim especially to emphasize, is there any *definable* objective which properly characterizes any of it. It simply is not finally directed to the satisfaction of any desires or the achievement of any ends external or internal which can be formulated in propositions and made the subject of logical discourse. All ends and motives are economic in that they require the use of objective resources in their realization; all are ideal, conventional, or sentimental in that the attempt to define objective ends breaks down. Behind them all is "the restless spirit of man," who is an aspiring rather than a desiring being; and such a scientifically undescriptive and unsatisfactory characterization is the best we can give.

---

1. [Whoever strives with all his power, we are allowed to save. *Faust*, part 2. Goethe.]

For the purpose of defining economics the correct procedure would appear to be to start from the ordinary meaning of the verb "to economize," that is, to use resources wisely in the achievement of *given* ends. Insofar as the ends are viewed as given, as data, then all activity is economic. The question of the effectiveness of the adaptation of means is the only question to be asked regarding conduct, and economics is the one and all-inclusive science of conduct. From this point of view the problem of life becomes simply the economic problem, how to employ the existing and available supplies of all sorts of resources, human and material, natural and artificial, in producing the maximum *amount* of *want-satisfaction* including the provision of new resources for increased value production insofar as the present population finds itself actually desiring future progress. The assumption that wants or ends are data reduces life to economics and raises again the question with which we started out, Is life all economics or does this view require supplementing by an ethical view of value?

The conception of economics outlined above is in harmony with the traditions of economic literature. The "economic man," the familiar subject of theoretical discussion, has been much mistreated by both friends and foes, but such a conception, explicit or implicit, underlies all economic speculation. The economic man is the individual who obeys economic laws, which is merely to say that he obeys *some* laws of conduct, it being the task of the science to find out what the laws are. He is the *rational* man, the man who knows what he wants and orders his conduct intelligently with a view to getting it. In no other sense can there be laws of conduct or a science of conduct; the only possible "science" of conduct is that which treats the behavior of the economic man, i.e., economics in the very broad sense in which we have used the term. A scientific principle necessarily takes the form that under given conditions certain things can be counted upon to happen; in the field of conduct the given conditions are the desires or ends and the rationale or technique for achieving them.

The objections raised to the notion of the economic man, are however also sound in their own way. They reduce to the proposition that *there is no such man*, and this is literally true. Human beings do not in their conscious behavior act according to laws, and in the concrete sense a science of conduct is an impossibility. They neither know what they want—to say nothing of what is "good" for them—nor act very intelligently to secure the things that they have decided to try to get. The limitation on intelligence—knowledge of technique—is not fatal to the conception of a scientific treatment of behavior, since people are "more or less" intelligent, and "tend" to act intelligently, and all science involves a large measure of abstraction. Far more essentially is the limitation due to the fact that the "given conditions," the causes at work, are not really given, that wants are

12

not ultimately data and the individual more or less completely recognizes that they are not.

The definition of economics must, therefore, be revised to state that it treats of conduct *insofar* as conduct is amenable to scientific treatment, insofar as it is controlled by definable conditions and can be reduced to law. But this, measured by the standard of natural science, is not very far. *There are no data* for a science of conduct in a sense analogous to natural science. The data of conduct are provisional, shifting, and special to individual, unique situations in so high a degree that generalization is relatively fruitless. *For the time being,* an individual acts (more or less) *as if* his conduct were directed to the realization of some end more or less ascertainable, but at best provisional and vague. The person himself is usually aware that it is not really final, not really an "end"; it is only the end of the particular act and not the ultimate end of that. A man engaged in a game of chess acts *as if* the supreme value in life were to capture his opponent's pieces; but this is obviously not a true or final end; the circumstances which have led the individual to accept it as end for the moment come largely under the head of accident and cannot be reduced to law—and the typical conduct situation in civilized life is analogous to the game in all the essential respects.

A science of conduct is, therefore, possible only if its subject matter is made abstract to the point of telling us little or nothing about actual behavior. Economics deals with the form of conduct rather than its substance or content. We can say that a man will in general prefer a larger quantity of wealth to a smaller (the principal trait of the economic man) because in the statement the term "wealth" has no definite concrete meaning; it is merely an abstract term covering everything which men do actually (provisionally) want. The only other important economic law of conduct, the law of diminishing utility, is almost as abstract; its objective content is covered by the statement that men strive to distribute income in some way most satisfactory to the person at the time among an indefinite number of wants and means of satisfaction rather than to concentrate upon one or a few. Such laws are unimportant because they deal with form only and say virtually nothing about content, but it is imperative to understand what they do and what they do not mean.

If one wishes to study the concrete content of motives and conduct he must turn from economic theory to biology, social psychology, and especially culture history. Culture history is not, therefore, a method of economics, as the historic quarrel would lead one to think, but a different field of inquiry. It gives a *genetic,* and not a *scientific* account of its subject matter. History has, indeed, tried to become a science and the effort has brought forth numerous "philosophies of history," but it is open to grave doubt whether "laws" of history exist and whether the entire project is not based on a misconception.

If a science of economics is limited to the abstract form of conduct and the treatment of conduct in the concrete takes the form of history, rather than science, what is to be said of ethics? In addition to the explanation of conduct in terms of motives and the explanation of the motives, common sense does raise another kind of question, that of the *evaluation* of motives. But we are met at the outset with the logically insuperable difficulty that the criticism of an end implies some standard, which can logically only be another end, which to enter into logical discourse must be viewed as a datum, like the first. Hence, scientifically we can never get beyond the question of whether one end conflicts with another and if so which is to be sacrificed. But this mere comparison of ends as given magnitudes belongs to the economic calculation involved in creating the maximum amount of value or want-satisfaction out of a given fund of resources; hence there seems to be no place for anything but economics in the field of value, and scientifically there is none. If we are to establish a place for ethics really distinct from economics and independent of it, it must be done by finding ends or standards which are something more than scientific data.

For those to whom ethics is only a more or less "glorified" economics, virtue is correspondingly reduced to an enlarged prudence. But the essential element in the moral common sense of mankind seems to be the conviction that there is a difference between virtue and prudence, between what one "really wants" to do and what one "ought" to do; even if some religious or other "sanction" makes it ultimately prudent to do right, at least it remains true that it is prudent because right, and not right because prudent, or because there is no difference between the two. A considerable part of the literature of ethics consists of debate over the validity of this distinction and of moral common sense, which is to say over whether there is any such thing as ethics or not, and the question creates perhaps the most fundamental division between schools of thought. There was no difficulty for the Greeks, who had no word for duty or conscience in their language, and there is none for the modern "pagan" who considers these things as outworn puritan superstitions. It must appear dogmatic to seem to take sides on the question without working out an entire philosophic system in justification of the position, but we wish to point out that *if* there is to be a real ethics it cannot be a science, and to cite a few reasons for believing in the possibility of a real ethics.

The first of these considerations is the argument developed in this paper that the view of ends as scientific data breaks down under examination. The second is that the rational, economic criticism of values gives results repugnant to all common sense. In this view the ideal man would be the economic man, the man who knows what he wants and "goes after it" with singleness of purpose. The fact is, of course, the reverse. The economic man is the selfish, ruthless object of moral condemnation.

Moreover, we do not bestow praise and affection on the basis of conduct alone or mainly, but quite irrationally on the motives themselves, the feelings to which we impute the conduct.

We cannot dwell on the moral habitability of the world under different hypotheses or argue the question whether such implications constitute "evidence" for the hypothesis in question. The disillusioned advocate of hardheadedness and clear thinking would usually admit that the "moral illusion" has stood the pragmatic test and concede its utility while contending that it is scientifically a hoax. But it is pertinent to observe that the brick-and-mortar world cannot be constructed for thought out of purely objective data. There is always a feeling element in any belief. Force and energy are notoriously feelings of ours which we read into things, yet we cannot think of anything as real without force as real. Apparently we are incapable of picturing anything as existing without putting a spark of our own consciousness into it. Behind every fact is a theory and behind that an interest. There is no purely objective reason for believing anything any more than there is for doing anything, and if our feelings tell us nothing about reality then we know and can know nothing about it. From this it is an easy step to see that the intolerable repugnance of the idea that not only duty and right, but all effort, aspiration, and sacrifice are delusions is, after all, as good a reason for believing that they are not as we have for believing that the solid earth exists in any other sense than seeming to us to do so.

But the main argument for the validity and necessity of a real, non-scientific, transcendental ethics comes out of the limitations of scientific explanation. We have seen that the "scientific" treatment of conduct is restricted to its abstract form, that its concrete content can only be explained "historically." But in dealing with human problems we are constantly thrown back upon categories still more remote from the scientific, upon relations which cannot be formulated in logical propositions at all, and we must admit that a large part of our "knowledge" is of this character. That figurative language does convey a meaning, however, is indisputable, and it is commonly a meaning which could not be expressed literally. When Burns says that his love is "like a red, red rose," etc., when Kipling tells us of Fuzzy-Wuzzy that " 'E's a daisy, 'e's a ducky, 'e's a lamb," their words mean something, though it is not what they say! William James has commented on the effectiveness of these comparisons whose physical basis is undiscoverable, illustrating by the statements that a certain author's style is like the atmosphere of a room in which pastilles have been burning. Let anyone take even a science textbook and try to translate all the figurative expressions into literal, purely logical form, and he will realize how impossible it is to describe the world in terms which mean definitely what they say.

Of this general description must be the criticism of values, as it is the character of aesthetic and literary criticism. Our values, our standards, are only more obviously of the same character which our desires reveal on examination—not describable because not stable, growing and changing by necessity of their inner nature. This is, of course, intellectually unsatisfactory. The scientific mind can rest only in one of two extreme positions, that there are absolute values, or that every individual desire is an absolute and one as "good" as another. But neither of these is true; we must learn to think in terms of "value-standards" which have validity of a more subtle kind. It is the higher goal of conduct to test and try these values, to define and improve them, rather than to accept and "satisfy" them. There are no rules for judging values, and it is the worst of errors to attempt to make rules—beyond the rule to "use good judgment"; but it is also most false to assert that one opinion is as good as another, that *de gustibus non disputandum est.* Professor Tufts has put the question in a neatly epigrammatic way that emphasizes its unsatisfactoriness from a rational, scientific standpoint: "The only test for goodness is that good persons on reflection approve and choose it—just as the test for good persons is that they choose and do the good."

If the suggestions above thrown out are sound, there is room in the field of conduct for three different kinds of treatment: first, a scientific view, or economics and technology; second, a genetic view, or culture history; and third, for a Criticism of Values. The discussion of the latter will, like literary and artistic criticism, run in terms of suggestion rather than logical statement, in figurative rather than literal language, and its principles will be available through sympathetic interpretation rather than intellectual cognition.

QUESTIONS

1. What does Knight mean when he says, "Men will give up their lives for the group, but not for its *mere life*"? (7)   *required and effective*

2. Why does Knight disagree with the view that "economics is the one and all-inclusive science of conduct"? (12)

3. What answer does Knight provide to his question, "Is life all economics or does this view require supplementing by an ethical view of value"? (12)

4. If Knight doesn't think economics is a science, what does he consider it to be?

5. Why does Knight argue for the necessity of a "real, nonscientific, transcendental ethics"? (15)

FOR FURTHER REFLECTION

1. Do you agree with Knight's proposition that the belief that men strive for happiness is a "palpable delusion"?

2. If Knight is correct that economics cannot tell us anything about human conduct, what is it good for?

3. To what extent should economic policies be governed by ethics?

DAVID HUME

One of the leading philosophers of the Enlightenment, David Hume (1711–1776) was born in Edinburgh, Scotland. Intellectually precocious, he enrolled in the University of Edinburgh when he was twelve years old, where he concentrated his studies on classics, literature, and philosophy. His first major work, *A Treatise of Human Nature* (1739–1740), was not a success, with the public's reaction ranging from indifference to bewilderment, and in some quarters it began to establish his reputation as a dangerous thinker inclined toward atheism.

Hume published *Essays, Moral and Political* (2 vols.; 1741–1742) with greater success, but his efforts to gain an academic appointment in philosophy at the University of Edinburgh were opposed due to his theological unorthodoxy. In 1751, he took a low-salaried job as librarian at the university. With access to the library's great resources, he wrote his *History of England* (6 vols.; 1754–1762), which was a critical and commercial success.

In 1763 Hume became secretary to the British embassy in France. He returned three years later with the philosopher Jean-Jacques Rousseau, who was fleeing persecution in Switzerland. Hume spent his last years in Edinburgh working on new editions of his writings, particularly his controversial *Dialogues Concerning Natural Religion* (1779).

Hume's work is generally associated with that of John Locke and George Berkeley. Like them, Hume was concerned with establishing the basis of knowledge in human psychology and the mind's direct experience of sense perceptions. In opposition to schools of philosophy that claim the existence of innate ideas, Hume is placed in the empiricist and skeptical-philosophical traditions. He was an influence on the philosopher Immanuel Kant, who wrote that Hume awakened him from his "dogmatic slumbers."

Hume's writings on economics comprise a small but significant portion of his published works and influenced his friend Adam Smith, author of *The Wealth of Nations* (1776). Among Hume's key ideas is his contention that a country does not achieve prosperity as a result of accumulating wealth alone, since prices change relative to changes in the money supply. In addition, he was a strong advocate of the idea that economic freedom is necessary for political freedom.

DAVID HUME

Of Money

M oney is not, properly speaking, one of the subjects of commerce; but only the instrument which men have agreed upon to facilitate the exchange of one commodity for another. It is none of the wheels of trade; it is the oil which renders the motion of the wheels more smooth and easy. If we consider any one kingdom by itself, it is evident that the greater or less plenty of money is of no consequence; since the prices of commodities are always proportioned to the plenty of money, and a crown in Harry VII's time served the same purpose as a pound does at present. It is only the *public* which draws any advantage from the greater plenty of money; and that only in its wars and negociations with foreign states. And this is the reason, why all rich and trading countries from Carthage to Great Britain and Holland have employed mercenary troops, which they hired from their poorer neighbors. Were they to make use of their native subjects, they would find less advantage from their superior riches, and from their great plenty of gold and silver; since the pay of all their servants must rise in proportion to the public opulence. Our small army of 20,000 men is maintained at as great expense, as a French army twice as numerous. The English fleet, during the late war, required as much money to support it as all the Roman legions, which kept the whole world in subjection, during the time of the emperors.

The greater number of people and their greater industry are service- able in all cases; at home and abroad, in private and in public. But the greater plenty of money is very limited in its use, and may even sometimes be a loss to a nation in its commerce with foreigners.

There seems to be a happy concurrence of causes in human affairs, which checks the growth of trade and riches, and hinders them from being confined entirely to one people; as might naturally at first be dreaded from the advantages of an established commerce. Where one nation has gotten the start of another in trade, it is very difficult for the latter to regain the ground it has lost; because of the superior industry and skill of the former, and the greater stocks, of which its merchants are possessed, and which enable them to trade on so much smaller profits. But these advantages are compensated, in some measure, by the low price of labor in every nation which has not an extensive commerce, and does not much abound in gold and silver. Manufactures therefore gradually shift their places, leaving those countries and provinces which they have already enriched, and flying to others, whither they are allured by the cheapness of provisions and labor; till they have enriched these also, and are again banished by the same causes. And, in general, we may observe that the dearness of every thing, from plenty of money, is a disadvantage, which attends an established commerce, and sets bounds to it in every country, by enabling the poorer states to undersell the richer in all foreign markets.

This has made me entertain a doubt concerning the benefit of *banks* and *paper credit*, which are so generally esteemed advantageous to every nation. That provisions and labor should become dear by the increase of trade and money is in many respects an inconvenience; but an inconvenience that is unavoidable, and the effect of that public wealth and prosperity which are the end of all our wishes. It is compensated by the advantages, which we reap from the possession of these precious metals, and the weight, which they give the nation in all foreign wars and negociations. But there appears no reason for increasing that inconvenience by a counterfeit money, which foreigners will not accept of in any payment, and which any great disorder in the state will reduce to nothing. There are, it is true, many people in every rich state, who, having large sums of money, would prefer paper with good security; as being of more easy transport and more safe custody. If the public provide not a bank, private bankers will take advantage of this circumstance; as the goldsmiths formerly did in London, or as the bankers do at present in Dublin: and therefore it is better, it may be thought, that a public company should enjoy the benefit of that paper credit, which always will have place in every opulent kingdom. But to endeavor artificially to increase such a credit can never be the interest of any trading nation; but must lay them under disadvantages, by increasing money beyond its natural proportion to labor and commodities, and thereby heightening their price to the merchant and manufacturer. And in this view, it must be allowed, that no bank could be more advantageous, than such a one as locked up all the money it received, and never augmented the circulating coin, as is usual, by returning part of its treasure into commerce. A public bank, by this expedient, might cut off much of the dealings of private bankers and money jobbers; and though the state bore the charge of salaries to the directors and tellers of this bank (for, according to the preceding supposition, it would have no profit from its dealings), the national advantage, resulting from the low price of labor and the destruction of paper credit, would be a sufficient compensation. Not to mention, that so large a sum, lying ready at command, would be a convenience in times of great public danger and distress; and what part of it was used might be replaced at leisure, when peace and tranquility was restored to the nation.

But of this subject of paper credit we shall treat more largely hereafter. And I shall finish this essay on money by proposing and explaining two observations, which may, perhaps, serve to employ the thoughts of our speculative politicians.

It was a shrewd observation of Anacharsis the Scythian, who had never seen money in his own country, that gold and silver seemed to him of no use to the Greeks, but to assist them in numeration and arithmetic. It is indeed evident, that money is nothing but the representation of labor and commodities, and serves only as a method of rating or estimating them. Where coin is in greater plenty—as a greater quantity of it is required to represent the same quantity of goods—it can have no effect, either good or bad, taking a nation within itself, any more than it would make an alteration on a merchant's books, if, instead of the Arabian method of notation, which requires few characters, he should make use of the Roman, which requires a great many. Nay, the greater quantity of money, like the Roman characters, is rather inconvenient, and requires greater trouble both to keep and transport it. But notwithstanding this conclusion, which must be allowed just, it is certain, that, since the discovery of the mines in America, industry has increased in all the nations of Europe, except in the possessors of those mines; and this may justly be ascribed, among other reasons, to the increase of gold and silver. Accordingly we find that, in every kingdom into which money begins to flow in greater abundance than formerly, every thing takes a new face: labor and industry gain life; the merchant becomes more enterprising, the manufacturer more diligent and skillful, and even the farmer follows his plow with greater alacrity and attention. This is not easily to be accounted for, if we consider only the influence which a greater abundance of coin has in the kingdom itself, by heightening the price of commodities, and obliging everyone to pay a greater number of these little yellow or white pieces for every thing he purchases. And as to foreign trade, it appears that great plenty of money is rather disadvantageous, by raising the price of every kind of labor.

To account, then, for this phenomenon, we must consider that though the high price of commodities be a necessary consequence of the increase of gold and silver, yet it follows not immediately upon that increase; but some time is required before the money circulates through the whole state, and makes its effect be felt on all ranks of people. At first, no alteration is perceived; by degrees the price rises, first of one commodity, then of another; till the whole at last reaches a just proportion with the new quantity of specie which is in the kingdom. In my opinion, it is only in this interval or intermediate situation, between the acquisition of money and rise of prices, that the increasing quantity of gold and silver is favorable to industry. When any quantity of money is imported into a nation, it is not at first dispersed into many hands, but is confined to the coffers of a few persons, who immediately seek to employ it to advantage. Here are a set of manufacturers or merchants, we shall suppose, who have received returns of gold and silver for goods which they sent to Cadiz. They are thereby enabled to employ more workmen than formerly, who never dream of demanding higher wages, but are glad of employment from such good pay-masters. If workmen become scarce, the manufacturer gives higher wages, but at first requires an increase of labor; and this is willingly submitted to by the artisan, who can now eat and drink better, to compensate his additional toil and fatigue. He carries his money to market, where he finds everything at the same price as formerly, but returns with greater quantity and of better kinds, for the use of his family. The farmer and gardener, finding that all their commodities are taken off, apply themselves with alacrity to the raising more; and at the same time can afford to take better and more cloths from their tradesmen, whose price is the same as for-merly, and their industry only whetted by so much new gain. It is easy to trace the money in its progress through the whole commonwealth; where we shall find that it must first quicken the diligence of every individual, before it increase the price of labor.

And that the specie may increase to a considerable pitch, before it have this latter effect, appears, among other instances, from the frequent operations of the French king on the money; where it was always found that the augmenting of the numerary value did not produce a proportional rise of the prices, at least for some time. In the last year of Louis XIV, money was raised three-sevenths, but prices augmented only one. Corn in France is now sold at the same price, or for the same number of livres, it was in 1683; though silver was then at thirty livres the mark, and is now at fifty. Not to mention the great addition of gold and silver, which may have come into that kingdom since the former period.

From the whole of this reasoning we may conclude that it is of no manner of consequence, with regard to the domestic happiness of a state, whether money be in a greater or less quantity. The good policy of the magistrate consists only in keeping it, if possible, still increasing; because, by that means, he keeps alive a spirit of industry in the nation, and increases the stock of labor, in which consists all real power and riches. A nation whose money decreases is actually, at that time, weaker and more miserable than another nation which possesses no more money, but is on the increasing hand. This will be easily accounted for, if we consider that the alterations in the quantity of money, either on one side or the other, are not immediately attended with proportionable alterations in the price of commodities. There is always an interval before matters be adjusted to their new situation; and this interval is as pernicious to industry, when gold and silver are diminishing, as it is advantageous when these metals are increasing. The workman has not the same employment from the manufacturer and merchant; though he pays the same price for everything in the market. The farmer cannot dispose of his corn and cattle; though he must pay the same rent to his landlord. The poverty, and beggary, and sloth, which must ensue, are easily foreseen.

The second observation which I proposed to make with regard to money may be explained after the following manner. There are some kingdoms, and many provinces in Europe (and all of them were once in the same condition), where money is so scarce that the landlord can get none at all from his tenants; but is obliged to take his rent in kind, and either to consume it himself, or transport it to places where he may find a market. In those countries, the prince can levy few or no taxes, but in the same manner: and as he will receive small benefit from impositions so paid, it is evident that such a kingdom has little force even at home; and cannot maintain fleets and armies to the same extent, as if every part of it abounded in gold and silver. There is surely a greater disproportion between the force of Germany, at present, and what it was three centuries ago, than there is in its industry, people, and manufactures. The Austrian dominions in the empire are in general well peopled and well cultivated, and are of great extent; but have not a proportionable weight in the balance of Europe; proceeding, as is commonly supposed, from the scarcity of money. How do all these facts agree with that principle of reason, that the quantity of gold and silver is in itself altogether indifferent? According to that principle wherever a sovereign has numbers of subjects, and these have plenty of commodities, he should of course be great and powerful, and they rich and happy, independent of the greater or lesser abundance of the precious metals. These admit of divisions and subdivisions to a great extent; and where the pieces might become so small as to be in danger of being lost, it is easy to mix the gold or silver with a baser metal, as is practiced in some countries of Europe; and by that means raise the pieces to a bulk more sensible and convenient. They still serve the same purposes of exchange, whatever their number may be, or whatever color they may be supposed to have.

To these difficulties I answer that the effect, here supposed to flow from scarcity of money, really arises from the manners and customs of the people; and that we mistake, as is too usual, a collateral effect for a cause. The contradiction is only apparent; but it requires some thought and reflection to discover the principles, by which we can reconcile *reason* to *experience*.

It seems a maxim almost self-evident, that the prices of everything depend on the proportion between commodities and money, and that any considerable alteration on either has the same effect, either of heightening or lowering the price. Increase the commodities, they become cheaper; increase the money, they rise in their value. As, on the other hand, a diminution of the former, and that of the latter, have contrary tendencies.

It is also evident that the prices do not so much depend on the absolute quantity of commodities and that of money, which are in a nation, as on that of the commodities, which come or may come to market, and of the money which circulates. If the coin be locked up in chests, it is the same thing with regard to prices, as if it were annihilated; if the commodities be hoarded in magazines and granaries, a like effect follows. As the money and commodities, in these cases, never meet, they cannot affect each other. Were we, at any time, to form conjectures concerning the price of provisions, the corn, which the farmer must reserve for seed and for the maintenance of himself and family, ought never to enter into the estimation. It is only the overplus, compared to the demand, that determines the value.

To apply these principles, we must consider that, in the first and more uncultivated ages of any state, ere fancy has confounded her wants with those of nature, men, content with the produce of their own fields, or with those rude improvements which they themselves can work upon them, have little occasion for exchange, at least for money, which, by agreement, is the common measure of exchange. The wool of the farmer's own flock, spun in his own family, and wrought by a neighboring weaver, who receives his payment in corn or wool, suffices for furniture and clothing. The carpenter, the smith, the mason, the tailor, are retained by wages of a like nature; and the landlord himself, dwelling in the neighborhood, is content to receive his rent in the commodities raised by the farmer. The greater part of these he consumes at home, in rustic hospitality: the rest, perhaps, he disposes of for money to the neighboring town, whence he draws the few materials of his expense and luxury.

But after men begin to refine on all these enjoyments, and live not always at home, nor are content with what can be raised in their neighborhood, there is more exchange and commerce of all kinds, and more money enters into that exchange. The tradesmen will not be paid in corn; because they want something more than barley to eat. The farmer goes beyond his own parish for the commodities he purchases, and cannot always carry his commodities to the merchant who supplies him. The landlord lives in the capital, or in a foreign country; and demands his rent in gold and silver, which can easily be transported to him. Great undertakers, and manufacturers, and merchants, arise in every commodity; and these can conveniently deal in nothing but in specie. And consequently, in this situation of society, the coin enters into many more contracts, and by that means is much more employed than in the former.

The necessary effect is, that, provided the money increase not in the nation, everything must become much cheaper in times of industry and refinement, than in rude, uncultivated ages. It is the proportion between the circulating money, and the commodities in the market, which determines the prices. Goods that are consumed at home, or exchanged with other goods in the neighborhood, never come to market; they affect not in the least the current specie; with regard to it they are as if totally annihilated; and consequently this method of using them sinks the proportion on the side of the commodities, and increases the prices. But after money enters into all contracts and sales, and is everywhere the measure of exchange, the same national cash has a much greater task to perform; all commodities are then in the market; the sphere of circulation is enlarged; it is the same case as if that individual sum were to serve a larger kingdom; and therefore, the proportion being here lessened on the side of the money, every thing must become cheaper, and the prices gradually fall.

By the most exact computations that have been formed all over Europe, after making allowance for the alteration in the numerary value or the denomination, it is found that the prices of all things have only risen three, or at most, four times, since the discovery of the West Indies. But will anyone assert, that there is not much more than four times the coin in Europe, that was in the fifteenth century, and the centuries preceding it? The Spaniards and Portuguese from their mines, the English, French, and Dutch, by their African trade, and by their interlopers in the West Indies, bring home about six millions a year, of which not above a third goes to the East Indies. This sum alone, in ten years, would probably double the ancient stock of money in Europe. And no other satisfactory reason can be given, why all prices have not risen to a much more exorbitant height, except that which is derived from a change of customs and manners. Besides that more commodities are produced by additional industry, the same commodities come more to market, after men depart from their ancient simplicity of manners. And though this increase has not been equal to that of money, it has, however, been considerable, and has preserved the proportion between coin and commodities nearer the ancient standard.

Were the question proposed, Which of these methods of living in the people, the simple or refined, is the most advantageous to the state or public? I should, without much scruple, prefer the latter, in a view to politics at least; and should produce this as an additional reason for the encouragement of trade and manufactures.

While men live in the ancient simple manner, and supply all their necessaries from domestic industry or from the neighborhood, the sovereign can levy no taxes in money from a considerable part of his subjects; and if he will impose on them any burdens, he must take his payment in commodities, with which alone they abound; a method attended with such great and obvious inconveniencies, that they need not here be insisted on. All the money he can pretend to raise must be from his principal cities, where alone it circulates; and these, it is evident, cannot afford him so much as the whole state could, did gold and silver circulate throughout the whole. But besides this obvious diminution of the revenue, there is another cause of the poverty of the public in such a situation. Not only the sovereign receives less money, but the same money goes not so far as in times of industry and general commerce. Everything is dearer, where the gold and silver are supposed equal; and that because fewer commodities come to market, and the whole coin bears a higher proportion to what is to be purchased by it; whence alone the prices of every thing are fixed and determined.

Here then we may learn the fallacy of the remark, often to be met with in historians, and even in common conversation, that any particular state is weak, though fertile, populous, and well cultivated, merely because it wants money. It appears that the want of money can never injure any state within itself: for men and commodities are the real strength of any community. It is the simple manner of living which here hurts the public, by confining the gold and silver to few hands, and preventing its universal diffusion and circulation. On the contrary, industry and refinements of all kinds incorporate it with the whole state, however small its quantity may be: they digest it into every vein, so to speak; and make it enter into every transaction and contract. No hand is entirely empty of it. And as the prices of every thing fall by that means, the sovereign has a double advantage: he may draw money by his taxes from every part of the state; and what he receives, goes farther in every purchase and payment.

We may infer, from a comparison of prices, that money is not more plentiful in China, than it was in Europe three centuries ago: but what immense power is that empire possessed of, if we may judge by the civil and military establishment maintained by it? Polybius tells us that provisions were so cheap in Italy during his time, that in some places the stated price for a meal at the inns was a *semis* a head, little more than a farthing! Yet the Roman power had even then subdued the whole known world. About a century before that period, the Carthaginian ambassador said, by way of raillery, that no people lived more sociably amongst themselves than the Romans; for that, in every entertainment, which, as foreign ministers, they received, they still observed the same plate at every table. The absolute quantity of the precious metals is a matter of great indifference. There are only two circumstances of any importance, namely, their gradual increase, and their thorough concoction and circulation through the state; and the influence of both these circumstances has here been explained.

QUESTIONS

1. What does Hume mean when he says that "money is nothing but the representation of labor and commodities, and serves only as a method of rating or estimating them"? (22)

2. Why does Hume maintain that "the quantity of gold and silver is in itself altogether indifferent"? (24)

3. In Hume's opinion, what determines the price of commodities?

4. According to Hume, why are prices determined by the proportion between money circulating in the economy and the commodities in the market?

5. What does Hume mean when he says that "the want of money can never injure any state within itself"? (27)

FOR FURTHER DISCUSSION

1. Is Hume's explanation of the effect on industry of the interval between the acquisition of money and the direction of prices still applicable?

2. How do you think Hume might explain the role of money in the United States economy today?

3. What remedy do you think Hume might endorse to improve the current economic situation in the United States?

private property, in religion, trade,
Thought that equal dist. of
property would lead to poverty

ADAM SMITH

A dam Smith (1723–1790) was born in Kirkcaldy, near Edinburgh, Scotland. He entered the University of Glasgow at age fourteen, where he was deeply influenced by the philosopher Francis Hutcheson and later became a close friend of the philosopher David Hume. Hutcheson, Hume, and Smith himself were major figures in the Enlightenment. After subsequent study at the University of Oxford, Smith returned to the University of Glasgow where he taught logic and moral philosophy for some dozen years. During this period, he wrote *The Theory of Moral Sentiments* (1759). In this work, he identifies the basis of moral behavior with the tendency of human beings to identify with the feelings of others, a sentiment he calls "sympathy."

In 1763 Smith resigned his professorship to accompany a young duke to France as his paid tutor. There, Smith met many prominent *philosophes*, the intellectual leaders of the French Enlightenment. Among these were the economic theorists—known as physiocrats—François Quesnay and Anne-Robert-Jacques Turgot. It is likely that from them he first encountered the ideas of the self-regulating nature of markets (the "invisible hand") and the economic benefits of free trade and government nonintervention generally ("laissez-faire"). In 1766 Smith returned to England where he spent the next decade working on *The Wealth of Nations,* published in 1776, and often considered the foundational text of modern economics. The principal achievement of this hugely ambitious work is the way it combines the many diverse subjects of political economy into a precise and systematic whole. It used to be supposed that the crucial role that self-interest plays in *The Wealth of Nations* represents a radical departure from Smith's earlier focus on sympathy in *The Theory of Moral Sentiments*. However, it is more likely he believed human nature reposes in both character traits, and so viewed these books as complementary.

The following selection, taken from *The Wealth of Nations*, raises fundamental questions about the relation of foreign trade to the prosperity of a nation as well as the more general question of how much, if any, government regulation of trade is desirable.

Of Restraints upon the Importation from Foreign Countries

B y restraining, either by high duties or by absolute prohibitions, the importation of such goods from foreign countries as can be produced at home, the monopoly of the home market is more or less secured to the domestic industry employed in producing them. Thus the prohibition of importing either live cattle or salt provisions from foreign countries secures to the graziers of Great Britain the monopoly of the home market for butcher's meat. The high duties upon the importation of corn, which in times of moderate plenty amount to a prohibition, give a like advantage to the growers of that commodity. The prohibition of the importation of foreign woollens is equally favorable to the woollen manufacturers. The silk manufacture, though altogether employed upon foreign materials, has lately obtained the same advantage. The linen manufacture has not yet obtained it, but is making great strides toward it. Many other sorts of manufacturers have, in the same manner, obtained in Great Britain, either altogether or very nearly, a monopoly against their countrymen. The variety of goods of which the importation into Great Britain is prohibited, either absolutely, or under certain circumstances, greatly exceeds what can easily be suspected by those who are not well acquainted with the laws of the customs.

That this monopoly of the home market frequently gives great encouragement to that particular species of industry which enjoys it, and frequently turns toward that employment a greater share of both the labor and stock of the society than would otherwise have gone to it, cannot be doubted. But whether it tends either to increase the general industry of

This selection is taken from chapter 2, "Of Restraints upon the Importation from Foreign Countries of Such Goods as Can Be Produced at Home," of book 4 of The Wealth of Nations.

the society, or to give it the most advantageous direction, is not, perhaps, altogether so evident.

The general industry of the society never can exceed what the capital of the society can employ. As the number of workmen that can be kept in employment by any particular person must bear a certain proportion to his capital, so the number of those that can be continually employed by all the members of a great society must bear a certain proportion to the whole capital of that society, and never can exceed that proportion. No regulation of commerce can increase the quantity of industry in any society beyond what its capital can maintain. It can only divert a part of it into a direction into which it might not otherwise have gone; and it is by no means certain that this artificial direction is likely to be more advantageous to the society than that into which it would have gone of its own accord.

Every individual is continually exerting himself to find out the most advantageous employment for whatever capital he can command. It is his own advantage, indeed, and not that of the society, which he has in view. But the study of his own advantage naturally, or rather necessarily, leads him to prefer that employment which is most advantageous to the society.

First, every individual endeavors to employ his capital as near home as he can, and consequently as much as he can in the support of domestic industry; provided always that he can thereby obtain the ordinary, or not a great deal less than the ordinary profits of stock.

Thus, upon equal or nearly equal profits, every wholesale merchant naturally prefers the home trade to the foreign trade of consumption, and the foreign trade of consumption to the carrying trade. In the home trade his capital is never so long out of his sight as it frequently is in the foreign trade of consumption. He can know better the character and situation of the persons whom he trusts, and if he should happen to be deceived, he knows better the laws of the country from which he must seek redress. In the carrying trade, the capital of the merchant is, as it were, divided between two foreign countries, and no part of it is ever necessarily brought home, or placed under his own immediate view and command. The capital which an Amsterdam merchant employs in carrying corn from Konigsberg to Lisbon, and fruit and wine from Lisbon to Konigsberg, must generally be the one half of it at Konigsberg and the other half at Lisbon. No part of it need ever come to Amsterdam. The natural residence of such a merchant should either be at Konigsberg or Lisbon, and it can only be some very particular circumstances which can make him prefer the residence of Amsterdam. The uneasiness, however, which he feels at being separated so far from his capital generally determines him to bring part both of the Konigsberg goods which he destines for the market of Lisbon, and of the Lisbon goods which he destines for that of Konigsberg, to Amsterdam: and though this necessarily subjects him to a double charge of loading and unloading, as well as to the payment of some duties and customs, yet for the sake of having some part of his capital always under his own view and command, he willingly submits to this extraordinary charge; and it is in this manner that every country which has any considerable share of the carrying trade becomes always the emporium, or general market, for the goods of all the different countries whose trade it carries on. The merchant, in order to save a second loading and unloading, endeavors always to sell in the home market as much of the goods of all those different countries as he can, and thus, so far as he can, to convert his carrying trade into a foreign trade of consumption. A merchant, in the same manner, who is engaged in the foreign trade of consumption, when he collects goods for foreign markets, will always be glad, upon equal or nearly equal profits, to sell as great a part of them at home as he can. He saves himself the risk and trouble of exportation, when, so far as he can, he thus converts his foreign trade of consumption into a home trade. Home is in this manner the center, if I may say so, round which the capitals of the inhabitants of every country are continually circulating, and toward which they are always tending, though by particular causes they may sometimes be driven off and repelled from it toward more distant employments. But a capital employed in the home trade, it has already been shown, necessarily puts into motion a greater quantity of domestic industry, and gives revenue and employment to a greater number of the inhabitants of the country, than an equal capital employed in the foreign trade of consumption: and one employed in the foreign trade of consumption has the same advantage over an equal capital employed in the carrying trade. Upon equal, or only nearly equal profits, therefore, every individual naturally inclines to employ his capital in the manner in which it is likely to afford the greatest support to domestic industry, and to give revenue and employment to the greatest number of people of his own country.

Secondly, every individual who employs his capital in the support of domestic industry, necessarily endeavors so to direct that industry that its produce may be of the greatest possible value.

The produce of industry is what it adds to the subject or materials upon which it is employed. In proportion as the value of this produce is great or small, so will likewise be the profits of the employer. But it is only for the sake of profit that any man employs a capital in the support of industry; and he will always, therefore, endeavor to employ it in the support of that industry of which the produce is likely to be of the greatest value, or to exchange for the greatest quantity either of money or of other goods.

But the annual revenue of every society is always precisely equal to the exchangeable value of the whole annual produce of its industry, or rather is precisely the same thing with that exchangeable value. As every individual, therefore, endeavors as much as he can both to employ his capital in the support of domestic industry, and so to direct that industry that its produce may be of the greatest value; every individual necessarily labors to render the annual revenue of the society as great as he can. He generally, indeed, neither intends to promote the public interest, nor knows how much he is promoting it. By preferring the support of domestic to that of foreign industry, he intends only his own security; and by directing that industry in such a manner as its produce may be of the greatest value, he intends only his own gain, and he is in this, as in many other cases, led by an invisible hand to promote an end which was no part of his intention. Nor is it always the worse for the society that it was no part of it. By pursuing his own interest he frequently promotes that of the society more effectually than when he really intends to promote it. I have never known much good done by those who affected to trade for the public good. It is an affectation, indeed, not very common among merchants, and very few words need be employed in dissuading them from it.

What is the species of domestic industry which his capital can employ, and of which the produce is likely to be of the greatest value, every individual, it is evident, can, in his local situation, judge much better than any statesman or lawgiver can do for him. The statesman who should attempt to direct private people in what manner they ought to employ their capitals would not only load himself with a most unnecessary attention, but assume an authority which could safely be trusted, not only to no single person, but to no council or senate whatever, and which would nowhere be so dangerous as in the hands of a man who had folly and presumption enough to fancy himself fit to exercise it.

To give the monopoly of the home market to the produce of domestic industry, in any particular art or manufacture, is in some measure to direct private people in what manner they ought to employ their capitals, and must, in almost all cases, be either a useless or a hurtful regulation. If the produce of domestic can be brought there as cheap as that of foreign industry, the regulation is evidently useless. If it cannot, it must generally be hurtful. It is the maxim of every prudent master of a family never to attempt to make at home what it will cost him more to make than to buy. The tailor does not attempt to make his own shoes, but buys them of the shoemaker. The shoemaker does not attempt to make his own clothes, but employs a tailor. The farmer attempts to make neither the one nor the other, but employs those different artificers. All of them find it for their interest to employ their whole industry in a way in which they have some advantage over their neighbors, and to purchase with a part of its produce, or what is the same thing, with the price of a part of it, whatever else they have occasion for.

What is prudence in the conduct of every private family can scarce be folly in that of a great kingdom. If a foreign country can supply us with a commodity cheaper than we ourselves can make it, better buy it of them with some part of the produce of our own industry employed in a way in which we have some advantage. The general industry of the country, being always in proportion to the capital which employs it, will not thereby be diminished, no more than that of the above-mentioned artificers; but only left to find out the way in which it can be employed with the greatest advantage. It is certainly not employed to the greatest advantage when it is thus directed toward an object which it can buy cheaper than it can make. The value of its annual produce is certainly more or less diminished when it is thus turned away from producing commodities evidently of more value than the commodity which it is directed to produce. According to the supposition, that commodity could be purchased from foreign countries cheaper than it can be made at home. It could, therefore, have been purchased with a part only of the commodities, or, what is the same thing, with a part only of the price of the commodities, which the industry employed by an equal capital would have produced at home, had it been left to follow its natural course. The industry of the country, therefore, is thus turned away from a more to a less advantageous employment, and the exchangeable value of its annual produce, instead of being increased, according to the intention of the lawgiver, must necessarily be diminished by every such regulation.

By means of such regulations, indeed, a particular manufacture may sometimes be acquired sooner than it could have been otherwise, and after a certain time may be made at home as cheap or cheaper than in the foreign country. But though the industry of the society may be thus carried with advantage into a particular channel sooner than it could have been otherwise, it will by no means follow that the sum total, either of its industry, or of its revenue, can ever be augmented by any such regulation. The industry of the society can augment only in proportion as its capital augments, and its capital can augment only in proportion to what can be gradually saved out of its revenue. But the immediate effect of every such regulation is to diminish its revenue, and what diminishes its revenue is certainly not very likely to augment its capital faster than it would have augmented of its own accord had both capital and industry been left to find out their natural employments.

Though for want of such regulations the society should never acquire the proposed manufacture, it would not, upon that account, necessarily be the poorer in any one period of its duration. In every period of its duration its whole capital and industry might still have been employed, though upon different objects, in the manner that was most advantageous at the time. In every period its revenue might have been the greatest which its capital could afford, and both capital and revenue might have been augmented with the greatest possible rapidity.

The natural advantages which one country has over another in producing particular commodities are sometimes so great that it is acknowledged by all the world to be in vain to struggle with them. By means of glasses, hotbeds, and hot walls, very good grapes can be raised in Scotland, and very good wine too can be made of them at about thirty times the expense for which at least equally good can be brought from foreign countries. Would it be a reasonable law to prohibit the importation of all foreign wines merely to encourage the making of claret and burgundy in Scotland? But if there would be a manifest absurdity in turning toward any employment thirty times more of the capital and industry of the country than would be necessary to purchase from foreign countries an equal quantity of the commodities wanted, there must be an absurdity, though not altogether so glaring, yet exactly of the same kind, in turning toward any such employment a thirtieth, or even a three-hundredth part more of either. Whether the advantages which one country has over another be natural or acquired is in this respect of no consequence. As long as the one country has those advantages, and the other wants them, it will always be more advantageous for the latter rather to buy of the former than to make. It is an acquired advantage only, which one artificer has over his neighbor, who exercises another trade; and yet they both find it more advantageous to buy of one another than to make what does not belong to their particular trades.

Merchants and manufacturers are the people who derive the greatest advantage from this monopoly of the home market. The prohibition of the importation of foreign cattle, and of salt provisions, together with the high duties upon foreign corn, which in times of moderate plenty amount to a prohibition, are not near so advantageous to the graziers and farmers of Great Britain as other regulations of the same kind are to its merchants and manufacturers. Manufactures, those of the finer kind especially, are more easily transported from one country to another than corn or cattle. It is in the fetching and carrying manufactures, accordingly, that foreign trade is chiefly employed. In manufactures, a very small advantage will enable foreigners to undersell our own workmen, even in the home market. It will require a very great one to enable them to do so in the rude produce of the soil. If the free importation of foreign manufactures were permitted, several of the home manufactures would probably suffer, and some of them, perhaps, go to ruin altogether, and a considerable part of the stock and industry at present employed in them would be forced to find out some other employment. But the freest importation of the rude produce of the soil could have no such effect upon the agriculture of the country.

If the importation of foreign cattle, for example, were made ever so free, so few could be imported that the grazing trade of Great Britain could be little affected by it. Live cattle are, perhaps, the only commodity of which the transportation is more expensive by sea than by land. By land they carry themselves to market. By sea, not only the cattle, but their food and their water too, must be carried at no small expense and inconveniency. The short sea between Ireland and Great Britain, indeed, renders the importation of Irish cattle more easy. But though the free importation of them, which was lately permitted only for a limited time, were rendered perpetual, it could have no considerable effect upon the interest of the graziers of Great Britain. Those parts of Great Britain which border upon the Irish Sea are all grazing countries. Irish cattle could never be imported for their use, but must be driven through those very extensive countries, at no small expense and inconveniency, before they could arrive at their proper market. Fat cattle could not be driven so far. Lean cattle, therefore, only could be imported, and such importation could interfere, not with the interest of the feeding or fattening countries, to which, by reducing the price of lean cattle, it would rather be advantageous, but with that of the breeding countries only. The small number of Irish cattle imported since their importation was permitted, together with the good price at which lean cattle still continue to sell, seem to demonstrate that even the breeding countries of Great Britain are never likely to be much affected by the free importation of Irish cattle. The common people of Ireland, indeed, are said to have sometimes opposed with violence the exportation of their cattle. But if the exporters had found any great advantage in continuing the trade, they could easily, when the law was on their side, have conquered this mobbish opposition.

Feeding and fattening countries, besides, must always be highly improved, whereas breeding countries are generally uncultivated. The high price of lean cattle, by augmenting the value of uncultivated land, is like a bounty against improvement. To any country which was highly improved throughout, it would be more advantageous to import its lean cattle than to breed them. The province of Holland, accordingly, is said to follow this maxim at present. The mountains of Scotland, Wales, and Northumberland, indeed, are countries not capable of much improvement, and seem destined by nature to be the breeding countries of Great Britain. The freest importation of foreign cattle could have no other effect than to hinder those breeding countries from taking advantage of the increasing population and improvement of the rest of the kingdom, from raising their price to an exorbitant height, and from laying a real tax upon all the more improved and cultivated parts of the country.

The freest importation of salt provisions, in the same manner, could have as little effect upon the interest of the graziers of Great Britain as that of live cattle. Salt provisions are not only a very bulky commodity, but when compared with fresh meat, they are a commodity both of worse quality, and as they cost more labor and expense, of higher price. They could never, therefore, come into competition with the fresh meat, though they might with the salt provisions of the country. They might be used for victualing ships for distant voyages and such like uses, but could never make any considerable part of the food of the people. The small quantity of salt provisions imported from Ireland since their importation was rendered free is an experimental proof that our graziers have nothing to apprehend from it. It does not appear that the price of butcher's meat has ever been sensibly affected by it.

Even the free importation of foreign corn could very little affect the interest of the farmers of Great Britain. Corn is a much more bulky commodity than butcher's meat. A pound of wheat at a penny is as dear as a pound of butcher's meat at fourpence. The small quantity of foreign corn imported even in times of the greatest scarcity may satisfy our farmers that they can have nothing to fear from the freest importation. The average quantity imported, one year with another, amounts only, according to the very well-informed author of the tracts upon the corn trade, to twenty-three thousand seven hundred and twenty-eight quarters of all sorts of grain, and does not exceed the five hundred and seventy-one part of the annual consumption But as the bounty upon corn occasions a greater exportation in years of plenty, so it must of consequence occasion a greater importation in years of scarcity than in the actual state of tillage would otherwise take place. By means of it the plenty of one year does not compensate the scarcity of another, and as the average quantity exported is necessarily augmented by it, so must likewise, in the actual state of tillage, the average quantity imported. If there were no bounty, as less corn would be exported, so it is probable that, one year with another, less would be imported than at present. The corn merchants, the fetchers and carriers of corn between Great Britain and foreign countries would have much less employment, and might suffer considerably; but the country gentlemen and farmers could suffer very little. It is in the corn merchants accordingly, rather than in the country gentlemen and farmers, that I have observed the greatest anxiety for the renewal and continuation of the bounty.

Country gentlemen and farmers are, to their great honor, of all people, the least subject to the wretched spirit of monopoly. The undertaker of a great manufactory is sometimes alarmed if another work of the same kind is established within twenty miles of him. The Dutch undertaker of the woollen manufacture at Abbeville stipulated that no work of the same kind should be established within thirty leagues of that city. Farmers and country gentlemen, on the contrary, are generally disposed rather to promote than to obstruct the cultivation and improvement of their neighbors' farms and estates. They have no secrets such as those of the greater part of manufacturers, but are generally rather fond of communicating to their neighbors and of extending as far as possible any new practice which they have found to be advantageous. *Pius Questus*, says old Cato, *stabilissimusque, minimeque invidiosus; minimeque male cogitantes sunt, qui in eo studio occupati sunt.*[1] Country gentlemen and farmers, dispersed in different parts of the country, cannot so easily combine as merchants and manufacturers, who, being collected into towns, and accustomed to that exclusive corporation spirit which prevails in them, naturally endeavor to obtain against all their countrymen the same exclusive privilege which they generally possess against the inhabitants of their respective towns. They accordingly seem to have been the original inventors of those restraints upon the importation of foreign goods which secure to them the monopoly of the home market. It was probably in imitation of them, and to put themselves upon a level with those who, they found, were disposed to oppress them, that the country gentlemen and farmers of Great Britain insofar forgot the generosity which is natural to their station as to demand the exclusive privilege of supplying their countrymen with corn and butcher's meat. They did not perhaps take time to consider how much less their interest could be affected by the freedom of trade than that of the people whose example they followed.

To prohibit by a perpetual law the importation of foreign corn and cattle is in reality to enact that the population and industry of the country shall at no time exceed what the rude produce of its own soil can maintain.

There seem, however, to be two cases in which it will generally be advantageous to lay some burden upon foreign for the encouragement of domestic industry.

The first is, when some particular sort of industry is necessary for the defense of the country. The defense of Great Britain, for example, depends very much upon the number of its sailors and shipping. The act of navigation, therefore, very properly endeavors to give the sailors and shipping of Great Britain the monopoly of the trade of their own country in some cases by absolute prohibitions and in others by heavy burdens upon the shipping of foreign countries. The following are the principal dispositions of this act.

First, all ships, of which the owners and three-fourths of the mariners are not British subjects, are prohibited, upon pain of forfeiting ship and cargo, from trading to the British settlements and plantations, or from being employed in the coasting trade of Great Britain.

Second, a great variety of the most bulky articles of importation can be brought into Great Britain only, either in such ships as are above

---

1. [A god-fearing occupation is stablest, and least invites envy; and those engaged in it are least unwholesome in their outlook. Cato, *De ve rustica*.]

described, or in ships of the country where those goods are purchased, and of which the owners, masters, and three-fourths of the mariners are of that particular country; and when imported even in ships of this latter kind, they are subject to double aliens duty. If imported in ships of any other country, the penalty is forfeiture of ship and goods. When this act was made, the Dutch were, what they still are, the great carriers of Europe, and by this regulation they were entirely excluded from being the carriers to Great Britain, or from importing to us the goods of any other European country.

Third, a great variety of the most bulky articles of importation are prohibited from being imported, even in British ships, from any country but that in which they are produced, under pains of forfeiting ship and cargo. This regulation, too, was probably intended against the Dutch. Holland was then, as now, the great emporium for all European goods, and by this regulation British ships were hindered from loading in Holland the goods of any other European country.

Fourth, salt fish of all kinds, whale fins, whalebone, oil, and blubber, not caught by and cured on board British vessels, when imported into Great Britain, are subjected to double aliens duty. The Dutch, as they are they the principal, were then the only fishers in Europe that attempted to supply foreign nations with fish. By this regulation, a very heavy burden was laid upon their supplying Great Britain.

When the act of navigation was made, though England and Holland were not actually at war, the most violent animosity subsisted between the two nations. It had begun during the government of the Long Parliament, which first framed this act, and it broke out soon after in the Dutch wars during that of the Protector and of Charles the Second. It is not impossible, therefore, that some of the regulations of this famous act may have proceeded from national animosity. They are as wise, however, as if they had all been dictated by the most deliberate wisdom. National animosity at that particular time aimed at the very same object which the most deliberate wisdom would have recommended, the diminution of the naval power of Holland, the only naval power which could endanger the security of England.

The act of navigation is not favorable to foreign commerce, or to the growth of that opulence which can arise from it. The interest of a nation in its commercial relations to foreign nations is, like that of a merchant with regard to the different people with whom he deals, to buy as cheap and to sell as dear as possible. But it will be most likely to buy cheap, when by the most perfect freedom of trade it encourages all nations to bring to it the goods which it has occasion to purchase; and, for the same reason, it will be most likely to sell dear, when its markets are thus filled with the greatest number of buyers. The act of navigation, it is true, lays no burden upon foreign ships that come to export the produce of British industry. Even the ancient aliens duty, which used to be paid upon all goods exported as well as imported, has, by several subsequent acts, been taken off from the greater part of the articles of exportation. But if foreigners, either by prohibitions or high duties, are hindered from coming to sell, they cannot always afford to come to buy; because coming without a cargo, they must lose the freight from their own country to Great Britain. By diminishing the number of sellers, therefore, we necessarily diminish that of buyers, and are thus likely not only to buy foreign goods dearer, but to sell our own cheaper, than if there was a more perfect freedom of trade. As defense, however it is of much more importance than opulence, the act of navigation is, perhaps, the wisest of all the commercial regulations of England.

The second case, in which it will generally be advantageous to lay some burden upon foreign for the encouragement of domestic industry is, when some tax is imposed at home upon the produce of the latter. In this case, it seems reasonable that an equal tax should be imposed upon the like produce of the former. This would not give the monopoly of the home market to domestic industry, nor turn toward a particular employment a greater share of the stock and labor of the country than what would naturally go to it. It would only hinder any part of what would naturally go to it from being turned away by the tax into a less natural direction, and would leave the competition between foreign and domestic industry, after the tax, as nearly as possible upon the same footing as before it. In Great Britain, when any such tax is laid upon the produce of domestic industry, it is usual at the same time, in order to stop the clamorous complaints of our merchants and manufacturers that they will be undersold at home, to lay a much heavier duty upon the importation of all foreign goods of the same kind.

This second limitation of the freedom of trade according to some people should, upon some occasions, be extended much farther than to the precise foreign commodities which could come into competition with those which had been taxed at home. When the necessaries of life have been taxed any country, it becomes proper, they pretend, to tax not only the like necessaries of life imported from other countries, but all sorts of foreign goods which can come into competition with anything that is the produce of domestic industry. Subsistence, they say, becomes necessarily dearer in consequence of such taxes; and the price of labor must always rise with the price of the laborers' subsistence. Every commodity, therefore, which is the produce of domestic industry, though not immediately taxed itself, becomes dearer in consequence of such taxes, because the labor which produces it becomes so. Such taxes, therefore, are really equivalent, they say, to a tax upon every particular commodity produced at home.

In order to put domestic upon the same footing with foreign industry, therefore, it becomes necessary, they think, to lay some duty upon every foreign commodity equal to this enhancement of the price of the home commodities with which it can come into competition.

Whether taxes upon the necessaries of life, such as those in Great Britain upon soap, salt, leather, candles, etc., necessarily raise the price of labor, and consequently that of all other commodities, I shall consider hereafter, when I come to treat of taxes. Supposing, however, in the meantime, that they have this effect, and they have it undoubtedly, this general enhancement of the price of all commodities, in consequence of that of labor, is a case which differs in the two following respects from that of a particular commodity of which the price was enhanced by a particular tax immediately imposed upon it.

First, it might always be known with great exactness how far the price of such a commodity could be enhanced by such a tax: but how far the general enhancement of the price of labor might affect that of every different commodity about which labor was employed could never be known with any tolerable exactness. It would be impossible, therefore, to proportion with any tolerable exactness the tax upon every foreign to this enhancement of the price of every home commodity.

Second, taxes upon the necessaries of life have nearly the same effect upon the circumstances of the people as a poor soil and a bad climate. Provisions are thereby rendered dearer in the same manner as if it required extraordinary labor and expense to raise them. As in the natural scarcity arising from soil and climate it would be absurd to direct the people in what manner they ought to employ their capitals and industry, so is it likewise in the artificial scarcity arising from such taxes. To be left to accommodate, as well as they could, their industry to their situation, and to find out those employments in which, notwithstanding their unfavorable circumstances, they might have some advantage either in the home or in the foreign market, is what in both cases would evidently be most for their advantage. To lay a new tax upon them, because they are already overburdened with taxes, and because they already pay too dear for the necessaries of life, to make them likewise pay too dear for the greater part of other commodities, is certainly a most absurd way of making amends.

Such taxes, when they have grown up to a certain height, are a curse equal to the barrenness of the earth and the inclemency of the heavens; and yet it is in the richest and most industrious countries that they have been most generally imposed. No other countries could support so great a disorder. As the strongest bodies only can live and enjoy health under an unwholesome regimen, so the nations only that in every sort of industry have the greatest natural and acquired advantages can subsist and prosper under such taxes. Holland is the country in Europe in which they abound most, and which from peculiar circumstances continues to prosper, not by means of them, as has been most absurdly supposed, but in spite of them.

As there are two cases in which it will generally be advantageous to lay some burden upon foreign for the encouragement of domestic industry, so there are two others in which it may sometimes be a matter of deliberation; in the one, how far it is proper to continue the free importation of certain foreign goods; and in the other, how far, or in what manner, it may be proper to restore that free importation after it has been for some time interrupted.

The case in which it may sometimes be a matter of deliberation how far it is proper to continue the free importation of certain foreign goods is, when some foreign nation restrains by high duties or prohibitions the importation of some of our manufactures into their country. Revenge in this case naturally dictates retaliation, and that we should impose the like duties and prohibitions upon the importation of some or all of their manufactures into ours. Nations, accordingly, seldom fail to retaliate in this manner. The French have been particularly forward to favor their own manufactures by restraining the importation of such foreign goods as could come into competition with them. In this consisted a great part of the policy of Mr. Colbert, who, notwithstanding his great abilities, seems in this case to have been imposed upon by the sophistry of merchants and manufacturers, who are always demanding a monopoly against their countrymen. It is at present the opinion of the most intelligent men in France that his operations of this kind have not been beneficial to his country. That minister, by the tariff of 1667, imposed very high duties upon a great number of foreign manufactures. Upon his refusing to moderate them in favor of the Dutch, they in 1671 prohibited the importation of the wines, brandies, and manufactures of France. The war of 1672 seems to have been in part occasioned by this commercial dispute. The peace of Nimeguen put an end to it in 1678 by moderating some of those duties in favor of the Dutch, who in consequence took off their prohibition. It was about the same time that the French and English began mutually to oppress each other's industry by the like duties and prohibitions, of which the French, however, seem to have set the first example. The spirit of hostility which has subsisted between the two nations ever since has hitherto hindered them from being moderated on either side. In 1697 the English prohibited the importation of bonelace, the manufacture of Flanders. The government of that country, at that time under the dominion of Spain, prohibited in return the importation of English woollens. In 1700, the prohibition of importing bonelace into England was taken off upon condition that the importance of English woollens into Flanders should be put on the same footing as before.

There may be good policy in retaliations of this kind, when there is a probability that they will procure the repeal of the high duties or prohibitions complained of. The recovery of a great foreign market will generally more than compensate the transitory inconveniency of paying dearer during a short time for some sorts of goods. To judge whether such retaliations are likely to produce such an effect does not, perhaps, belong so much to the science of a legislator, whose deliberations ought to be governed by general principles which are always the same, as to the skill of that insidious and crafty animal, vulgarly called a statesman or politician, whose councils are directed by the momentary fluctuations of affairs. When there is no probability that any such repeal can be procured, it seems a bad method of compensating the injury done to certain classes of our people to do another injury ourselves, not only to those classes, but to almost all the other classes of them. When our neighbors prohibit some manufacture of ours, we generally prohibit, not only the same, for that alone would seldom affect them considerably, but some other manufacture of theirs. This may no doubt give encouragement to some particular class of workmen among ourselves, and by excluding some of their rivals, may enable them to raise their price in the home market. Those workmen, however, who suffered by our neighbors' prohibition will not be benefited by ours. On the contrary, they and almost all the other classes of our citizens will thereby be obliged to pay dearer than before for certain goods. Every such law, therefore, imposes a real tax upon the whole country, not in favor of that particular class of workmen who were injured by our neighbors' prohibition, but of some other class.

The case in which it may sometimes be a matter of deliberation, how far, or in what manner, it is proper to restore the free importation of foreign goods, after it has been for some time interrupted, is, when particular manufactures, by means of high duties or prohibitions upon all foreign goods which can come into competition with them, have been so far extended as to employ a great multitude of hands. Humanity may in this case require that the freedom of trade should be restored only by slow gradations, and with a good deal of reserve and circumspection. Were those high duties and prohibitions taken away all at once, cheaper foreign goods of the same kind might be poured so fast into the home market as to deprive all at once many thousands of our people of their ordinary employment and means of subsistence. The disorder which this would occasion might no doubt be very considerable. It would in all probability, however, be much less than is commonly imagined, for the two following reasons:

First, all those manufactures, of which any part is commonly exported to other European countries without a bounty, could be very little affected by the freest importation of foreign goods. Such manufactures must be sold as cheap abroad as any other foreign goods of the same quality and kind, and consequently must be sold cheaper at home. They would still, therefore, keep possession of the home market, and though a capricious man of fashion might sometimes prefer foreign wares, merely because they were foreign, to cheaper and better goods of the same kind that were made at home, this folly could, from the nature of things, extend to so few that it could make no sensible impression upon the general employment of the people. But a great part of all the different branches of our woollen manufacture, of our tanned leather, and of our hardware are annually exported to other European countries without any bounty, and these are the manufactures which employ the greatest number of hands. The silk, perhaps, is the manufacture which would suffer the most by this freedom of trade, and after it the linen, though the latter much less than the former.

Second, though a great number of people should, by thus restoring the freedom of trade, be thrown all at once out of their ordinary employment and common method of subsistence, it would by no means follow that they would thereby be deprived either of employment or subsistence. By the reduction of the army and navy at the end of the late war, more than a hundred thousand soldiers and seamen, a number equal to what is employed in the greatest manufactures, were all at once thrown out of their ordinary employment; but, though they no doubt suffered some inconveniency, they were not thereby deprived of all employment and subsistence. The greater part of the seamen, it is probable, gradually betook themselves to the merchant service as they could find occasion, and in the meantime both they and the soldiers were absorbed in the great mass of the people, and employed in a great variety of occupations. Not only no great convulsion, but no sensible disorder arose from so great a change in the situation of more than a hundred thousand men, all accustomed to the use of arms, and many of them to rapine and plunder. The number of vagrants was scarce anywhere sensibly increased by it, even the wages of labor were not reduced by it in any occupation, so far as I have been able to learn, except in that of seamen in the merchant-service. But if we compare together the habits of a soldier and of any sort of manufacturer, we shall find that those of the latter do not tend so much to disqualify him from being employed in a new trade, as those of the former from being employed in any. The manufacturer has always been accustomed to look for his subsistence from his labor only: the soldier to expect it from his pay. Application and industry have been familiar to the one; idleness and dissipation to the other. But it is surely much easier to change the direction of industry from one sort of labor to another than to turn idleness and dissipation to any. To the greater part of manufactures besides, it has already been observed, there are other collateral manufactures of so similar a nature that a workman can easily transfer his industry from one of them to another. The greater part of such workmen too are occasionally employed in country labor. The stock which employed them in a particular manufacture before will still remain in the country to employ an equal number of people in some other way. The capital of the country remaining the same, the demand for labor will likewise be the same, or very nearly the same, though it may be exerted in different places and for different occupations. Soldiers and seamen, indeed, when discharged from the king's service, are at liberty to exercise any trade, within any town or place of Great Britain or Ireland. Let the same natural liberty of exercising what species of industry they please, be restored to all his Majesty's subjects, in the same manner as to soldiers and seamen; that is, break down the exclusive privileges of corporations, and repeal the statute of apprenticeship, both which are real encroachments upon natural liberty, and add to these the repeal of the law of settlements, so that a poor workman, when thrown out of employment either in one trade or in one place, may seek for it in another trade or in another place without the fear either of a prosecution or of a removal, and neither the public nor the individuals will suffer much more from the occasional disbanding some particular classes of manufacturers than from that of soldiers. Our manufacturers have no doubt great merit with their country, but they cannot have more than those who defend it with their blood, nor deserve to be treated with more delicacy.

To expect, indeed, that the freedom of trade should ever be entirely restored in Great Britain is as absurd as to expect that an Oceana or Utopia should ever be established in it. Not only the prejudices of the public, but what is much more unconquerable, the private interests of many individuals, irresistibly oppose it. Were the officers of the army to oppose with the same zeal and unanimity any reduction in the numbers of forces with which master manufacturers set themselves against every law that is likely to increase the number of their rivals in the home market; were the former to animate their soldiers in the same manner as the latter enflame their workmen to attack with violence and outrage the proposers of any such regulation, to attempt to reduce the army would be as dangerous as it has now become to attempt to diminish in any respect the monopoly which our manufacturers have obtained against us. This monopoly has so much increased the number of some particular tribes of them that, like an overgrown standing army, they have become formidable to the government, and upon many occasions intimidate the legislature. The Member of Parliament who supports every proposal for strengthening this monopoly is sure to acquire not only the reputation of understanding trade, but great popularity and influence with an order of men whose numbers and wealth render them of great importance. If he opposes them, on the contrary, and still more if he has authority enough to be able to thwart them, neither the most acknowledged probity, nor the highest rank, nor the greatest public services can protect him from the most infamous abuse and detraction, from personal insults, nor sometimes from real danger, arising from the insolent outrage of furious and disappointed monopolists.

The undertaker of a great manufacture, who, by the home markets being suddenly laid open to the competition of foreigners, should be obliged to abandon his trade, would no doubt suffer very considerably. That part of his capital which had usually been employed in purchasing materials and in paying his workmen might, without much difficulty, perhaps, find another employment. But that part of it which was fixed in workhouses, and in the instruments of trade, could scarce be disposed of without considerable loss. The equitable regard, therefore, to his interest requires that changes of this kind should never be introduced suddenly, but slowly, gradually, and after a very long warning. The legislature, were it possible that its deliberations could be always directed, not by the clamorous importunity of partial interests, but by an extensive view of the general good, ought upon this very account, perhaps, to be particularly careful neither to establish any new monopolies of this kind, nor to extend further those which are already established. Every such regulation introduces some degree of real disorder into the constitution of the state, which it will be difficult afterwards to cure without occasioning another disorder.

How far it may be proper to impose taxes upon the importation of foreign goods, in order not to prevent their importation but to raise a revenue for government, I shall consider hereafter when I come to treat of taxes. Taxes imposed with a view to prevent, or even to diminish importation, are evidently as destructive of the revenue of the customs as of the freedom of trade.

QUESTIONS

1. What does Smith mean when he says that "the study of his own advantage naturally, or rather necessarily, leads [the individual] to prefer that employment which is most advantageous to the society"? (31)

2. What does Smith mean by the "invisible hand"? (33)

3. Why does Smith oppose most government policies that regulate trade with other countries?

4. What does Smith mean when he says an importation tax on certain goods imposes a "real tax upon the whole country"? (43)

5. Why is Smith opposed to monopolies?

FOR FURTHER REFLECTION

1. In matters of international trade, should nations today attempt to adhere to Smith's theory of natural advantage?

2. What are the advantages and disadvantages of Smith's theories of free trade in today's global economy?

3. If Smith assumes that the demand for labor is roughly equal to the capital of a country, how might he account for high levels of unemployment in today's developed economies?

THOMAS ROBERT MALTHUS

Thomas Robert Malthus (1766–1834), along with his close friend David Ricardo, was a prominent member of the younger generation of economic thinkers who built upon the foundation established by Adam Smith in his *Wealth of Nations*. Malthus also helped found the science of demographics. He is best known for claiming that population increase must inevitably outstrip food production, miring the working class forever in misery.

Malthus was born in Surrey, England. His father was a member of the landed gentry who counted David Hume among his acquaintances. Malthus was educated at home, then sent to Jesus College, Cambridge, where he studied for the ministry and took prizes in the classics. He was ordained in the Anglican Church and was active as a country curate in the parish of his birth during the 1790s. His real interests, however, lay in philosophy and political economy, and he began publishing a series of pamphlets on economic questions, beginning with his *Essay on the Principle of Population* (1798). Two years later he published "High Price of Provisions." Excerpts from both of these essays follow. Many more pamphlets on both particular and general topics in economics followed over the next three decades, as well as several new, heavily augmented editions of the *Essay* and a general treatise, *Principles of Political Economy* (1820). Due to the success of the *Essay* and his other writings, in 1805 Malthus was appointed a professor of history and political economy at a training college run by the East India Company for its staff members—in effect, the first paid professorship in economics in the English-speaking world.

Malthus wrote the *Essay* as an antidote to what he considered the unwarranted optimism of the Age of Enlightenment concerning the inevitable progress of humanity toward universal economic prosperity. The questions he raised lie at the heart of controversies in our own day surrounding the "carrying capacity" of the earth. Charles Darwin was strongly influenced by Malthus's depiction of human populations in conflict with each other for scarce resources when he was forming his theory of natural selection, by which species of plants and animals compete, successfully or not, for survival.

Selected Essays

An Essay on the Principle of Population

The great and unlooked-for discoveries that have taken place of late years in natural philosophy, the increasing diffusion of general knowledge from the extension of the art of printing, the ardent and unshackled spirit of inquiry that prevails throughout the lettered and even unlettered world, the new and extraordinary lights that have been thrown on political subjects which dazzle and astonish the understanding, and particularly that tremendous phenomenon in the political horizon, the French Revolution, which, like a blazing comet, seems destined either to inspire with fresh life and vigor, or to scorch up and destroy the shrinking inhabitants of the earth, have all concurred to lead many able men into the opinion that we were touching on a period big with the most important changes, changes that would in some measure be decisive of the future fate of mankind.

It has been said that the great question is now at issue, whether man shall henceforth start forward with accelerated velocity toward illimitable, and hitherto unconceived improvement, or be condemned to a perpetual oscillation between happiness and misery, and after every effort remain still at an immeasurable distance from the wished-for goal.

Yet, anxiously as every friend of mankind must look forward to the termination of this painful suspense, and eagerly as the inquiring mind would hail every ray of light that might assist its view into futurity, it is much to be lamented that the writers on each side of this momentous question still keep far aloof from each other. Their mutual arguments do not meet with a candid examination. The question is not brought to rest on fewer points, and even in theory scarcely seems to be approaching to a decision.

This selection is taken from chapter 1 of Malthus's Essay on the Principle of Population.

The advocate for the present order of things is apt to treat the sect of speculative philosophers either as a set of artful and designing knaves who preach up ardent benevolence and draw captivating pictures of a happier state of society only the better to enable them to destroy the present establishments and to forward their own deep-laid schemes of ambition, or as wild and mad-headed enthusiasts whose silly speculations and absurd paradoxes are not worthy the attention of any reasonable man.

The advocate for the perfectibility of man, and of society, retorts on the defender of establishments a more than equal contempt. He brands him as the slave of the most miserable and narrow prejudices; or as the defender of the abuses of civil society only because he profits by them. He paints him either as a character who prostitutes his understanding to his interest, or as one whose powers of mind are not of a size to grasp any thing great and noble, who cannot see above five yards before him, and who must therefore be utterly unable to take in the views of the enlightened benefactor of mankind.

In this unamicable contest the cause of truth cannot but suffer. The really good arguments on each side of the question are not allowed to have their proper weight. Each pursues his own theory, little solicitous to correct or improve it by an attention to what is advanced by his opponents.

The friend of the present order of things condemns all political speculations in the gross. He will not even condescend to examine the grounds from which the perfectibility of society is inferred. Much less will he give himself the trouble in a fair and candid manner to attempt an exposition of their fallacy.

The speculative philosopher equally offends against the cause of truth. With eyes fixed on a happier state of society, the blessings of which he paints in the most captivating colors, he allows himself to indulge in the most bitter invectives against every present establishment, without applying his talents to consider the best and safest means of removing abuses and without seeming to be aware of the tremendous obstacles that threaten, even in theory, to oppose the progress of man toward perfection.

It is an acknowledged truth in philosophy that a just theory will always be confirmed by experiment. Yet so much friction, and so many minute circumstances occur in practice, which it is next to impossible for the most enlarged and penetrating mind to foresee, that on few subjects can any theory be pronounced just, till all the arguments against it have been maturely weighed and clearly and consistently refuted.

I have read some of the speculations on the perfectibility of man and of society with great pleasure. I have been warmed and delighted with the enchanting picture which they hold forth. I ardently wish for such happy improvements. But I see great, and to my understanding, unconquerable difficulties in the way to them. These difficulties it is my present purpose to state, declaring at the same time that so far from exulting in them, as a cause of triumph over the friends of innovation, nothing would give me greater pleasure than to see them completely removed.

The most important argument that I shall adduce is certainly not new. The principles on which it depends have been explained in part by Hume, and more at large by Dr. Adam Smith. It has been advanced and applied to the present subject, though not with its proper weight, or in the most forcible point of view, by Mr. Wallace, and it may probably have been stated by many writers that I have never met with. I should certainly therefore not think of advancing it again, though I mean to place it in a point of view in some degree different from any that I have hitherto seen, if it had ever been fairly and satisfactorily answered.

The cause of this neglect on the part of the advocates for the perfectibility of mankind is not easily accounted for. I cannot doubt the talents of such men as Godwin and Condorcet. I am unwilling to doubt their candor. To my understanding, and probably to that of most others, the difficulty appears insurmountable. Yet these men of acknowledged ability and penetration scarcely deign to notice it, and hold on their course in such speculations with unabated ardor and undiminished confidence. I have certainly no right to say that they purposely shut their eyes to such arguments. I ought rather to doubt the validity of them, when neglected by such men, however forcibly their truth may strike my own mind. Yet in this respect it must be acknowledged that we are all of us too prone to err. If I saw a glass of wine repeatedly presented to a man, and he took no notice of it, I should be apt to think that he was blind or uncivil. A juster philosophy might teach me rather to think that my eyes deceived me and that the offer was not really what I conceived it to be.

In entering upon the argument I must premise that I put out of the question, at present, all mere conjectures, that is, all suppositions, the probable realization of which cannot be inferred upon any just philosophical grounds. A writer may tell me that he thinks man will ultimately become an ostrich. I cannot properly contradict him. But before he can expect to bring any reasonable person over to his opinion, he ought to show that the necks of mankind have been gradually elongating, that the lips have grown harder and more prominent, that the legs and feet are daily altering their shape, and that the hair is beginning to change into stubs of feathers. And till the probability of so wonderful a conversion can be shewn, it is surely lost time and lost eloquence to expatiate on the happiness of man in such a state; to describe his powers, both of running and flying, to paint him in a condition where all narrow luxuries would be condemned, where he would be employed only in collecting the necessaries of life, and where, consequently, each man's share of labor would be light, and his portion of leisure ample.

I think I may fairly make two postulations.

First, that food is necessary to the existence of man.

Second, that the passion between the sexes is necessary and will remain nearly in its present state.

These two laws, ever since we have had any knowledge of mankind, appear to have been fixed laws of our nature, and, as we have not hitherto seen any alteration in them, we have no right to conclude that they will ever cease to be what they now are, without an immediate act of power in that Being who first arranged the system of the universe, and for the advantage of his creatures, still executes, according to fixed laws, all its various operations.

I do not know that any writer has supposed that on this earth man will ultimately be able to live without food. But Mr. Godwin has conjectured that the passion between the sexes may in time be extinguished. As, however, he calls this part of his work a deviation into the land of conjecture, I will not dwell longer upon it at present than to say that the best arguments for the perfectibility of man are drawn from a contemplation of the great progress that he has already made from the savage state and the difficulty of saying where he is to stop. But toward the extinction of the passion between the sexes, no progress whatever has hitherto been made. It appears to exist in as much force at present as it did two thousand or four thousand years ago. There are individual exceptions now as there always have been. But, as these exceptions do not appear to increase in number, it would surely be a very unphilosophical mode of arguing to infer, merely from the existence of an exception, that the exception would in time become the rule, and the rule the exception.

Assuming then my postulations as granted, I say that power of population is indefinitely greater than the power in the earth to produce subsistence for man.

Population, when unchecked, increases in a geometrical ratio. Subsistence increases only in an arithmetical ratio. A slight acquaintance with numbers will show the immensity of the first power in comparison of the second.

By that law of our nature which makes food necessary to the life of man, the effects of these two unequal powers must be kept equal.

This implies a strong and constantly operating check on population from the difficulty of subsistence. This difficulty must fall somewhere and must necessarily be severely felt by a large portion of mankind.

Through the animal and vegetable kingdoms, nature has scattered the seeds of life abroad with the most profuse and liberal hand. She has been comparatively sparing in the room and the nourishment necessary to rear them. The germs of existence contained in this spot of earth, with ample food, and ample room to expand in, would fill millions of worlds in the course of a few thousand years. Necessity, that imperious, all-pervading law of nature, restrains them within the prescribed bounds. The race of plants and the race of animals shrink under this great restrictive law. And the race of man cannot, by any efforts of reason, escape from it. Among plants and animals its effects are waste of seed, sickness, and premature death. Among mankind, misery and vice. The former, misery, is an absolutely necessary consequence of it. Vice is a highly probable consequence, and we therefore see it abundantly prevail, but it ought not, perhaps, to be called an absolutely necessary consequence. The ordeal of virtue is to resist all temptation to evil.

This natural inequality of the two powers of population and of production in the earth, and that great law of our nature which must constantly keep their effects equal, form the great difficulty that to me appears insurmountable in the way to the perfectibility of society. All other arguments are of slight and subordinate consideration in comparison of this. I see no way by which man can escape from the weight of this law which pervades all animated nature. No fancied equality, no agrarian regulations in their utmost extent could remove the pressure of it even for a single century. And it appears, therefore, to be decisive against the possible existence of a society, all the members of which should live in ease, happiness, and comparative leisure; and feel no anxiety about providing the means of subsistence for themselves and families.

Consequently, if the premises are just, the argument is conclusive against the perfectibility of the mass of mankind.

I have thus sketched the general outline of the argument, but I will examine it more particularly, and I think it will be found that experience—the true source and foundation of all knowledge—invariably confirms its truth.

High Price of Provisions

Among the many causes that have been assigned of the present high price of provisions, I am much inclined to suspect that the principal one has hitherto escaped detection; at least, in the discussions on the subject, either in print or conversation, which have fallen within my knowledge, the cause—which I conceive to have operated most strongly toward increasing the price of the necessaries of life—has not yet been suggested. There are some disorders, which, though they scarcely admit of a cure, or even of any considerable mitigation, are still capable of being made greatly worse. In such misfortunes it is of great importance to know the desperate nature of

This selection is taken from "High Price of Provisions."

the disease. The next step to the alleviation of pain is the bearing it with composure, and not aggravating it by impatience and irritation.

It cannot admit of a doubt with persons of sense and information that, during the last year, there was a scarcity, to a certain extent, of all sorts of grain; but it must be at the same time acknowledged that the price was higher than the degree of that scarcity would at first sight appear to warrant.

In the summer of 1799, in the course of a northern tour, I passed through Sweden. There was at that time a general dearth of corn throughout the country, owing to a long drought the preceding year. In the province of Värmland, adjoining to Norway, it approached almost to a famine, and the lower classes of people suffered most severe distress. At the time we were passing through that part of the country, which was in July, they were reduced to two most miserable substitutes for bread: one made of the inner bark of the fir, and the other of the common sorrel dried, and powdered. These substances, though made into the usual shape of their rye bread, had no affinity to it whatever in taste, and but very little, I believe, in nourishment, as the effects of this miserable food were but too visible in their pallid and unhealthy countenances.

There could be little doubt that the degree of scarcity then prevailing in that part of Sweden was considerably greater than any we have hitherto experienced here; and yet, as far as we could learn, the price of rye, which is the grain principally used for bread, had not risen above double its usual average; whereas in this country last year, in a scarcity that must be acknowledged to be very greatly inferior in degree, wheat rose to above three times its former price.

The continuation of extraordinary high prices, after a harvest that was at one time looked forward to as abundant, has contributed still more to astonish and perplex the public mind. Many men of sense have joined in the universal cry of the common people, that there must be roguery somewhere; and the general indignation has fallen upon monopolizers, forestallers, and regraters—words that are vented from every mouth with fearful execrations, and are applied indiscriminately to all middlemen whatever, to every kind of trader that goes between the grower of the commodity and the consumer.

This popular clamor, headed by the lord chief justice and enforced throughout the country by the instructions of the grand juries, must make every reflecting mind tremble for the future supply of our markets. I cannot but think, therefore, that I should do an acceptable service if I could succeed in accounting for the present high price of the necessaries of life, without criminating a class of men who, I believe, have been accused unjustly and who, every political economist must know, are absolutely necessary in the complicated machinery that distributes the provisions and other commodities of a large nation.

I ought first to premise, however, that I am not interested in this question, further than as a lover of truth, and a well-wisher to my country. I have no sort of connection whatever with any of these middlemen or great farmers, who are now the objects of public indignation; and, as an individual with a small fixed income, I am certainly among that class of persons on whom the high price of provisions must fall the heaviest.

To proceed to the point: I am most strongly inclined to suspect that the attempt in most parts of the kingdom to increase the parish allowances in proportion to the price of corn, combined with the riches of the country—which have enabled it to proceed as far as it has done in this attempt—is, comparatively speaking, the sole cause which has occasioned the price of provisions in this country to rise so much higher than the degree of scarcity would seem to warrant so much higher than it would do in any other country where this cause did not operate.

It may appear, perhaps, at first, to the reader, that this cause is inadequate to the effect we experience; but, if he will kindly allow me a few minutes of patient and candid attention, I hope I shall be able to convince him that it is not only adequate to produce the present high price of provisions of which we complain; but, admitting a real scarcity, that the attempt to carry it actually into execution might raise the quartern loaf before the expiration of a year, to as many shillings as it is now pence.

Adam Smith has most justly stated that the actual price at which a commodity is sold is compounded of its natural price, the price at which it can be brought to market, allowing the usual profit in times of moderate plenty, and the proportion of the supply to the demand. When any commodity is scarce, its natural price is necessarily forgotten, and its actual price is regulated by the excess of the demand above the supply.

Let us suppose a commodity in great request by fifty people, but of which, from some failure in its production, there is only sufficient to supply forty. If the fortieth man from the top have two shillings which he can spend in this commodity, and the thirty-nine above him more in various proportions, and the ten below all less, the actual price of the article, according to the genuine principles of trade, will be two shillings. If more be asked, the whole will not be sold, because there are only forty who have as much as two shillings to spend on the article; and there is no reason for asking less, because the whole may be disposed of at that sum.

Let us suppose, now, that somebody gives the ten poor men, who were excluded, a shilling apiece. The whole fifty can now offer two shillings, the price which was before asked. According to every genuine principle of fair trading, the commodity must immediately rise. If it does not, I would ask, upon what principle are ten—out of the fifty who are all able to offer two shillings—to be rejected? For still, according to the supposition, there is only enough for forty. The two shillings of a poor man are just as good as the two shillings of a rich one; and, if we interfere to prevent the commodity from rising out of the reach of the poorest ten, whoever they may be, we must toss up, draw lots, raffle, or fight to determine who are to be excluded. It would be beyond my present purpose to enter into the question whether any of these modes would be more eligible, for the distribution of the commodities of a country, than the sordid distinction of money; but certainly, according to the customs of all civilized and enlightened nations, and according to every acknowledged principle of commercial dealing, the price must be allowed to rise to that point which will put it beyond the power of ten out of the fifty to purchase. This point will, perhaps, be half a crown or more, which will now become the price of the commodity. Let another shilling apiece be given to the excluded ten: all will now be able to offer half a crown. The price must in consequence immediately rise to three shillings or more, and so on *toties quoties*.

In the progress of this operation the ten excluded would not be always entirely the same. The richest of the ten first excluded would probably be raised above the poorest of the first forty. Small changes of this kind must take place. The additional allowances to the poorest, and the weight of the high prices on those above them, would tend to level the two orders; but, till a complete level had taken place, ten must be always excluded, and the price would always be fixed, as nearly as possible, at that sum which the fortieth man at the top could afford to give. This, if the donatives were continued, would raise the commodity to an extraordinary price, without the supposition of any combination and conspiracy among the vendors, or any kind of unfair dealing whatever.

The rise in the price of corn and of other provisions in this country has been effected exactly in the same manner, though the operation may be a little more complicated; and I am firmly convinced that it never could have reached its present height, but from the system of poor laws and parish allowances, which have operated precisely in the same mode as the donatives of a shilling in the instance I have just adduced.

The harvest of 1799 was bad, both in quality and quantity. Few people could deny that there appeared to be a very considerable deficiency of produce; and the price of the load of wheat rose in consequence almost immediately to £20. I returned from the north in the beginning of November, and found the alarm so great and general, and the price of corn so high, that I remember thinking that it was probably fully adequate to the degree of the deficiency, and, taking into consideration the prospect of importation from the very early alarm, that it would not rise much higher during the year. In this conjecture, it appears that I was much mistaken; but I have very little doubt that in any other country equally rich, yet without the system of poor laws and parish allowances, the price would never have exceeded £25 the load of wheat; and that this sum would have been sufficiently high to have excluded such a number of people from their usual consumption as to make the deficient crop, with the quantity imported, last throughout the year.

The system of poor laws and parish allowances in this country—and I will add, to their honor, the humanity and generosity of the higher and middle classes of society—naturally and necessarily altered this state of things. The poor complained to the justices that their wages would not enable them to supply their families in the single article of bread. The justices very humanely, and I am far from saying improperly, listened to their complaints, inquired what was the smallest sum on which they could support their families, at the then price of wheat, and gave an order of relief on the parish accordingly. The poor were now enabled, for a short time, to purchase nearly their usual quantity of flour; but the stock in the country was not sufficient, even with the prospect of importation, to allow of the usual distribution to all its members. The crop was consuming too fast. Every market day the demand exceeded the supply; and those whose business it was to judge on these subjects felt convinced that in a month or two the scarcity would be greater than it was at that time. Those who were able, therefore, kept back their corn. In so doing, they undoubtedly consulted their own interest; but they, as undoubtedly—whether with the intention or not is of no consequence—consulted the true interest of the state; for if they had not kept it back, too much would have been consumed, and there would have been a famine instead of a scarcity at the end of the year.

The corn, therefore, naturally rose. The poor were again distressed. Fresh complaints were made to the justices, and a further relief granted; but, like the water from the mouth of Tantalus, the corn still slipped from the grasp of the poor; and rose again so as to disable them from purchasing a sufficiency to keep their families in health. The alarm now became still greater, and more general.[1] The justices in their individual capacities were not thought competent to determine the proper modes of relief in the present crisis; a general meeting of the magistrates was called, aided by the united wisdom of other gentlemen of the county; but the result was merely the continuation and extension of the former system of relief; and, to say the truth, I hardly see what else could have been done. In some parishes this relief was given in the shape of flour; in others, which was certainly better, in money, accompanied with a recommendation not to spend the whole of it in wheaten bread, but to adopt some other kind of food. All, however, went upon the principle of inquiring what was the

---

1. I am describing what took place in the neighborhood where I then lived; and I have reason to believe that something nearly similar took place in most counties of the kingdom.

usual consumption of flour in the different families, and of enabling them to purchase nearly the same quantity that they did before the scarcity. With this additional command of money in the lower classes, and the consequent increased consumption, the number of purchasers at the then price would naturally exceed the supply. The corn would in consequence continue rising. The poor's rates in many parishes increased from four shillings in the pound to fourteen; the price of wheat necessarily kept pace with them; and before the end of the year was at near £40 a load; when probably without the operation of this cause it would not have exceeded £20 or £25.

Some of the poor would naturally make use of their additional command of money to purchase butter, cheese, bacon, pickled pork, rice, potatoes, etc. These commodities are all more limited in quantity than corn; and would, therefore, more suddenly feel the increased demand. If butter, cheese, bacon, pickled pork, and the coarser parts of meat had continued at their usual price, they would have been purchased by so many, to come in aid of an inferior kind of bread, or to give a relish and additional nourishment to their potatoes and rice, that the supply would not have been half adequate to the quantity of these articles that was wanted. These commodities, therefore, rose as naturally and as necessarily as the corn; and, according to the genuine principles of fair trade, their price was fixed at that sum which only such a number could afford to give, as would enable the supply to answer the demand.

To fix upon this sum is the great object of every dealer and speculator in every commodity whatever, and about which he must, of course, exercise his private judgment. A reflecting mind, far from being astonished that there are now and then errors in speculation, must feel much greater astonishment that there are so few; and that the supplies of a large nation, whether plentiful or scanty, should be distributed so equally throughout the year. Most happily for society, individual interest is, in these cases, so closely and intimately interwoven with the public interest that one cannot gain or lose without a gain or loss to the other. The man who refuses to send his corn to market when it is at £20 a load, because he thinks that in two months time it will be at £30, if he be right in his judgment and succeed in his speculation, is a positive and decided benefactor to the state, because he keeps his supply to that period when the state is much more in want of it; and if he and some others did not keep it back in that manner, instead of its being £30 in two months, it would be £40 or £50.

If he be wrong in his speculation, he loses perhaps very considerably himself, and the state suffers a little; because, had he brought his corn to market at £20, the price would have fallen sooner, and the event showed that there was corn enough in the country to allow of it; but the slight evil that the state suffers in this case is almost wholly compensated by the glut in the market, when the corn is brought out, which makes the price fall below what it would have been otherwise.

I am far from saying that there can be no such thing as monopoly, and the other hard words that have been so much talked of. In a commodity of a confined nature, within the purchase of two or three large capitals, or of a company of merchants, we all know that it has often existed; and, in a very few instances, the article may have been in part destroyed to enhance the price, as the Dutch Company destroyed the nutmeg trees in their spice islands; but in an article which is in so many hands as corn is, in this country, monopoly—to any pernicious extent—may safely be pronounced impossible. Where are the capitals, or where is the company of merchants rich enough to buy such a quantity of corn, as would make it answer to them to destroy, or—which is the same thing—not to sell a great part of it? As they could not, by the greatest of exertions, purchase one-fourth of all the corn in the country, it is evident that, if any considerable part of their stock remained unsold, they would have enriched all the other dealers in corn at their own expense, and would not have gained half so much in proportion to their capital as the rest of the farmers and cornfactors. If on the contrary all their stock sold, it would be a proof that the speculation had been just, and that the country had really benefited by it.

It seems now to be universally agreed that the stock of old corn remaining on hand at the beginning of the harvest this year was unusually small, notwithstanding that the harvest came on nearly a month sooner than could have been expected in the beginning of June. This is a clear, decided, and unanswerable proof that there had been no speculations in corn that were prejudicial to the country. All that the large farmers and cornfactors had done was to raise the corn to that price which excluded a sufficient number from their usual consumption, to enable the supply to last throughout the year. This price, however, has been most essentially and powerfully affected by the ability that has been given to the laboring poor, by means of parish allowances, of continuing to purchase wheat notwithstanding its extraordinary rise; and this ability must necessarily prevent the price of corn from falling very materially, till there is an actual glut in the market; for, while the whole stock will go off at £30 a load, it cannot, on any regular principle of trade, sink lower. I was in very great hopes, just before the harvest, that such a glut was about to take place; but it is now to be feared, from the nature of the present crop, that no such happy event can be hoped for during the year.

I do not know whether I have convinced my reader that the cause which I have assigned of the present extraordinary price of provisions is adequate to the effect; but I certainly feel most strongly convinced of it myself; and I cannot but believe that, if he differ from me, it can only be in degree, and from thinking that the principle of parish allowances has not yet been carried far enough to produce any material effect. With regard to the principle itself, if it were really carried into execution, it appears to me capable almost of mathematical demonstration: that, granting a real scarcity of one-fourth, which could not be remedied by importation, it is adequate to the effecting any height of price that the proportion of the circulating medium to the quantity of corn daily consumed would admit.

QUESTIONS

1. When Malthus argues that the price of corn rose because of the parish allowance, is he contradicting his theory of population growth from *An Essay on the Principle of Population*?

No

2. If Malthus recognizes the role of the market in causing the price of corn to rise out of proportion to the degree of scarcity, why does he blame the parish allowance for causing the price to rise?

there is a greater money supply

3. Why does Malthus argue that, in times of food scarcity, market demand should be made equal to supply by allowing prices to rise beyond the purchasing power of the poorest members of society?

rise in price will result in price in ... rise in ... as demand drops.

4. According to Malthus, why will market prices be determined by the ability of the maximum number of people who can pay in times of shortage?

5. Why does Malthus claim that the middlemen who seek to profit from food scarcity are acting in "the true interest of the state"? (58)

they act as a store house when producing scarcity and as price relief when predicting abundance.

FOR FURTHER REFLECTION

1. Are you convinced by Malthus's "clear, decided, and unanswerable proof that there had been no speculations in corn that were prejudicial to the country"? *No*

2. Have scientific advances in agricultural production invalidated Malthus's theory that population growth will outstrip food production? *So far! and partly*

3. Do you agree with Malthus that the interests of dealers and speculators are "intimately interwoven with the public interest"? *? yes but not always to the positive.*

J ean-Baptiste Say (1767–1832) was a French economist and follower of Adam Smith, often credited with the insight that supply, or production, is the main driving force of the economy, rather than demand, a principle known as "Say's Law." During his lifetime, Say's reputation stood very high. Thomas Jefferson claimed that Say's *Treatise on Political Economy* (1803) was sounder and more easily understood than Smith's *Wealth of Nations*.

Say was born in Lyon, France, into a family of merchants, who had hopes that Say would join the family business. To develop his business skills, he spent two years in England, working for an insurance company. During this time, he learned English and read *The Wealth of Nations*. Later in life, his command of English allowed him to befriend and correspond with the economists Thomas Malthus and David Ricardo. After returning to France, he worked for a time for a life insurance company. However, Say's career was disrupted by the French Revolution, during which he worked as a writer, editor, soldier, and eventually a finance minister, serving under Napoleon as a member of the Tribunate from 1799 to 1806. It was during this time that he wrote the first edition of his *Treatise*. His political career came to an end, however, when Napoleon dismissed him over his refusal to amend his *Treatise* to reflect Napoleon's economic policies. After retiring to private life, Say spent several years as an entrepreneur—a term he coined—founding a successful spinning mill employing some five hundred workers and the latest English technology. He sold the business in 1813. After Napoleon's fall in 1815, he became a professor, ending his career with an appointment to a chair in political economy at the Collège de France.

Say's *Treatise*, from which the following selection is taken, was soon translated into English and quickly became a standard text on the subject in the United States, remaining so for many years. Say's contributions to economics broke new ground in a number of areas, emphasizing such subjects as entrepreneurship, the theory that the value of goods is based on their usefulness to the purchaser and not on the resources that went into producing them, and the importance in economic thinking of empirical observation and experience as opposed to abstract theorizing.

Of the Demand or Market for Products

I t is common to hear adventurers in the different channels of industry assert that their difficulty lies not in production, but in the disposal of commodities; that products would always be abundant, if there were but a ready demand, or market for them. When the demand for their commodities is slow, difficult, and productive of little advantage, they pronounce money to be scarce; the grand object of their desire is a consumption brisk enough to quicken sales and keep up prices. But ask them what peculiar causes and circumstances facilitate the demand for their products, and you will soon perceive that most of them have extremely vague notions of these matters; that their observation of facts is imperfect, and their explanation still more so; that they treat doubtful points as matter of certainty, often pray for what is directly opposite to their interests, and importunately solicit from authority a protection of the most mischievous tendency.

To enable us to form clear and correct practical notions in regard to markets for the products of industry, we must carefully analyze the best established and most certain facts, and apply to them the inferences we have already deduced from a similar way of proceeding; and thus perhaps we may arrive at new and important truths, that may serve to enlighten the views of the agents of industry, and to give confidence to the measures of governments anxious to afford them encouragement.

A man who applies his labor to the investing of objects with value by the creation of utility of some sort, cannot expect such a value to be appreciated and paid for, unless where other men have the means of purchasing it. Now, of what do these means consist? Of other values of other products, likewise the fruits of industry, capital, and land. Which leads us to a conclusion that may at first sight appear paradoxical, namely, that it is a production which opens a demand for products.

This selection is taken from book 1, chapter 15 of A Treatise on Political Economy.

Should a tradesman say, "I do not want other products for my woollens, I want money," there could be little difficulty in convincing him that his customers could not pay him in money, without having first procured it by the sale of some other commodities of their own. "Yonder farmer," he may be told, "will buy your woollens, if his crops be good, and will buy more or less according to their abundance or scantiness; he can buy none at all, if his crops fail altogether. Neither can you buy his wool nor his corn yourself, unless you contrive to get woollens or some other article to buy withal. You say, you only want money; I say, you want other commodities, and not money. For what, in point of fact, do you want the money? Is it not for the purchase of raw materials or stock for your trade, or victuals for your support? Wherefore, it is products that you want, and not money. The silver coin you will have received on the sale of your own products, and given in the purchase of those of other people, will the next moment execute the same office between other contracting parties, and so from one to another to infinity; just as a public vehicle successively transports objects one after another. If you cannot find a ready sale for your commodity, will you say, it is merely for want of a vehicle to transport it? For, after all, money is but the agent of the transfer of values. Its whole utility has consisted in conveying to your hands the value of the commodities, which your customer has sold, for the purpose of buying again from you; and the very next purchase you make, it will again convey to a third person the value of the products you may have sold to others. So that you will have bought, and everybody must buy, the objects of want or desire, each with the value of his respective products transformed into money for the moment only. Otherwise, how could it be possible that there should now be bought and sold in France five or six times as many commodities, as in the miserable reign of Charles VI? Is it not obvious that five or six times as many commodities must have been produced, and that they must have served to purchase one or the other?"

Thus, to say that sales are dull, owing to the scarcity of money, is to mistake the means for the cause; an error that proceeds from the circumstance, that almost all produce is in the first instance exchanged for money, before it is ultimately converted into other produce: and the commodity, which recurs so repeatedly in use, appears to vulgar apprehensions the most important of commodities, and the end and object of all transactions, whereas it is only the medium. Sales cannot be said to be dull because money is scarce, but because other products are so. There is always money enough to conduct the circulation and mutual interchange of other values, when those values really exist. Should the increase of traffic require more money to facilitate it, the want is easily supplied, and is a strong indication of prosperity—a proof that a great abundance of values has been created, which it is wished to exchange for other values. In such cases, merchants know well enough how to find substitutes for the product serving as the medium of exchange or money: and money itself soon pours in, for this reason, that all produce naturally gravitates to that place where it is most in demand. It is a good sign when the business is too great for the money; just in the same way as it is a good sign when the goods are too plentiful for the warehouses.

When a superabundant article can find no vent, the scarcity of money has so little to do with the obstruction of its sale that the sellers would gladly receive its value in goods for their own consumption at the current price of the day: they would not ask for money, or have any occasion for that product, since the only use they could make of it would be to convert it forthwith into articles of their own consumption.

This observation is applicable to all cases, where there is a supply of commodities or of services in the market. They will universally find the most extensive demand in those places, where the most of values are produced; because in no other places are the sole means of purchase created, that is, values. Money performs but a momentary function in this double exchange; and when the transaction is finally closed, it will always be found that one kind of commodity has been exchanged for another.

It is worth while to remark that a product is no sooner created than it, from that instant, affords a market for other products to the full extent of its own value. When the producer has put the finishing hand to his product, he is most anxious to sell it immediately, lest its value should diminish in his hands. Nor is he less anxious to dispose of the money he may get for it; for the value of money is also perishable. But the only way of getting rid of money is in the purchase of some product or other. Thus, the mere circumstance of the creation of one product immediately opens a vent for other products.

For this reason, a good harvest is favorable, not only to the agriculturist, but likewise to the dealers in all commodities generally. The greater the crop, the larger are the purchases of the growers. A bad harvest, on the contrary, hurts the sale of commodities at large. And so it is also with the products of manufacture and commerce. The success of one branch of commerce supplies more ample means of purchase, and consequently opens a market for the products of all the other branches; on the other hand, the stagnation of one channel of manufacture, or of commerce, is felt in all the rest.

But it may be asked, if this be so, how does it happen, that there is at times so great a glut of commodities in the market, and so much difficulty in finding a vent for them? Why cannot one of these superabundant commodities be exchanged for another? I answer that the glut of a particular commodity arises from its having outrun the total demand for it in one or two ways; either because it has been produced in excessive abundance, or because the production of other commodities has fallen short.

It is because the production of some commodities has declined, that other commodities are superabundant. To use a more hackneyed phrase, people have bought less, because they have made less profit; and they have made less profit for one or two causes; either they have found difficulties in the employment of their productive means, or these means have themselves been deficient.

It is observable, moreover, that precisely at the same time that one commodity makes a loss, another commodity is making excessive profit. And, since such profits must operate as a powerful stimulus to the cultivation of that particular kind of products, there must needs be some violent means, or some extraordinary cause, a political or natural convulsion, or the avarice or ignorance of authority, to perpetuate this scarcity on the one hand, and consequent glut on the other. No sooner is the cause of this political disease removed than the means of production feel a natural impulse toward the vacant channels, the replenishment of which restores activity to all the others. One kind of production would seldom outstrip every other, and its products be disproportionately cheapened, were production left entirely free.

Should a producer imagine, that many other classes, yielding no material products, are his customers and consumers equally with the classes that raise themselves a product of their own; as, for example, public functionaries, physicians, lawyers, churchmen, etc., and thence infer that there is a class of demand other than that of the actual producers, he would but expose the shallowness and superficiality of his ideas. A priest goes to a shop to buy a gown or a surplice; he takes the value, that is to make the purchase, in the form of money. Whence had he that money? From some tax gatherer who has taken it from a taxpayer. But whence did this latter derive it? From the value he has himself produced. This value, first produced by the taxpayer, and afterward turned into money, and given to the priest for his salary, has enabled him to make the purchase. The priest stands in the place of the producer, who might himself have laid the value of his product on his own account, in the purchase, perhaps, not of a gown or surplice, but of some other more serviceable product. The consumption of the particular product, the gown or surplice, has but supplanted that of some other product. It is quite impossible that the purchase of one product can be affected, otherwise than by the value of another.

From this important truth may be deduced the following important conclusions:

1. That in every community the more numerous are the producers, and the more various their productions, the more prompt, numerous, and extensive are the markets for those productions; and, by a natural consequence, the more profitable are they to the producers; for price rises with the demand. But this advantage is to be derived from real production

alone, and not from a forced circulation of products; for a value once created is not augmented in its passage from one hand to another, nor by being seized and expended by the government, instead of by an individual. The man that lives upon the productions of other people originates no demand for those productions; he merely puts himself in the place of the producer, to the great injury of production, as we shall presently see.

2. That each individual is interested in the general prosperity of all, and that the success of one branch of industry promotes that of all the others. In fact, whatever profession or line of business a man may devote himself to, he is the better paid and the more readily finds employment, in proportion as he sees others thriving equally around him. A man of talent that scarcely vegetates in a retrograde state of society would find a thousand ways of turning his faculties to account in a thriving community that could afford to employ and reward his ability. A merchant established in a rich and populous town, sells to a much larger amount than one who sets up in a poor district, with a population sunk in indolence and apathy. What could an active manufacturer, or an intelligent merchant, do in a small deserted and semibarbarous town in a remote corner of Poland or Westphalia? Though in no fear of a competitor, he could sell but little, because little was produced; while at Paris, Amsterdam, or London, in spite of the competition of a hundred dealers in his own line, he might do business on the largest scale. The reason is obvious: he is surrounded with people who produce largely in an infinity of ways, and who make purchases, each with his respective products, that is to say, with the money arising from the sale of what he may have produced.

This is the true source of the gains made by the townspeople out of the country people, and again by the latter out of the former; both of them have wherewith to buy more largely, the more amply they themselves produce. A city, standing in the center of a rich surrounding country, feels no want of rich and numerous customers; and, on the other hand, the vicinity of an opulent city gives additional value to the produce of the country. The division of nations into agricultural, manufacturing, and commercial, is idle enough. For the success of a people in agriculture is a stimulus to its manufacturing and commercial prosperity; and the flourishing condition of its manufacture and commerce reflects a benefit upon its agriculture also.

The position of a nation, in respect of its neighbors, is analogous to the relation of one of its provinces to the others, or of the country to the town; it has an interest in their prosperity, being sure to profit by their opulence. The government of the United States, therefore, acted most wisely, in their attempt, about the year 1802, to civilize their savage neighbors, the Creek Indians. The design was to introduce habits of industry among them, and make them producers capable of carrying on a barter trade with the States of the Union; for there is nothing to be got by deal-ing with a people that have nothing to pay. It is useful and honorable to mankind that one nation among so many should conduct itself uniformly upon liberal principles. The brilliant results of this enlightened policy will demonstrate that the systems and theories really destructive and fallacious are the exclusive and jealous maxims acted upon by the old European governments, and by them most impudently styled *practical truths*, for no other reason, as it would seem, than because they have the misfortune to put them in practice. The United States will have the honor of proving experimentally that true policy goes hand in hand with moderation and humanity.

3. From this fruitful principle, we may draw this further conclusion, that it is no injury to the internal or national industry and production to buy and import commodities from abroad; for nothing can be bought from strangers, except with native products, which find a vent in this external traffic. Should it be objected, that this foreign produce may have been bought with specie, I answer, specie is not always a native product, but must have been bought itself with the products of native industry; so that whether the foreign articles be paid for in specie or in home products, the vent for national industry is the same in both cases.

4. The same principle leads to the conclusion that the encouragement of mere consumption is no benefit to commerce; for the difficulty lies in supplying the means, not in stimulating the desire of consumption; and we have seen that production alone, furnishes those means. Thus, it is the aim of good government to stimulate production, of bad government to encourage consumption.

For the same reason that the creation of a new product is the opening of a new market for other products, the consumption or destruction of a product is the stoppage of a vent for them. This is no evil where the end of the product has been answered by its destruction, which end is the satisfying of some human want, or the creation of some new product designed for such a satisfaction. Indeed, if the nation be in a thriving condition, the gross national reproduction exceeds the gross consumption. The consumed products have fulfilled their office, as it is natural and fitting they should; the consumption, however, has opened no new market, but just the reverse.

Having once arrived at the clear conviction that the general demand for products is brisk in proportion to the activity of production, we need not trouble ourselves much to inquire toward what channel of industry production may be most advantageously directed. The products created give rise to various degrees of demand, according to the wants, the man-ners, the comparative capital, industry, and natural resources of each country; the article most in request, owing to the competition of buyers, yields the best interest of money to the capitalist, the largest profits to the adventurer, and the best wages to the laborer; and the agency of their respective services is naturally attracted by these advantages toward those particular channels.

In a community, city, province, or nation that produces abundantly, and adds every moment to the sum of its products, almost all the branches of commerce, manufacture, and generally of industry, yield handsome profits, because the demand is great, and because there is always a large quantity of products in the market, ready to bid for new productive services. And, vice versa, wherever, by reason of the blunders of the nation or its government, production is stationary, or does not keep pace with consumption, the demand gradually declines, the value of the product is less than the charges of its production; no productive exertion is properly rewarded; profits and wages decrease; the employment of capital becomes less advantageous and more hazardous; it is consumed piecemeal, not through extravagance, but through necessity, and because the sources of profit are dried up. The laboring classes experience a want of work; families before in tolerable circumstances are more cramped and confined; and those before in difficulties are left altogether destitute. Depopulation, misery, and returning barbarism occupy the place of abundance and happiness.

Such are the concomitants of declining production, which are only to be remedied by frugality, intelligence, activity, and freedom.

QUESTIONS

1. Why does Say believe that it is the availability of goods in the marketplace, not the availability of money, that determines consumer demand?

2. According to Say, what is the mechanism by which "the mere circumstance of the creation of one product immediately opens a vent for other products"? (66)

3. What kind of situation is Say referring to when he says, "The priest stands in the place of the producer?" (67)

4. What does Say mean when he claims that "each individual is interested in the general prosperity of all, and that the success of one branch of industry promotes that of all the others"? (68)

5. Why does Say maintain that "it is the aim of good government to stimulate production, of bad government to encourage consumption"? (69)

FOR FURTHER REFLECTION

1. Was Say's prediction correct, that "The United States will have the honor of proving experimentally that true policy goes hand in hand with moderation and humanity"?

2. If, as Say maintains, production and not lack of money determines demand, why are many people in today's developed economies unable to afford even basic commodities?

3. During a recession, should governments intervene to stimulate production and encourage consumption?

DAVID RICARDO

David Ricardo (1772–1823) was, after Adam Smith, one of the most important exponents of classical economics. His abstract models of economic behavior and extensive employment of mathematical formulas had a profound influence on the subsequent development of economic theory. Ricardo's work represents the trend away from viewing economics as a branch of philosophy and the movement toward economics as a mathematically-based science.

Ricardo was born in London into a Jewish family whose Spanish-Portuguese ancestors had settled in the Netherlands after they were forced out of Spain in the late fifteenth century. Ricardo's father, a successful stockbroker, moved his family to England in 1760. After two years at a Hebrew school in Amsterdam, Ricardo went to work for his father on the London Stock Exchange. When he was twenty-one, he married a young Quaker woman, as a result of which his family disinherited him. Nevertheless, he went on to amass a very sizable fortune (estimated at more than $100 million in today's money) by, among other things, helping the British government finance its wars with Napoleon.

After reading of *The Wealth of Nations* in 1799, Ricardo became very interested in economic theory, and in 1810 he published *The High Price of Bullion*. In it, he argued that the inflation then raging was caused by the Bank of England printing too many bank notes. A controversy ensued, eventually causing the Bank of England to reform its policies. It also brought Ricardo the friendship of such notable thinkers as Jeremy Bentham, Thomas Malthus, and James Mill, the father of John Stuart Mill. Retiring from business shortly before Napoleon's defeat to devote himself to writing, Ricardo published *On the Principles of Political Economy and Taxation* (1817) from which the following selection is taken. In 1819, he entered the House of Commons, where he was an effective advocate for free trade.

Ricardo was centrally important in originating several ideas that became fundamental in economic theory, including the law of diminishing returns, the law of comparative advantage, and the labor theory of value. The latter formed the basis for Karl Marx's analysis of an inevitable class struggle under capitalism.

On Machinery

n the present chapter I shall enter into some inquiry respecting the
influence of machinery on the interests of the different classes of society,
a subject of great importance, and one which appears never to have been
investigated in a manner to lead to any certain or satisfactory results. It is
more incumbent on me to declare my opinion on this question, because
they have, on further reflection, undergone a considerable change; and
although I am not aware that I have ever published anything respecting
machinery which it is necessary for me to retract, yet I have in other ways
given my support to doctrines which I now think erroneous; it, therefore,
becomes a duty in me to submit my present views to examination, with
my reasons for entertaining them.

Ever since I first turned my attention to questions of political economy, I have been of opinion that such an application of machinery to any
branch of production, as should have the effect of saving labor, was a general good, accompanied only with that portion of inconvenience which in
most cases attends the removal of capital and labor from one employment
to another. It appeared to me that provided the landlords had the same
money rents, they would be benefited by the reduction in the prices of
some of the commodities on which those rents were expended, and which
reduction of price could not fail to be the consequence of the employment
of machinery. The capitalist, I thought, was eventually benefited precisely
in the same manner. He, indeed, who made the discovery of the machine,
or who first usefully applied it, would enjoy an additional advantage, by
making great profits for a time; but, in proportion as the machine came
into general use, the price of the commodity produced, would, from the
effects of competition, sink to its cost of production, when the capitalist
would get the same money profits as before, and he would only participate in the general advantage, as a consumer, by being enabled, with the
same money revenue, to command an additional quantity of comforts and

This selection is taken from chapter 31 of On the Principles of Political Economy and Taxation.

enjoyments. The class of laborers also, I thought, was equally benefited by the use of machinery, as they would have the means of buying more commodities with the same money wages, and I thought that no reduction of wages would take place, because the capitalist would have the power of demanding and employing the same quantity of labor as before, although he might be under the necessity of employing it in the production of a new, or at any rate, of a different commodity. If, by improved machinery, with the employment of the same quantity of labor, the quantity of stockings could be quadrupled, and the demand for stockings were only doubled, some laborers would necessarily be discharged from the stocking trade; but as the capital which employed them was still in being, and as it was the interest of those who had it to employ it productively, it appeared to me that it would be employed on the production of some other commodity, useful to the society, for which there could not fail to be a demand; for I was, and am, deeply impressed with the truth of the observation of Adam Smith, that "the desire for food is limited in every man, by the narrow capacity of the human stomach, but the desire of the conveniences, and ornaments of building, dress, equipage and household furniture, seems to have no limit or certain boundary." As, then, it appeared to me that there would be the same demand for labor as before, and that wages would be no lower, I thought that the laboring class would, equally with the other classes, participate in the advantage, from the general cheapness of commodities arising from the use of machinery.

These were my opinions, and they continue unaltered, as far as regards the landlord and the capitalist; but I am convinced, that the substitution of machinery for human labor, is often very injurious to the interests of the class of laborers.

My mistake arose from the supposition that whenever the net income of a society increased, its gross income would also increase; I now, however, see reason to be satisfied that the one fund, from which landlords and capitalists derive their revenue, may increase, while the other, that upon which the laboring class mainly depend, may diminish, and therefore it follows, if I am right, that the same cause which may increase the net revenue of the country may at the same time render the population redundant, and deteriorate the condition of the laborer.

A capitalist we will suppose employs a capital of the value of £20,000 and that he carries on the joint business of a farmer, and a manufacturer of necessaries. We will further suppose that £7,000 of this capital is invested in fixed capital, viz., in buildings, implements, etc., etc., and that the remaining £13,000 is employed as circulating capital in the support of labor. Let us suppose, too, that profits are 10 percent, and consequently that the capitalist's capital is every year put into its original state of efficiency, and yields a profit of £2,000.

Each year the capitalist begins his operations, by having food and necessaries in his possession of the value of £13,000, all of which he sells in the course of the year to his own workmen for that sum of money, and, during the same period, he pays them the like amount of money for wages: at the end of the year they replace in his possession food and necessaries of the value of £15,000, £2,000 of which he consumes himself, or disposes of as may best suit his pleasure and gratification. As far as these products are concerned, the gross produce for that year is £15,000, and the net produce £2,000. Suppose now that the following year the capitalist employs half his men in constructing a machine, and the other half in producing food and necessaries as usual. During that year he would pay the sum of £13,000 in wages as usual, and would sell food and necessaries to the same amount to his workmen; but what would be the case the following year?

While the machine was being made, only one-half of the usual quantity of food and necessaries would be obtained, and they would be only one-half the value of the quantity which was produced before. The machine would be worth £7,500, and the food and necessaries £7,500, and, therefore, the capital of the capitalist would be as great as before; for he would have besides these two values, his fixed capital worth £7,000, making in the whole £20,000 capital, and £2,000 profit. After deducting this latter sum for his own expenses, he would have a no greater circulating capital than £5,500 with which to carry on his subsequent operations; and, therefore, his means of employing labor would be reduced in the proportion of £13,000 to £5,500, and, consequently, all the labor which was before employed by £7,500 would become redundant.

The reduced quantity of labor which the capitalist can employ must, indeed, with the assistance of the machine, and after deductions for its repairs, produce a value equal to £7,500, it must replace the circulating capital with a profit of £2,000 on the whole capital; but if this be done, if the net income be not diminished, of what importance is it to the capitalist whether the gross income be of the value of £3,000, of £10,000, or of £15,000?

In this case, then, although the net produce will not be diminished in value, although its power of purchasing commodities may be greatly increased, the gross produce will have fallen from a value of £15,000 to a value of £7,500, and as the power of supporting a population, and employing labor, depends always on the gross produce of a nation, and not on its net produce, there will necessarily be a diminution in the demand for labor, population will become redundant, and the situation of the laboring classes will be that of distress and poverty.

As, however, the power of saving from revenue to add to capital must depend on the efficiency of the net revenue, to satisfy the wants of the capitalist, it could not fail to follow from the reduction in the price of commodities consequent on the introduction of machinery, that with the same wants he would have increased means of saving—increased facility of transferring revenue into capital. But with every increase of capital he would employ more laborers; and, therefore, a portion of the people thrown out of work in the first instance, would be subsequently employed; and if the increased production, in consequence of the employment of the machine, was so great as to afford, in the shape of net produce, as great a quantity of food and necessaries as existed before in the form of gross produce, there would be the same ability to employ the whole population, and, therefore, there would not necessarily be any redundancy of people.

All I wish to prove is that the discovery and use of machinery may be attended with a diminution of gross produce; and whenever that is the case, it will be injurious to the laboring class, as some of their number will be thrown out of employment, and population will become redundant, compared with the funds which are to employ it.

The case which I have supposed is the most simple that I could select; but it would make no difference in the result, if we supposed that the machinery was applied to the trade of any manufacturer—that of a clothier, for example, or of a cotton manufacturer. If in the trade of a clothier, less cloth would be produced after the introduction of machinery; for a part of that quantity which is disposed of for the purpose of paying a large body of workmen, would not be required by their employer. In consequence of using the machine, it would be necessary for him to reproduce a value, only equal to the value consumed, together with the profits on the whole capital. £7,500 might do this as effectually as £15,000 did before, the case differing in no respect from the former instance. It may be said, however, that the demand for cloth would be as great as before, and it may be asked, from whence would this supply come? But by whom would the cloth be demanded? By the farmers and the other producers of necessaries, who employed their capitals in producing these necessaries as a means of obtaining cloth: they gave corn and necessaries to the clothier for cloth, and he bestowed them on his workmen for the cloth which their work afforded him.

This trade would now cease; the clothier would not want the food and clothing, having fewer men to employ and having less cloth to dispose of. The farmers and others, who only produced necessaries as means to an end, could no longer obtain cloth by such an application of their capitals, and, therefore, they would either themselves employ their capitals in producing cloth, or would lend them to others, in order that the commodity really wanted might be furnished; and that for which no one had the means of paying, or for which there was no demand, might cease to be produced. This, then, leads us to the same result; the demand for labor would diminish, and the commodities necessary to the support of labor would not be produced in the same abundance.

If these views be correct, it follows:

1. That the discovery, and useful application of machinery, always leads to the increase of the net produce of the country, although it may not, and will not, after an inconsiderable interval, increase the value of that net produce.

2. That an increase of the net produce of a country is compatible with a diminution of the gross produce, and that the motives for employing machinery are always sufficient to insure its employment, if it will increase the net produce, although it may, and frequently must, diminish both the quantity of the gross produce, and its value.

3. That the opinion entertained by the laboring class, that the employment of machinery is frequently detrimental to their interests, is not founded on prejudice and error, but is conformable to the correct principles of political economy.

4. That if the improved means of production, in consequence of the use of machinery, should increase the net produce of a country in a degree so great as not to diminish the gross produce (I mean always quantity of commodities and not value), then the situation of all classes will be improved. The landlord and capitalist will benefit, not by an increase of rent and profit, but by the advantages resulting from the expenditure of the same rent, and profit, on commodities, very considerably reduced in value, while the situation of the laboring classes will also be considerably improved; first, from the increased demand for menial servants; second, from the stimulus to savings from revenue, which such an abundant net produce will afford; and third, from the low price of all articles of consumption on which their wages will be expended.

Independently of the consideration of the discovery and use of machinery, to which our attention has been just directed, the laboring class have no small interest in the manner in which the net income of the country is expended, although it should, in all cases, be expended for the gratification and enjoyments of those who are fairly entitled to it.

If a landlord, or a capitalist, expends his revenue in the manner of an ancient baron, in the support of a great number of retainers, or menial servants, he will give employment to much more labor, than if he expended it on fine clothes, or costly furniture; on carriages, on horses, or in the purchase of any other luxuries.

In both cases the net revenue would be the same, and so would be the gross revenue, but the former would be realized in different commodities. If my revenue were £10,000, the same quantity nearly of productive labor would be employed, whether I realized it in fine clothes and costly furniture, etc., etc., or in a quantity of food and clothing of the same value. If, however, I realized my revenue in the first set of commodities, no more labor would be *consequently* employed—I should enjoy my furniture and my clothes, and there would be an end of them; but if I realized my revenue in food and clothing, and my desire was to employ menial servants, all those whom I could so employ with my revenue of £10,000, or with the food and clothing which it would purchase, would be to be added to the former demand for laborers, and this addition would take place only because I chose this mode of expending my revenue. As the laborers, then, are interested in the demand for labor, they must naturally desire that as much of the revenue as possible should be diverted from expenditure on luxuries, to be expended in the support of menial servants.

In the same manner, a country engaged in war, and which is under the necessity of maintaining large fleets and armies, employs a great many more men than will be employed when the war terminates, and the annual expenses which it brings with it, cease.

If I were not called upon for a tax of £500 during the war, and which is expended on men in the situations of soldiers and sailors, I might probably expend that portion of my income on furniture, clothes, books, etc., etc., and whether it was expended in the one way or in the other, there would be the same quantity of labor employed in production; for the food and clothing of the soldier and sailor would require the same amount of industry to produce it as the more luxurious commodities; but in the case of the war, there would be the additional demand for men as soldiers and sailors; and, consequently, a war which is supported out of the revenue, and not from the capital of a country, is favorable to the increase of population.

At the termination of the war, when part of my revenue reverts to me, and is employed as before in the purchase of wine, furniture, or other luxuries, the population which it before supported, and which the war called into existence, will become redundant, and by its effect on the rest of the population, and its competition with it for employment, will sink the value of wages, and very materially deteriorate the condition of the laboring classes.

There is one other case that should be noticed of the possibility of an increase in the amount of the net revenue of a country, and even of its gross revenue, with a diminution of demand for labor, and that is when the labor of horses is substituted for that of man. If I employed one hundred men on my farm, and if I found that the food bestowed on fifty of those men could be diverted to the support of horses, and afford me a greater return of raw produce, after allowing for the interest of the capital which the purchase of the horses would absorb, it would be advantageous to me to substitute the horses for the men, and I should accordingly do so; but this would not be for the interest of the men, and unless the income I obtained, was so much increased as to enable me to employ the men as well as the horses, it is evident that the population would become redundant, and the laborers' condition would sink in the general scale. It is evident he could not, under any circumstances, be employed in agriculture; but if the produce of the land were increased by the substitution of horses for men, he might be employed in manufactures, or as a menial servant.

The statements which I have made will not, I hope, lead to the inference that machinery should not be encouraged. To elucidate the principle, I have been supposing, that improved machinery is *suddenly* discovered, and extensively used; but the truth is that these discoveries are gradual, and rather operate in determining the employment of the capital which is saved and accumulated, than in diverting capital from its actual employment.

With every increase of capital and population, food will generally rise, on account of its being more difficult to produce. The consequence of a rise of food will be a rise of wages, and every rise of wages will have a tendency to determine the saved capital in a greater proportion than before to the employment of machinery. Machinery and labor are in constant competition, and the former can frequently not be employed until labor rises.

In America and many other countries, where the food of man is easily provided, there is not nearly such great temptation to employ machinery as in England, where food is high, and costs much labor for its production. The same cause that raises labor does not raise the value of machines, and, therefore, with every augmentation of capital, a greater proportion of it is employed on machinery. The demand for labor will continue to increase with an increase of capital, but not in proportion to its increase; the ratio will necessarily be a diminishing ratio.

I have before observed, too, that the increase of net incomes, estimated in commodities, which is always the consequence of improved machinery, will lead to new savings and accumulations. These savings, it must be remembered, are annual, and must soon create a fund, much greater than the gross revenue, originally lost by the discovery of the machine, when the demand for labor will be as great as before, and the situation of the people will be still further improved by the increased savings which the increased net revenue will still enable them to make.

The employment of machinery could never be safely discouraged in a state, for if a capital is not allowed to get the greatest net revenue that the use of machinery will afford here, it will be carried abroad, and this must be a much more serious discouragement to the demand for labor, than the most extensive employment of machinery; for, while a capital is employed in this country, it must create a demand for some labor; machinery cannot be worked without the assistance of men, it cannot be made but with the contribution of their labor. By investing part of a capital in improved machinery, there will be a diminution in the progressive demand for labor; by exporting it to another country, the demand will be wholly annihilated.

The prices of commodities, too, are regulated by their cost of production. By employing improved machinery, the cost of production of commodities is reduced, and, consequently, you can afford to sell them in foreign markets at a cheaper price. If, however, you were to reject the use of machinery, while all other countries encouraged it, you would be obliged to export your money, in exchange for foreign goods, till you sunk the natural prices of your goods to the prices of other countries. In making your exchanges with those countries, you might give a commodity which cost two days' labor, here, for a commodity which cost one, abroad, and this disadvantageous exchange would be the consequence of your own act, for the commodity which you export, and which cost you two days' labor, would have cost you only one if you had not rejected the use of machinery, the services of which your neighbors had more wisely appropriated to themselves.

QUESTIONS

1. If machines result in distress and poverty for the laboring classes, why does Ricardo conclude that machinery should not be discouraged?

2. According to Ricardo, why does the power to support a population and employ labor depend on "gross produce" and not "net produce"? (76)

3. Under what conditions does Ricardo assume that "the situation of all classes will be improved" by the use of machines? (78)

4. What does Ricardo mean by the statement, "Machinery and labor are in constant competition"? (80)

5. Does Ricardo think that wages for labor should be kept as low as possible?

FOR FURTHER REFLECTION

1. If unemployment is a consequence of technological developments, should governments take measures to relieve the resulting unemployment and poverty of those affected?

2. Is a certain level of unemployment an inevitable consequence of technological change?

3. What factors should a manufacturer take into consideration in determining how much capital to invest in improved technology?

FRÉDÉRIC BASTIAT

Frédéric Bastiat (1801–1850) was a gentleman farmer, businessman, and politician who wrote a series of highly original works on political economy remarkable for their incisive wit and literary brilliance. He was born into a family of businessmen and farmers in southwestern France and raised in the thriving port city of Bayonne and on his family's country estate near Mugron. At seventeen he went to work in the family exporting business. He later inherited the family estate and was able to devote himself to scholarly pursuits. Largely self-taught in economics, Bastiat was intellectually voracious, reading widely in philosophy, history, and literature. He was also active in public affairs, holding local and regional offices before becoming a member of the National Assembly in Paris in 1948.

As a writer, Bastiat achieved renown chiefly as an advocate of free trade and a spirited defender of laissez-faire market principles. His first article, published in 1834, addressed a petition by French merchants to eliminate tariffs on agricultural products, while maintaining them on manufactured goods. Bastiat ridiculed the merchants' blatant hypocrisy in demanding free trade for others and protection for themselves. This article was followed by others vigorously attacking various kinds of taxation. In 1844 he wrote an essay carefully analyzing the deleterious effects of tariffs on both French and English trade. Despite Bastiat's lack of academic training, this essay was accepted by a prestigious journal and brought him to national attention. From then until his death, six years later, he played an important role in public life in France, founding a free-trade association, editing a free-trade newspaper, and debating the famous socialist Pierre-Joseph Proudhon. During this period, Bastiat produced his most well-known works, including *Economic Sophisms* (1845), *Economic Harmonies* (1850), and the essay "That Which Is Seen and That Which Is Not Seen" (1850). In the latter work, from which excerpts follow, Bastiat first clearly articulated the important economic concept of "opportunity cost," that is, the cost of any activity measured in terms of the value of the next best alternative not chosen.

That Which Is Seen,
and That Which Is Not Seen

I n the department of economy, an act, a habit, an institution, a law, gives birth not only to an effect, but to a series of effects. Of these effects, the first only is immediate; it manifests itself simultaneously with its cause—*it is seen*. The others unfold in succession—*they are not seen*: it is well for us, if they are *foreseen*. Between a good and a bad economist this constitutes the whole difference—the one takes account of the *visible* effect; the other takes account both of the effects which are *seen*, and also of those which it is necessary to *foresee*. Now this difference is enormous, for it almost always happens that when the immediate consequence is favorable, the ultimate consequences are fatal, *and the converse*. Hence it follows that the bad economist pursues a small present good, which will be followed by a great evil to come, while the true economist pursues a great good to come, at the risk of a small present evil.

In fact, it is the same in the science of health, arts, and in that of morals. It often happens, that the sweeter the first fruit of a habit is, the more bitter are the consequences. Take, for example, debauchery, idleness, prodigality. When, therefore, a man, absorbed in the effect which *is seen*, has not yet learned to discern those which are not seen, he gives way to fatal habits, not only by inclination, but by calculation.

This explains the fatally grievous condition of mankind. Ignorance surrounds its cradle: then its actions are determined by their first consequences, the only ones which, in its first stage, it can see. It is only in the long run that it learns to take account of the others. It has to learn this lesson from two very different masters—experience and foresight. Experience teaches effectually, but brutally. It makes us acquainted with all the effects of an action, by causing us to feel them; and we cannot fail to finish by knowing that fire burns, if we have burned ourselves. For this rough teacher, I should like, if possible, to substitute a more gentle one. I mean foresight. For this purpose I shall examine the consequences of certain economical phenomena, by placing in opposition to each other those *which are seen*, and those *which are not seen*.

The Broken Window

Have you ever witnessed the anger of the good shopkeeper, James B., when his careless son happened to break a square of glass? If you have been present at such a scene, you will most assuredly bear witness to the fact, that every one of the spectators, were there even thirty of them, by common consent apparently, offered the unfortunate owner this invariable consolation—"It is an ill wind that blows nobody good. Everybody must live, and what would become of the glaziers if panes of glass were never broken?"

Now, this form of condolence contains an entire theory, which it will be well to show up in this simple case, seeing that it is precisely the same as that which, unhappily, regulates the greater part of our economical institutions.

Suppose it cost six francs to repair the damage, and you say that the accident brings six francs to the glazier's trade—that it encourages that trade to the amount of six francs—I grant it; I have not a word to say against it; you reason justly. The glazier comes, performs his task, receives his six francs, rubs his hands, and, in his heart, blesses the careless child. All this is *that which is seen*.

But if, on the other hand, you come to the conclusion, as is too often the case, that it is a good thing to break windows, that it causes money to circulate, and that the encouragement of industry in general will be the result of it, you will oblige me to call out, "Stop there! your theory is confined to that *which is seen*; it takes no account of that *which is not seen*."

It is not seen that as our shopkeeper has spent six francs upon one thing, he cannot spend them upon another. *It is not seen* that if he had not had a window to replace, he would, perhaps, have replaced his old shoes, or added another book to his library. In short, he would have employed his six francs in some way, which this accident has prevented.

Let us take a view of industry in general, as affected by this circumstance. The window being broken, the glazier's trade is encouraged to the amount of six francs; *this is that which is seen*.

If the window had not been broken, the shoemaker's trade (or some other) would have been encouraged to the amount of six francs; this is *that which is not seen*.

And if *that which is not seen* is taken into consideration, because it is a negative fact, as well as that which is seen, because it is a positive fact, it will be understood that neither industry *in general*, nor the sum total of *national labor*, is affected, whether windows are broken or not.

Now let us consider James B. himself. In the former supposition, that of the window being broken, he spends six francs, and has neither more nor less than he had before, the enjoyment of a window.

In the second, where we suppose the window not to have been broken, he would have spent six francs in shoes, and would have had at the same time the enjoyment of a pair of shoes and of a window.

Now, as James B. forms a part of society, we must come to the conclusion that, taking it altogether and making an estimate of its enjoyments and its labors, it has lost the value of the broken window.

Whence we arrive at this unexpected conclusion: "Society loses the value of things which are uselessly destroyed;" and we must assent to a maxim which will make the hair of protectionists stand on end—to break, to spoil, to waste is not to encourage national labor; or, more briefly, "destruction is not profit."

What will you say, *Moniteur Industriel*—what will you say, disciples of good M. F. Chamans, who has calculated with so much precision how much trade would gain by the burning of Paris, from the number of houses it would be necessary to rebuild?

I am sorry to disturb these ingenious calculations, as far as their spirit has been introduced into our legislation; but I beg him to begin them again, by taking into the account *that which is not seen*, and placing it alongside of *that which is seen*.

The reader must take care to remember that there are not two persons only, but three concerned in the little scene which I have submitted to his attention. One of them, James B., represents the consumer, reduced, by an act of destruction, to one enjoyment instead of two. Another, under the title of the glazier, shows us the producer, whose trade is encouraged by the accident. The third is the shoemaker (or some other tradesman), whose labor suffers proportionably by the same cause. It is this third person who is always kept in the shade, and who, personating *that which is not seen*, is a necessary element of the problem. It is he who shows us how absurd it is to think we see a profit in an act of destruction. It is he who will soon teach us that it is not less absurd to see a profit in a restriction, which is, after all, nothing else than a partial destruction. Therefore, if you will only go to the root of all the arguments which are adduced in its favor, all you will find will be the paraphrase of this vulgar saying—*What would become of the glaziers, if nobody ever broke windows?* . . .

Taxes

Have you never chanced to hear it said, "There is no better investment than taxes. Only see what a number of families it maintains, and consider how it reacts upon industry; it is an inexhaustible stream, it is life itself."

In order to combat this doctrine, I must refer to my preceding refutation. Political economy knew well enough that its arguments were not so amusing that it could be said of them, *repetitions please*. It has, therefore, turned the proverb to its own use, well convinced that, in its mouth, *repetitions teach*.

The advantages which officials advocate are *those which are seen*. The benefit which accrues to the providers *is still that which is seen*. This blinds all eyes.

But the disadvantages which the taxpayers have to get rid of are *those which are not seen*. And the injury which results from it to the providers, is still that *which is not seen*, although this ought to be self-evident.

When an official spends for his own profit an extra hundred sous, it implies that a taxpayer spends for his profit a hundred sous less. But the expense of the official *is seen*, because the act is performed, while that of the taxpayer *is not seen*, because, alas! he is prevented from performing it.

You compare the nation, perhaps, to a parched tract of land, and the tax to a fertilizing rain. Be it so. But you ought also to ask yourself where the sources of this rain are, and whether it is not the tax itself that draws away the moisture from the ground and dries it up.

Again, you ought to ask yourself whether it is possible that the soil can receive as much of this precious water by rain as it loses by evaporation.

There is one thing very certain, that when James B. counts out a hundred sous for the tax gatherer, he receives nothing in return. Afterward, when an official spends these hundred sous, and returns them to James B., it is for an equal value in corn or labor. The final result is a loss to James B. of five francs.

It is very true that often, perhaps very often, the official performs for James B. an equivalent service. In this case there is no loss on either side; there is merely an exchange. Therefore, my arguments do not at all apply to useful functionaries. All I say is: if you wish to create an office, prove its utility. Show that its value to James B., by the services which it performs for him, is equal to what it costs him. But, apart from this intrinsic utility, do not bring forward as an argument the benefit which it confers upon the official, his family, and his providers; do not assert that it encourages labor.

When James B. gives a hundred pence to a government officer for a really useful service, it is exactly the same as when he gives a hundred sous to a shoemaker for a pair of shoes.

But when James B. gives a hundred sous to a government officer, and receives nothing for them unless it be annoyances, he might as well give them to a thief. It is nonsense to say that the government officer will spend these hundred sous to the great profit of *national labor*; the thief would do the same; and so would James B., if he had not been stopped on the road by the extralegal parasite, nor by the lawful sponger.

Let us accustom ourselves, then, to avoid judging of things by *what is seen* only, but to judge of them by *that which is not seen.*

Last year I was on the Committee of Finance, for under the constituency the members of the opposition were not systematically excluded from all the commissions: in that the constituency acted wisely. We have heard M. Thiers say, "I have passed my life in opposing the legitimist party, and the priest party. Since the common danger has brought us together, now that I associate with them and know them, and now that we speak face to face, I have found out that they are not the monsters I used to imagine them."

Yes, distrust is exaggerated, hatred is fostered among parties who never mix; and if the majority would allow the minority to be present at the commissions, it would perhaps be discovered that the ideas of the different sides are not so far removed from each other, and, above all, that their intentions are not so perverse as is supposed. However, last year I was on the Committee of Finance. Every time that one of our colleagues spoke of fixing at a moderate figure the maintenance of the president of the republic, that of the ministers, and of the ambassadors, it was answered—

"For the good of the service, it is necessary to surround certain offices with splendor and dignity, as a means of attracting men of merit to them. A vast number of unfortunate persons apply to the president of the republic, and it would be placing him in a very painful position to oblige him to be constantly refusing them. A certain style in the ministerial saloons is a part of the machinery of constitutional governments."

Although such arguments may be controverted, they certainly deserve a serious examination. They are based upon the public interest, whether rightly estimated or not; and as far as I am concerned, I have much more respect for them than many of our Catos have, who are actuated by a narrow spirit of parsimony or of jealousy.

But what revolts the economical part of my conscience, and makes me blush for the intellectual resources of my country, is when this absurd relic of feudalism is brought forward, which it constantly is, and it is favorably received too—

"Besides, the luxury of great government officers encourages the arts, industry, and labor. The head of the state and his ministers cannot give banquets and soirées without causing life to circulate through all the veins of the social body. To reduce their means, would starve Parisian industry, and consequently that of the whole nation."

I must beg you, gentlemen, to pay some little regard to arithmetic, at least; and not to say before the National Assembly in France, lest to its shame it should agree with you, that an addition gives a different sum, according to whether it is added up from the bottom to the top, or from the top to the bottom of the column.

For instance, I want to agree with a drainer to make a trench in my field for a hundred sous. Just as we have concluded our arrangement, the tax gatherer comes, takes my hundred sous, and sends them to the minister of the Interior; my bargain is at end, but the minister will have another dish added to his table. Upon what ground will you dare to affirm that this official expense helps the national industry? Do you not see, that in this there is only a reversing of satisfaction and labor? A minister has his table better covered, it is true, but it is just as true that an agriculturist has his field worse drained. A Parisian tavern keeper has gained a hundred sous, I grant you; but then you must grant me that a drainer has been prevented from gaining five francs. It all comes to this—that the official and the tavern keeper being satisfied, is *that which is seen*; the field undrained, and the drainer deprived of his job, is *that which is not seen*. Dear me! how much trouble there is in proving that two and two make four; and if you succeed in proving it, it is said, "The thing is so plain it is quite tiresome," and they vote as if you had proved nothing at all. . . .

Public Works

Nothing is more natural than that a nation, after having assured itself than an enterprise will benefit the community, should have it executed by means of a general assessment. But I lose patience, I confess, when I hear this economic blunder advanced in support of such a project—"Besides, it will be a means of creating labor for the workmen."

The state opens a road, builds a palace, straightens a street, cuts a canal; and so gives work to certain workmen—*this is what is seen*: but it deprives certain other workmen of work, and this is what *is not seen*.

The road is begun. A thousand workmen come every morning, leave every evening, and take their wages—this is certain. If the road had not been decreed, if the supplies had not been voted, these good people would have had neither work nor salary there; this also is certain.

But is this all? Does not the operation, as a whole, contain something else? At the moment when M. Dupin pronounces the emphatic words, "The Assembly has adopted," do the millions descend miraculously on a moonbeam into the coffers of MM. Fould and Bineau? In order that the evolution may be complete, as it is said, must not the state organize the receipts as well as the expenditure? Must it not set its tax gatherers and taxpayers to work, the former to gather, and the latter to pay?

Study the question, now, in both its elements. While you state the destination given by the state to the millions voted, do not neglect to state also the destination which the taxpayer would have given, but cannot now give, to the same. Then you will understand that a public enterprise is a coin with two sides. Upon one is engraved a laborer at work, with this device, *that which is seen*; on the other is a laborer out of work, with the device, *that which is not seen*.

The sophism which this work is intended to refute is the more dangerous when applied to public works, inasmuch as it serves to justify the most wanton enterprises and extravagance. When a railroad or a bridge are of real utility, it is sufficient to mention this utility. But if it does not exist, what do they do? Recourse is had to this mystification: "We must find work for the workmen."

Accordingly, orders are given that the drains in the Champ de Mars be made and unmade. The great Napoleon, it is said, thought he was doing a very philanthropic work by causing ditches to be made and then filled up. He said, therefore, "What signifies the result? All we want is to see wealth spread among the laboring classes."

But let us go to the root of the matter. We are deceived by money. To demand the cooperation of all the citizens in a common work, in the form of money, is in reality to demand a concurrence in kind; for every one procures, by his own labor, the sum to which he is taxed. Now, if all the citizens were to be called together, and made to execute, in conjunction, a work useful to all, this would be easily understood; their reward would be found in the results of the work itself.

But after having called them together, if you force them to make roads which no one will pass through, palaces which no one will inhabit, and this under the pretext of finding them work, it would be absurd, and they would have a right to argue, "With this labor we have nothing to do; we prefer working on our own account."

A proceeding which consists in making the citizens cooperate in giving money but not labor, does not, in any way, alter the general results. The only thing is, that the loss would react upon all parties. By the former, those whom the state employs, escape their part of the loss, by adding it to that which their fellow citizens have already suffered.

There is an article in our constitution which says, "Society favors and encourages the development of labor—by the establishment of public works, by the state, the departments, and the parishes, as a means of employing persons who are in want of work."

As a temporary measure, on any emergency, during a hard winter, this interference with the taxpayers may have its use. It acts in the same way as securities. It adds nothing either to labor or to wages, but it takes labor and wages from ordinary times to give them, at a loss it is true, to times of difficulty.

As a permanent, general, systematic measure, it is nothing else than a ruinous mystification, an impossibility, that shows a little excited labor *which is seen*, and hides a great deal of prevented labor *which is not seen*.

The Intermediates

Society is the total of the forced or voluntary services which men perform for each other; that is to say, of *public services* and *private services*.

The former, imposed and regulated by the law, which it is not always easy to change, even when it is desirable, may survive with it their own usefulness, and still preserve the name of *public services*, even when they are no longer services at all, but rather *public annoyances*. The latter belong to the sphere of the will, of individual responsibility. Everyone gives and receives what he wishes, and what he can, after a debate. They have always the presumption of real utility, in exact proportion to their comparative value.

This is the reason why the former description of services so often become stationary, while the latter obey the law of progress.

While the exaggerated development of public services, by the waste of strength which it involves, fastens upon society a fatal sycophancy, it is a singular thing that several modern sects, attributing this character to free and private services, are endeavoring to transform professions into functions.

These sects violently oppose what they call intermediates. They would gladly suppress the capitalist, the banker, the speculator, the projector, the merchant, and the trader, accusing them of interposing between production and consumption, to extort from both, without giving either anything in return. Or rather, they would transfer to the state the work which they accomplish, for this work cannot be suppressed.

The sophism of the Socialists on this point is, showing to the public what it pays to the intermediates in exchange for their services, and concealing from it what is necessary to be paid to the state. Here is the usual conflict between what is before our eyes, and what is perceptible to the mind only, between *what is seen*, and *what is not seen*.

It was at the time of the scarcity, in 1847, that the Socialist schools attempted and succeeded in popularizing their fatal theory. They knew very well that the most absurd notions have always a chance with people who are suffering: *malisunda fames*.

Therefore, by the help of the fine words "trafficking in men by men, speculation on hunger, monopoly," they began to blacken commerce, and to cast a veil over its benefits.

"What can be the use," they say, "of leaving to the merchants the care of importing food from the United States and the Crimea? Why do not the state, the departments, and the towns, organize a service for provisions, and a magazine for stores? They would sell at a *return price*, and the people, poor things, would be exempted from the tribute which they pay to free, that is, to egotistical, individual, and anarchical commerce."

The tribute paid by the people to commerce, is *that which is seen*. The tribute which the people would pay to the state, or to its agents, in the Socialist system, is *what is not seen*.

In what does this pretended tribute, which the people pay to commerce, consist? In this: that two men render each other a mutual service, in all freedom, and under the pressure of competition and reduced prices.

When the hungry stomach is at Paris, and corn which can satisfy it is at Odessa, the suffering cannot cease till the corn is brought into contact with the stomach. There are three means by which this contact may be effected: (1) the famished men may go themselves and fetch the corn, (2) they may leave this task to those to whose trade it belongs, and (3) they may club together, and give the office in charge to public functionaries. Which of these three methods possesses the greatest advantages? In every time, in all countries, and the more free, enlightened, and experienced they are, men have *voluntarily* chosen the second. I confess that this is sufficient, in my opinion, to justify this choice. I cannot believe that mankind, as a whole, is deceiving itself upon a point which touches it so nearly. But let us consider the subject.

For thirty-six millions of citizens to go and fetch the corn they want from Odessa is a manifest impossibility. The first means, then, goes for nothing. The consumers cannot act for themselves. They must, of necessity, have recourse to *intermediates*, officials or agents.

But, observe, that the first of these three means would be the most natural. In reality, the hungry man has to fetch his corn. It is a task which concerns himself; a service due to himself. If another person, on whatever ground, performs this service for him, takes the task upon himself, this latter has a claim upon him for a compensation. I mean by this to say that intermediates contain in themselves the principle of remuneration.

However that may be, since we must refer to what the Socialists call a parasite, I would ask, which of the two is the most exacting parasite, the merchant or the official?

Commerce (free, of course, otherwise I could not reason upon it), commerce, I say, is led by its own interests to study the seasons, to give daily statements of the state of the crops, to receive information from every part of the globe, to foresee wants, to take precautions beforehand. It has vessels always ready, correspondents everywhere; and it is its immediate interest to buy at the lowest possible price, to economize in all the details of its operations, and to attain the greatest results by the smallest efforts. It is not the French merchants only who are occupied in procuring provisions for France in time of need, and if their interest leads them irresistibly to accomplish their task at the smallest possible cost, the competition which they create among one another leads them no less irresistibly to cause the consumers to partake of the profits of those realized savings. The corn arrives; it is to the interest of commerce to sell it as soon as possible, so as to avoid risks, to realize its funds, and begin again the first opportunity.

Directed by the comparison of prices, it distributes food over the whole surface of the country, beginning always at the highest price, that is, where the demand is the greatest. It is impossible to imagine an organization more completely calculated to meet the interest of those who are in want; and the beauty of this organization, unperceived as it is by the Socialists, results from the very fact that it is free. It is true, the consumer is obliged to reimburse commerce for the expenses of conveyance, freight, storeroom, commission, etc.; but can any system be devised, in which he who eats corn is not obliged to defray the expenses, whatever they may be, of bringing it within his reach? The remuneration for the service performed has to be paid also: but as regards its amount, this is reduced to the smallest possible sum by competition; and as regards its justice, it would be very strange if the artisans of Paris would not work for the artisans of Marseilles, when the merchants of Marseilles work for the artisans of Paris.

If, according to the Socialist invention, the state were to stand in the stead of commerce, what would happen? I should like to be informed where the saving would be to the public? Would it be in the price of purchase? Imagine the delegates of 40,000 parishes arriving at Odessa on a given day, and on the day of need; imagine the effect upon prices. Would the saving be in the expenses? Would fewer vessels be required, fewer sailors, fewer transports, fewer sloops, or would you be exempt from the payment of all these things? Would it be in the profits of the merchants? Would your officials go to Odessa for nothing? Would they travel and work on the principle of fraternity? Must they not live? Must not they be paid for their time? And do you believe that these expenses would not exceed a thousand times the 2 or 3 percent the merchant gains, at the rate at which he is ready to treat?

And then consider the difficulty of levying so many taxes, and of dividing so much food. Think of the injustice, of the abuses inseparable from such an enterprise. Think of the responsibility which would weigh upon the government.

The Socialists who have invented these follies, and who, in the days of distress, have introduced them into the minds of the masses, take to themselves literally the title of *advanced men*; and it is not without some danger that custom, that tyrant of tongues, authorizes the term, and the sentiment which it involves. *Advanced!* This supposes that these gentlemen can see further than the common people; that their only fault is that they are too much in advance of their age, and if the time is not yet come for suppressing certain free services, pretended parasites, the fault is to be attributed to the public, which is in the rear of Socialism. I say, from my soul and my conscience, the reverse is the truth; and I know not to what barbarous age we should have to go back, if we would find the level of Socialist knowledge on this subject. These modern sectarians incessantly oppose association to actual society. They overlook the fact that society, under a free regulation, is a true association, far superior to any of those which proceed from their fertile imaginations.

Let me illustrate this by an example. Before a man, when he gets up in the morning, can put on a coat, ground must have been enclosed, broken up, drained, tilled, and sown with a particular kind of plant; flocks must have been fed, and have given their wool; this wool must have been spun, woven, dyed, and converted into cloth; this cloth must have been cut, sewed, and made into a garment. And this series of operations implies a number of others; it supposes the employment of instruments for plowing, etc., sheepfolds, sheds, coal, machines, carriages, etc.

If society were not a perfectly real association, a person who wanted a coat would be reduced to the necessity of working in solitude; that is, of performing for himself the innumerable parts of this series, from the first stroke of the pickaxe to the last stitch which concludes the work. But, thanks to the sociability which is the distinguishing character of our race, these operations are distributed among a multitude of workers; and they are further subdivided, for the common good, to an extent that, as the consumption becomes more active, one single operation is able to support a new trade.

Then comes the division of the profits, which operates according to the contingent value which each has brought to the entire work. If this is not association, I should like to know what is.

Observe, that as no one of these workers has obtained the smallest particle of matter from nothingness, they are confined to performing for one another mutual services, and to helping one another in a common object, and that all may be considered, with respect to others, *intermediates*. If, for instance, in the course of the operation, the conveyance becomes important enough to occupy one person, the spinning another, the weaving another, why should the first be considered a *parasite* more than the other two? The conveyance must be made, must it not? Does not he who performs it devote to it his time and trouble? And by so doing does he not spare that of his colleagues? Do these do more or other than this for him? Are they not equally dependent for remuneration, that is, for the division of the produce, upon the law of reduced price? Is it not in all liberty, for the common good, that this separation of work takes place, and that these arrangements are entered into? What do we want with a Socialist then, who, under pretence of organizing for us, comes despotically to break up our voluntary arrangements, to check the division of labor, to substitute isolated efforts for combined ones, and to send civilization back? Is association, as I describe it here, in itself less association, because everyone enters and leaves it freely, chooses his place in it, judges and bargains for himself on his own responsibility, and brings with him the spring and warrant of personal interest? That it may deserve this name, is it necessary that a pretended reformer should come and impose upon us his plan and his will, and, as it were, to concentrate mankind in himself?

The more we examine these *advanced schools*, the more do we become convinced that there is but one thing at the root of them: ignorance proclaiming itself infallible, and claiming despotism in the name of this infallibility.

I hope the reader will excuse this digression. It may not be altogether useless, at a time when declamations, springing from St. Simonian, Phalansterian, and Icarian books, are invoking the press and the tribune, and which seriously threaten the liberty of labor and commercial transactions. . . .

Machinery

"A curse on machines! Every year, their increasing power devotes millions of workmen to pauperism, by depriving them of work, and therefore of wages and bread. A curse on machines!"

This is the cry which is raised by vulgar prejudice, and echoed in the journals.

But to curse machines is to curse the spirit of humanity!

It puzzles me to conceive how any man can feel any satisfaction in such a doctrine.

For, if true, what is its inevitable consequence? That there is no activity, prosperity, wealth, or happiness possible for any people, except for those who are stupid and inert, and to whom God has not granted the fatal gift of knowing how to think, to observe, to combine, to invent, and to obtain the greatest results with the smallest means. On the contrary, rags, mean huts, poverty, and inanition are the inevitable lot of every nation which seeks and finds in iron, fire, wind, electricity, magnetism, the laws of chemistry and mechanics, in a word, in the powers of nature, an assistance to its natural powers. We might as well say with Rousseau, "Every man that thinks is a depraved animal."

This is not all; if this doctrine is true, since all men think and invent, since all, from first to last, and at every moment of their existence, seek the cooperation of the powers of nature, and try to make the most of a little, by reducing either the work of their hands or their expenses, so as to obtain the greatest possible amount of gratification with the smallest possible amount of labor, it must follow, as a matter of course, that the whole of mankind is rushing toward its decline, by the same mental aspiration toward progress, which torments each of its members.

Hence, it ought to be made known, by statistics, that the inhabitants of Lancashire, abandoning that land of machines, seek for work in Ireland, where they are unknown; and, by history, that barbarism darkens the epochs of civilization, and that civilization shines in times of ignorance and barbarism.

There is evidently in this mass of contradictions something which revolts us, and which leads us to suspect that the problem contains within it an element of solution which has not been sufficiently disengaged.

Here is the whole mystery: behind *that which is seen* lies something *which is not seen*. I will endeavor to bring it to light. The demonstration I shall give will only be a repetition of the preceding one, for the problems are one and the same.

Men have a natural propensity to make the best bargain they can, when not prevented by an opposing force; that is, they like to obtain as much as they possibly can for their labor, whether the advantage is obtained from a *foreign producer* or a skilful *mechanical producer.*

The theoretical objection which is made to this propensity is the same in both cases. In each case it is reproached with the apparent inactivity which it causes to labor. Now, labor rendered available, not inactive, is the very thing that determines it. And, therefore, in both cases, the same practical obstacle—force—is opposed to it also.

The legislator prohibits foreign competition, and forbids mechanical competition. For what other means can exist for arresting a propensity which is natural to all men, but that of depriving them of their liberty?

In many countries, it is true, the legislator strikes at only one of these competitions, and confines himself to grumbling at the other. This only proves one thing, that is, that the legislator is inconsistent.

We need not be surprised at this. On a wrong road, inconsistency is inevitable; if it were not so, mankind would be sacrificed. A false principle never has been, and never will be, carried out to the end.

Now for our demonstration, which shall not be a long one.

James B. had two francs which he had gained by two workmen; but it occurs to him that an arrangement of ropes and weights might be made which would diminish the labor by half. Thus he obtains the same advantage, saves a franc, and discharges a workman.

He discharges a workman: *this is that which is seen.*

And seeing this only, it is said, "See how misery attends civilization; this is the way that liberty is fatal to equality. The human mind has made a conquest, and immediately a workman is cast into the gulf of pauperism. James B. may possibly employ the two workmen, but then he will give them only half their wages, for they will compete with each other, and offer themselves at the lowest price. Thus the rich are always growing richer, and the poor, poorer. Society wants remodeling." A very fine conclusion, and worthy of the preamble.

Happily, preamble and conclusion are both false, because, behind the half of the phenomenon which is seen, lies the other half which is not seen.

The franc saved by James B. is not seen, no more are the necessary effects of this saving.

Since, in consequence of his invention, James B. spends only one franc on hand labor in the pursuit of a determined advantage, another franc remains to him.

If, then, there is in the world a workman with unemployed arms, there is also in the world a capitalist with an unemployed franc. These two elements meet and combine, and it is as clear as daylight, that between the supply and demand of labor, and between the supply and demand of wages, the relation is in no way changed.

The invention and the workman paid with the first franc now perform the work which was formerly accomplished by two workmen. The second workman, paid with the second franc, realizes a new kind of work.

What is the change, then, which has taken place? An additional national advantage has been gained; in other words, the invention is a gratuitous triumph—a gratuitous profit for mankind.

From the form which I have given to my demonstration, the following inference might be drawn: "It is the capitalist who reaps all the advantage from machinery. The working class, if it suffers only temporarily, never profits by it, since, by your own showing, they displace a portion of the national labor, without diminishing it, it is true, but also without increasing it."

I do not pretend, in this slight treatise, to answer every objection; the only end I have in view is to combat a vulgar, widely spread, and dangerous prejudice. I want to prove that a new machine only causes the discharge of a certain number of hands, when the remuneration which pays them is abstracted by force. These hands, and this remuneration, would combine to produce what it was impossible to produce before the invention; whence it follows, that the final result is *an increase of advantages for equal labor.*

Who is the gainer by these additional advantages?

First, it is true, the capitalist, the inventor; the first who succeeds in using the machine; and this is the reward of his genius and his courage. In this case, as we have just seen, he effects a saving upon the expense of production, which, in whatever way it may be spent (and it always is spent), employs exactly as many hands as the machine caused to be dismissed.

But soon competition obliges him to lower his prices in proportion to the saving itself; and then it is no longer the inventor who reaps the benefit of the invention—it is the purchaser of what is produced, the consumer, the public, including the workmen; in a word, mankind.

And *that which is not seen* is, that the saving thus procured for all consumers creates a fund whence wages may be supplied, and which replaces that which the machine has exhausted.

Thus, to recur to the forementioned example, James B. obtains a profit by spending two francs in wages. Thanks to his invention, the hand labor costs him only one franc. So long as he sells the thing produced at the same price, he employs one workman less in producing this particular thing, and that is *what is seen*; but there is an additional workman employed by the franc which James B. has saved. This is *that which is not seen*.

When, by the natural progress of things, James B. is obliged to lower the price of the thing produced by one franc, then he no longer realizes a saving; then he has no longer a franc to dispose of, to procure for the national labor a new production; but then another gainer takes his place, and this gainer is mankind. Whoever buys the thing he has produced pays a franc less, and necessarily adds this saving to the fund of wages; and this, again, is *what is not seen*.

Another solution, founded upon facts, has been given of this problem of machinery.

It was said, machinery reduces the expense of production, and lowers the price of the thing produced. The reduction of the profit causes an increase of consumption, which necessitates an increase of production, and, finally, the introduction of as many workmen, or more, after the invention as were necessary before it. As a proof of this, printing, weaving, etc., are instanced.

This demonstration is not a scientific one. It would lead us to conclude that if the consumption of the particular production of which we are speaking remains stationary, or nearly so, machinery must injure labor. This is not the case.

Suppose that in a certain country all the people wore hats; if, by machinery, the price could be reduced half, it would not *necessarily follow* that the consumption would be doubled.

Would you say, that in this case a portion of the national labor had been paralyzed? Yes, according to the vulgar demonstration; but, according to mine, no; for even if not a single hat more should be bought in the country, the entire fund of wages would not be the less secure. That which failed to go to the hat-making trade would be found to have gone to the economy realized by all the consumers, and would thence serve to pay for all the labor which the machine had rendered useless, and to excite a new development of all the trades. And thus it is that things go on. I have known newspapers to cost eighty francs, now we pay forty-eight: here is a saving of thirty-two francs to the subscribers. It is not certain, or, at least, necessary, that the thirty-two francs should take the direction of the journalist trade; but it is certain, and necessary too, that if they do not take this direction they will take another. One makes use of them for taking in more newspapers; another, to get better living; another, better clothes; another, better furniture. It is thus that the trades are bound together. They form a vast whole, whose different parts communicate by secret canals; what is saved by one, profits all. It is very important for us to understand, that savings never take place at the expense of labor and wages.

Credit

In all times, but more especially of late years, attempts have been made to extend wealth by the extension of credit.

I believe it is no exaggeration to say that since the revolution of February, the Parisian presses have issued more than 10,000 pamphlets, crying up this solution of the *social problem*.

The only basis, alas! of this solution, is an optical delusion—if, indeed, an optical delusion can be called a basis at all.

The first thing done is to confuse cash with produce, then paper money with cash; and from these two confusions it is pretended that a reality can be drawn.

It is absolutely necessary in this question to forget money, coin, bills, and the other instruments by means of which productions pass from hand to hand; our business is with the productions themselves, which are the real objects of the loan; for when a farmer borrows fifty francs to buy a plow, it is not, in reality, the fifty francs which are lent to him, but the plow; and when a merchant borrows 20,000 francs to purchase a house, it is not the 20,000 francs which he owes, but the house. Money only appears for the sake of facilitating the arrangements between the parties.

Peter may not be disposed to lend his plow, but James may be willing to lend his money. What does William do in this case? He borrows money of James, and with this money he buys the plow of Peter.

But, in point of fact, no one borrows money for the sake of the money itself; money is only the medium by which to obtain possession of productions. Now, it is impossible in any country to transmit from one person to another more productions than that country contains.

Whatever may be the amount of cash and of paper which is in circulation, the whole of the borrowers cannot receive more plows, houses, tools, and supplies of raw material, than the lenders altogether can furnish; for we must take care not to forget, that every borrower supposes a lender, and that what is once borrowed implies a loan.

This granted, what advantage is there in institutions of credit? It is that they facilitate, between borrowers and lenders, the means of finding and treating with each other; but it is not in their power to cause an instantaneous increase of the things to be borrowed and lent. And yet they ought to be able to do so, if the aim of the reformers is to be attained, since they aspire to nothing less than to place plows, houses, tools, and provisions in the hands of all those who desire them.

And how do they intend to effect this?

By making the state security for the loan.

Let us try and fathom the subject, for it contains *something which is seen*, and also *something which is not seen*. We must endeavor to look at both.

We will suppose that there is but one plow in the world, and that two farmers apply for it.

Peter is the possessor of the only plow which is to be had in France; John and James wish to borrow it. John, by his honesty, his property, and good reputation, offers security. He *inspires confidence*; he has *credit*. James inspires little or no confidence. It naturally happens that Peter lends his plow to John.

But now, according to the Socialist plan, the state interferes, and says to Peter, "Lend your plow to James, I will be security for its return, and this security will be better than that of John, for he has no one to be responsible for him but himself; and I, although it is true that I have nothing, dispose of the fortune of the taxpayers, and it is with their money that, in case of need, I shall pay you the principal and interest." Consequently, Peter lends his plow to James: *this is what is seen.*

And the Socialists rub their hands, and say, "See how well our plan has answered. Thanks to the intervention of the state, poor James has a plow. He will no longer be obliged to dig the ground; he is on the road to make a fortune. It is a good thing for him, and an advantage to the nation as a whole."

Indeed, gentlemen, it is no such thing; it is no advantage to the nation, for there is something behind *which is not seen*.

It is not seen, that the plow is in the hands of James, only because it is not in those of John.

It is not seen, that if James farms instead of digging, John will be reduced to the necessity of digging instead of farming.

That, consequently, what was considered an increase of loan is nothing but a displacement of loan. Besides, *it is not seen* that this displacement implies two acts of deep injustice.

It is an injustice to John, who, after having deserved and obtained *credit* by his honesty and activity, sees himself robbed of it.

It is an injustice to the taxpayers, who are made to pay a debt which is no concern of theirs.

Will any one say that government offers the same facilities to John as it does to James? But as there is only one plow to be had, two cannot be lent. The argument always maintains that, thanks to the intervention of the state, more will be borrowed than there are things to be lent; for the plow represents here the bulk of available capitals.

It is true, I have reduced the operation to the most simple expression of it, but if you submit the most complicated government institutions of credit to the same test, you will be convinced that they can have but one result; viz., to displace credit, not to augment it. In one country, and in a given time, there is only a certain amount of capital available, and all are employed. In guaranteeing the nonpayers, the state may, indeed, increase the number of borrowers, and thus raise the rate of interest (always to the prejudice of the taxpayer), but it has no power to increase the number of lenders, and the importance of the total of the loans.

There is one conclusion, however, which I would not for the world be suspected of drawing. I say, that the law ought not to favor, artificially, the power of borrowing, but I do not say that it ought not to restrain them artificially. If, in our system of mortgage, or in any other, there be obstacles to the diffusion of the application of credit, let them be got rid of; nothing can be better or more just than this. But this is all which is consistent with liberty, and it is all that any who are worthy of the name of reformers will ask. . . .

Frugality and Luxury

It is not only in the public expenditure that *what is seen* eclipses *what is not seen*. Setting aside what relates to political economy, this phenomenon leads to false reasoning. It causes nations to consider their moral and their material interests as contradictory to each other. What can be more discouraging, or more dismal?

For instance, there is not a father of a family who does not think it his duty to teach his children order, system, the habits of carefulness, of economy, and of moderation in spending money.

There is no religion which does not thunder against pomp and luxury. This is as it should be; but, on the other hand, how frequently do we hear the following remarks:

"To hoard is to drain the veins of the people."

"The luxury of the great is the comfort of the little."

"Prodigals ruin themselves, but they enrich the state."

"It is the superfluity of the rich which makes bread for the poor."

Here, certainly, is a striking contradiction between the moral and the social idea. How many eminent spirits, after having made the assertion, repose in peace. It is a thing I never could understand, for it seems to me that nothing can be more distressing than to discover two opposite tendencies in mankind. Why, it comes to degradation at each of the extremes: economy brings it to misery; prodigality plunges it into moral degradation. Happily, these vulgar maxims exhibit economy and luxury in a false light, taking account, as they do, of those immediate consequences *which are seen*, and not of the remote ones, *which are not seen*. Let us see if we can rectify this incomplete view of the case.

Mondor and his brother Aristus, after dividing the paternal inheritance, have each an income of 50,000 francs. Mondor practices the fashionable philanthropy. He is what is called a squanderer of money. He renews his furniture several times a year; changes his equipages every month. People talk of his ingenious contrivances to bring them sooner to an end: in short, he surpasses the fast livers of Balzac and Alexander Dumas.

Thus, everybody is singing his praises. It is, "Tell us about Mondor! Mondor forever! He is the benefactor of the workman; a blessing to the people. It is true, he revels in dissipation; he splashes the passersby; his own dignity and that of human nature are lowered a little; but what of that? He does good with his fortune, if not with himself. He causes money to circulate; he always sends the tradespeople away satisfied. Is not money made round that it may roll?"

Aristus has adopted a very different plan of life. If he is not an egotist, he is, at any rate, an *individualist*, for he considers expense, seeks only moderate and reasonable enjoyments, thinks of his children's prospects, and, in fact, he *economizes*.

And what do people say of him? "What is the good of a rich fellow like him? He is a skinflint. There is something imposing, perhaps, in the simplicity of his life; and he is humane, too, and benevolent, and generous, but he *calculates*. He does not spend his income; his house is neither brilliant nor bustling. What good does he do to the paper hangers, the carriage makers, the horse dealers, and the confectioners?"

These opinions, which are fatal to morality, are founded upon what strikes the eye—the expenditure of the prodigal; and another, which is out of sight, the equal and even superior expenditure of the economist.

But things have been so admirably arranged by the divine inventor of social order, that in this, as in everything else, political economy and morality, far from clashing, agree; and the wisdom of Aristus is not only more dignified, but still more *profitable*, than the folly of Mondor. And when I say profitable, I do not mean only profitable to Aristus, or even to society in general, but more profitable to the workmen themselves—to the trade of the time.

To prove it, it is only necessary to turn the mind's eye to those hidden consequences of human actions, which the bodily eye does not see.

Yes, the prodigality of Mondor has visible effects, in every point of view. Everybody can see his landaus, his phaetons, his berlins, the delicate paintings on his ceilings, his rich carpets, the brilliant effects of his house. Everyone knows that his horses run upon the turf. The dinners which he gives at the Hotel de Paris attract the attention of the crowds on the boulevards; and it is said, "That is a generous man; far from saving his income, he is very likely breaking into his capital." This is *what is seen*.

It is not so easy to see, with regard to the interest of workers, what becomes of the income of Aristus. If we were to trace it carefully, however, we should see that the whole of it, down to the last farthing, affords work to the laborers, as certainly as the fortune of Mondor. Only there is this difference: the wanton extravagance of Mondor is doomed to be constantly decreasing, and to come to an end without fail; while the wise expenditure of Aristus will go on increasing from year to year. And if this is the case, then, most assuredly, the public interest will be in unison with morality.

Aristus spends upon himself and his household 20,000 francs a year. If that is not sufficient to content him, he does not deserve to be called a wise man. He is touched by the miseries which oppress the poorer classes; he thinks he is bound in conscience to afford them some relief, and therefore he devotes 10,000 francs to acts of benevolence. Among the merchants, the manufacturers, and the agriculturists, he has friends who are suffering under temporary difficulties; he makes himself acquainted with their situation, that he may assist them with prudence and efficiency, and to this work he devotes 10,000 francs more. Then he does not forget that he has daughters to portion, and sons for whose prospects it is his duty to provide, and therefore he considers it a duty to lay by and put out to interest 10,000 francs every year.

The following is a list of his expenses:

1. Personal expenses	20,000 francs
2. Benevolent objects	10,000 francs
3. Offices of friendship	10,000 francs
4. Saving	10,000 francs

Let us examine each of these items, and we shall see that not a single farthing escapes the national labor.

1. Personal expenses: These, as far as workpeople and tradesmen are concerned, have precisely the same effect as an equal sum spent by Mondor. This is self-evident, therefore we shall say no more about it.

2. Benevolent objects: The 10,000 francs devoted to this purpose benefit trade in an equal degree; they reach the butcher, the baker, the tailor, and the carpenter. The only thing is that the bread, the meat, and the clothing are not used by Aristus, but by those whom he has made his substitutes. Now, this simple substitution of one consumer for another in no way affects trade in general. It is all one, whether Aristus spends a crown, or desires some unfortunate person to spend it instead.

3. Offices of friendship: The friend to whom Aristus lends or gives 10,000 francs does not receive them to bury them; that would be against the hypothesis. He uses them to pay for goods, or to discharge debts. In the first case, trade is encouraged. Will any one pretend to say that it gains more by Mondor's purchase of a thoroughbred horse for 10,000 francs, than by the purchase of 10,000 francs' worth of stuffs by Aristus or his friend? For, if this sum serves to pay a debt, a third person appears, viz. the creditor, who will certainly employ them upon something in his trade, his household, or his farm. He forms another medium between Aristus and the workmen. The names only are changed, the expense remains, and also the encouragement to trade.

4. Saving: There remains now the 10,000 francs saved; and it is here, as regards the encouragement to the arts, to trade, labor, and the workmen, that Mondor appears far superior to Aristus, although, in a moral point of view, Aristus shows himself, in some degree, superior to Mondor.

I can never look at these apparent contradictions between the great laws of nature without a feeling of physical uneasiness which amounts to suffering. Were mankind reduced to the necessity of choosing between two parties, one of whom injures his interest, and the other his conscience, we should have nothing to hope from the future. Happily, this is not the case; and to see Aristus regain his economical superiority, as well as his moral superiority, it is sufficient to understand this consoling maxim, which is no less true from having a paradoxical appearance, "To save is to spend."

What is Aristus's object in saving 10,000 francs? Is it to bury them in his garden? No, certainly; he intends to increase his capital and his income; consequently, this money, instead of being employed upon his own personal gratification, is used for buying land, a house, etc., or it is placed in the hands of a merchant or a banker. Follow the progress of this money in any one of these cases, and you will be convinced that through the medium of vendors or lenders, it is encouraging labor quite as certainly as if Aristus, following the example of his brother, had exchanged it for furniture, jewels, and horses.

For when Aristus buys lands or rents for 10,000 francs, he is determined by the consideration that he does not want to spend this money. This is why you complain of him.

But, at the same time, the man who sells the land or the rent is determined by the consideration that he does want to spend the 10,000 francs in some way; so that the money is spent in any case, either by Aristus, or by others in his stead.

With respect to the working class, to the encouragement of labor, there is only one difference between the conduct of Aristus and that of Mondor. Mondor spends the money himself, and around him, and therefore the effect *is seen*. Aristus, spending it partly through intermediate parties, and at a distance, the effect is *not seen*. But, in fact, those who know how to attribute effects to their proper causes, will perceive, that *what is not seen* is as certain as *what is seen*. This is proved by the fact that in both cases the money circulates and does not lie in the iron chest of the wise man, any more than it does in that of the spendthrift. It is, therefore, false to say that economy does actual harm to trade; as described above, it is equally beneficial with luxury.

But how far superior is it, if, instead of confining our thoughts to the present moment, we let them embrace a longer period!

Ten years pass away. What is become of Mondor and his fortune, and his great popularity? Mondor is ruined. Instead of spending 60,000 francs every year in the social body, he is, perhaps, a burden to it. In any case, he is no longer the delight of shopkeepers; he is no longer the patron of the arts and of trade; he is no longer of any use to the workmen, nor are his successors, whom he has brought to want.

At the end of the same ten years, Aristus not only continues to throw his income into circulation, but he adds an increasing sum from year to year to his expenses. He enlarges the national capital, that is, the fund which supplies wages, and as it is upon the extent of this fund that the demand for hands depends, he assists in progressively increasing the remuneration of the working class; and if he dies, he leaves children whom he has taught to succeed him in this work of progress and civilization.

In a moral point of view, the superiority of frugality over luxury is indisputable. It is consoling to think that it is so in political economy, to everyone who, not confining his views to the immediate effects of phenomena, knows how to extend his investigations to their final effects.

He Who Has a Right to Work Has a Right to Profit

"Brethren, you must club together to find me work at your own price." This is the right to work; i.e., elementary Socialism of the first degree.

"Brethren, you must club together to find me work at my own price." This is the right to profit; i.e., refined Socialism, or Socialism of the second degree.

Both of these live upon such of their effects as *are seen*. They will die by means of those effects *which are not seen*.

That *which is seen* is the labor and the profit excited by social combination. *That which is not seen* is the labor and the profit to which this same combination would give rise, if it were left to the taxpayers.

In 1848, the right to labor for a moment showed two faces. This was sufficient to ruin it in public opinion.

One of these faces was called *national workshops*. The other, *forty-five centimes*. Millions of francs went daily from the Rue Rivoli to the national workshops. This was the fair side of the medal.

And this is the reverse. If millions are taken out of a cashbox, they must first have been put into it. This is why the organizers of the right to public labor apply to the taxpayers.

Now, the peasants said, "I must pay forty-five centimes; then I must deprive myself of some clothing. I cannot manure my field; I cannot repair my house."

And the country workmen said, "As our townsman deprives himself of some clothing, there will be less work for the tailor; as he does not improve his field, there will be less work for the drainer; as he does not repair his house, there will be less work for the carpenter and mason."

It was then proved that two kinds of meal cannot come out of one sack, and that the work furnished by the government was done at the expense of labor, paid for by the taxpayer. This was the death of the right to labor, which showed itself as much a chimera as an injustice. And yet, the right to profit, which is only an exaggeration of the right to labor, is still alive and flourishing.

Ought not the protectionist to blush at the part he would make society play?

He says to it, "You must give me work, and, more than that, lucrative work. I have foolishly fixed upon a trade by which I lose ten percent. If you impose a tax of twenty francs upon my countrymen, and give it to me, I shall be a gainer instead of a loser. Now, profit is my right; you owe it me." Now, any society which would listen to this sophist, burden itself with taxes to satisfy him, and not perceive that the loss to which any trade is exposed is no less a loss when others are forced to make up for it—such a society, I say, would deserve the burden inflicted upon it.

Thus we learn, by the numerous subjects which I have treated, that to be ignorant of political economy is to allow ourselves to be dazzled by the immediate effect of a phenomenon; to be acquainted with it is to embrace in thought and in forethought the whole compass of effects.

I might subject a host of other questions to the same test; but I shrink from the monotony of a constantly uniform demonstration, and I conclude by applying to political economy what Chateaubriand says of history—

"There are," he says, "two consequences in history: an immediate one, which is instantly recognized, and one in the distance, which is not at first perceived. These consequences often contradict each other; the former are the results of our own limited wisdom, the latter, those of that wisdom which endures. The providential event appears after the human event. God rises up behind men. Deny, if you will, the supreme counsel; disown its action; dispute about words; designate, by the term, force of circumstances, or reason, what the vulgar call Providence; but look to the end of an accomplished fact, and you will see that it has always produced the contrary of what was expected from it, if it was not established at first upon morality and justice."[1]

---

1. [From Frances-René Chateaubriand's posthumous memoirs.]

QUESTIONS

1. What distinction does Bastiat draw between consequences that are seen and consequences that are not seen? (85)

2. Why is Bastiat strongly opposed to the "Socialists"? (91)

3. Why does Bastiat say that the "pressure of competition and reduced prices" will relieve hunger during times of food scarcity? (92)

4. What does Bastiat mean when he calls society "a perfectly real association"? (94)

5. According to Bastiat, how does the maxim "To save is to spend" result in both "seen" and "unseen" consequences"? (104)

FOR FURTHER REFLECTION

1. If, according to Bastiat, economic behavior results in consequences that cannot immediately be seen, is it possible to measure its long-term consequences with any degree of accuracy?

2. Which public services, if any, would Bastiat think are best delivered by governments?

3. Why are moral values often attached to a belief in a particular economic theory?

John Stuart Mill (1806–1873), perhaps the most important English philosopher of the nineteenth century, is principally known for his contributions to epistemology, ethics, and political theory. Nevertheless, his *Principles of Political Economy* (2 vols.; 1848) was a masterful elaboration on the economic theories of his predecessors Adam Smith and David Ricardo and became a leading university textbook on the subject for many decades.

Mill was born in London, the son of James Mill, who was a close friend of Jeremy Bentham and Ricardo and a distinguished philosopher and political thinker in his own right. The younger Mill was the subject of an extraordinary experiment in homeschooling, made famous through the account he gave of it in his *Autobiography* (1873). Under the supervision of his father, John began to read ancient Greek at the age of three and had mastered that language and many other subjects by the time he was eight. In his early teens, he began to study political economy, reading Smith, Ricardo, and his father's works. When he was eighteen, Mill followed his father into the East India Company, where he spent most of his career. After a great struggle to come out from under the influence of his father and find his own direction in life, he embarked upon an active life as a scholar and commentator on public affairs. In addition to numerous essays on political, economic, and literary topics, he published a stream of highly influential books, including *A System of Logic* (2 vols.; 1843); *On Liberty* (1859), containing the classic defense of the liberal political philosophy of noninterference by the state in the lives of individuals; and *Utilitarianism* (1863), defending and modifying the moral philosophy originated by Bentham and his father.

Mill's *Principles of Economic Theory* reformulates and improves upon several classical concepts, such as economies of scale, and emphasizes the spontaneous efficiency of markets and the principle of laissez faire. In the following excerpts, Mill discusses the ways in which the basic operations of government—protecting the well-being of individuals and their property, levying taxes, and legislating—affect a nation's economy, for better and for worse. He then proceeds to investigate the optimal degree of "noninterference" by government in the economy.

JOHN STUART MILL

Principles of Political Economy (selection)

The Ordinary Functions of Government

1

Before we discuss the line of demarcation between the things with which government should, and those with which they should not, directly interfere, it is necessary to consider the economical effects, whether of a bad or of a good complexion, arising from the manner in which they acquit themselves of the duties which devolve on them in all societies, and which no one denies to be incumbent on them.

The first of these is the protection of person and property. There is no need to expatiate on the influence exercised over the economical interests of society by the degree of completeness with which this duty of government is performed. Insecurity of person and property is as much as to say uncertainty of the connection between all human exertion or sacrifice and the attainment of the ends for the sake of which they are undergone. It means, uncertainty whether they who sow shall reap, whether they who produce shall consume, and they who spare today shall enjoy tomorrow. It means, not only that labor and frugality are not the road to acquisition, but that violence is. When person and property are to a certain degree insecure, all the possessions of the weak are at the mercy of the strong. No one can keep what he has produced, unless he is more capable of defending it, than others who give no part of their time and exertions to useful industry are of taking it from him. The productive classes, therefore, when the insecurity surpasses a certain point, being unequal to their own protection against the predatory population, are obliged to place themselves individually in a state of dependence on some member of the predatory class, that

This selection is taken from chapters 8 and 11 of book 5 of Principles of Political Economy.

it may be his interest to shield them from all depredation except his own. In this manner, in the Middle Ages, allodial property generally became feudal, and numbers of the poorer freemen voluntarily made themselves and their posterity serfs of some military lord.

Nevertheless, in attaching to this great requisite, security of person and property, the importance which is justly due to it, we must not forget that even for economical purposes there are other things quite as indispensable, the presence of which will often make up for a very considerable degree of imperfection in the protective arrangements of government. . . . The free cities of Italy, Flanders, and the Hanseatic league were habitually in a state of such internal turbulence, varied by such destructive external wars, that person and property enjoyed very imperfect protection; yet during several centuries they increased rapidly in wealth and prosperity, brought many of the industrial arts to a high degree of advancement, carried on distant and dangerous voyages of exploration and commerce with extraordinary success, became an overmatch in power for the greatest feudal lords, and could defend themselves even against the sovereigns of Europe: because in the midst of turmoil and violence, the citizens of those towns enjoyed a certain rude freedom, under conditions of union and cooperation, which, taken together, made them a brave, energetic, and high-spirited people, and fostered a great amount of public spirit and patriotism. The prosperity of these and other free states in a lawless age shows that a certain degree of insecurity, in some combinations of circumstances, has good as well as bad effects, by making energy and practical ability the conditions of safety. Insecurity paralyzes only when it is such in nature and in degree that no energy of which mankind in general are capable affords any tolerable means of self-protection. And this is a main reason why oppression by the government, whose power is generally irresistible by any efforts that can be made by individuals, has so much more baneful an effect on the springs of national prosperity, than almost any degree of lawlessness and turbulence under free institutions. Nations have acquired some wealth, and made some progress in improvement, in states of social union so imperfect as to border on anarchy: but no countries in which the people were exposed without limit to arbitrary exactions from the officers of government ever yet continued to have industry or wealth. A few generations of such a government never fail to extinguish both. Some of the fairest, and once the most prosperous, regions of the earth, have, under the Roman and afterward under the Turkish dominion, been reduced to a desert, solely by that cause. I say solely, because they would have recovered with the utmost rapidity, as countries always do, from the devastations of war, or any other temporary calamities. Difficulties and hardships are often but an incentive to exertion: what is fatal to it, is the belief that it will not be suffered to produce its fruits.

2

Simple overtaxation by government, though a great evil, is not comparable in the economical part of its mischiefs to exactions much more moderate in amount, which either subject the contributor to the arbitrary mandate of government officers, or are so laid on as to place skill, industry, and frugality at a disadvantage. The burthen of taxation in our own country is very great, yet as everyone knows its limit, and is seldom made to pay more than he expects and calculates on, and as the modes of taxation are not of such a kind as much to impair the motives to industry and economy, the sources of prosperity are little diminished by the pressure of taxation; they may even, as some think, be increased, by the extra exertions made to compensate for the pressure of the taxes. But in the barbarous despotisms of many countries of the East, where taxation consists in fastening upon those who have succeeded in acquiring something, in order to confiscate it, unless the possessor buys its release by submitting to give some large sum as a compromise, we cannot expect to find voluntary industry, or wealth derived from any source but plunder. And even in comparatively civilized countries, bad modes of raising a revenue have had effects similar in kind, though in an inferior degree. French writers before the Revolution represented the *taille* as a main cause of the backward state of agriculture, and of the wretched condition of the rural population; not from its amount, but because, being proportioned to the visible capital of the cultivator, it gave him a motive for appearing poor, which sufficed to turn the scale in favor of indolence. The arbitrary powers also of fiscal officers, of *intendants* and *subdélégués*, were more destructive of prosperity than a far larger amount of exactions, because they destroyed security: there was a marked superiority in the condition of the *pays d'états*, which were exempt from this scourge. The universal venality ascribed (1848) to Russian functionaries must be an immense drag on the capabilities of economical improvement possessed so abundantly by the Russian empire: since the emoluments of public officers must depend on the success with which they can multiply vexations, for the purpose of being bought off by bribes.

Yet mere excess of taxation, even when not aggravated by uncertainty, is, independently of its injustice, a serious economical evil. It may be carried so far as to discourage industry by insufficiency of reward. Very long before it reaches this point it prevents or greatly checks accumulation, or causes the capital accumulated to be sent for investment to foreign countries. Taxes which fall on profits, even though that kind of income may not pay more than its just share, necessarily diminish the motive to any saving, except for investment in foreign countries where profits are higher. Holland, for example, seems to have long ago reached the practical minimum of profits: already in the last century her wealthy capitalists had a great part of their fortunes invested in the loans and joint-stock speculations of other countries: and this low rate of profit is ascribed to the heavy taxation, which had been in some measure forced on her by the circumstances of her position and history. The taxes indeed, besides their great amount, were many of them on necessaries, a kind of tax peculiarly injurious to industry and accumulation. But when the aggregate amount of taxation is very great, it is inevitable that recourse must be had for part of it to taxes of an objectionable character. And any taxes on consumption, when heavy, even if not operating on profits, have something of the same effect, by driving persons of moderate means to live abroad, often taking their capital with them. Although I by no means join with those political economists who think no state of national existence desirable in which there is not a rapid increase of wealth, I cannot overlook the many disadvantages to an independent nation from being brought prematurely to a stationary state, while the neighboring countries continue advancing.

3

The subject of protection to person and property, considered as afforded by government, ramifies widely, into a number of indirect channels. It embraces, for example, the whole subject of the perfection or inefficiency of the means provided for the ascertainment of rights and the redress of injuries. Person and property cannot be considered secure where the administration of justice is imperfect, either from defect of integrity or capacity in the tribunals, or because the delays, vexation, and expense accompanying their operation impose a heavy tax on those who appeal to them, and make it preferable to submit to any endurable amount of the evils which they are designed to remedy. In England there is no fault to be found with the administration of justice, in point of pecuniary integrity; a result which the progress of social improvement may also be supposed to have brought about in several other nations of Europe. But legal and judicial imperfections of other kinds are abundant; and, in England especially, are a large abatement from the value of the services which the government renders back to the people in return for our enormous taxation. In the first place, the incognoscibility (as Bentham termed it) of the law, and its extreme uncertainty, even to those who best know it, render a resort to the tribunals often necessary for obtaining justice, when, there being no dispute as to facts, no litigation ought to be required. In the next place, the procedure of the tribunals is so replete with delay, vexation, and expense that the price at which justice is at last obtained is an evil outweighing a very considerable amount of injustice; and the wrong side, even that which the law considers such, has many chances of gaining its point, through the abandonment of litigation by the other party for want of funds, or through a compromise in which a sacrifice is made of just rights to terminate the suit, or through some technical quirk, whereby a decision is obtained on some other ground than the merits. This last detestable incident often happens without blame to the judge, under a system of law of which a great part rests on no rational principles adapted to the present state of society, but was originally founded partly on a kind of whims and conceits, and partly on the principles and incidents of feudal tenure (which now survive only as legal fictions); and has only been very imperfectly adapted, as cases arose, to the changes which had taken place in society. Of all parts of the English legal system, the Court of Chancery, which has the best substantive law, has been incomparably the worst as to delay, vexation, and expense; and this is the only tribunal for most of the classes of cases which are in their nature the most complicated, such as cases of partnership, and the great range and variety of cases which come under the denomination of trust. The recent reforms in this court have abated the mischief, but are still far from having removed it.

Fortunately for the prosperity of England, the greater part of the mercantile law is comparatively modern, and was made by the tribunals, by the simple process of recognizing and giving force of law to the usages which, from motives of convenience, had grown up among merchants themselves: so that this part of the law, at least, was substantially made by those who were most interested in its goodness: while the defects of the tribunals have been the less practically pernicious in reference to commercial transactions, because the importance of credit, which depends on character, renders the restraints of opinion (though, as daily experience proves, an insufficient) yet a very powerful, protection against those forms of mercantile dishonesty which are generally recognized as such.

The imperfections of the law, both in its substance and in its procedure, fall heaviest upon the interests connected with what is technically called *real* property; in the general language of European jurisprudence, immoveable property. With respect to all this portion of the wealth of the community, the law fails egregiously in the protection which it undertakes to provide. It fails, first, by the uncertainty, and the maze of technicalities, which make it impossible for anyone, at however great an expense, to possess a title to land which he can positively know to be unassailable. It fails, secondly, in omitting to provide due evidence of transactions, by a proper registration of legal documents. It fails, thirdly, by creating a necessity for operose and expensive instruments and formalities (independently of fiscal burthens) on occasion of the purchase and sale, or even the lease or mortgage, of immoveable property. And, fourthly, it fails by the intolerable expense and delay of law proceedings, in almost all cases in which real property is concerned. There is no doubt that the greatest sufferers by the defects of the higher courts of civil law are the landowners. Legal expenses, either those of actual litigation, or of the preparation of legal instruments, form, I apprehend, no inconsiderable item in the annual expenditure of most persons of large landed property, and the saleable value of their land is greatly impaired, by the difficulty of giving to the buyer complete confidence in the title; independently of the legal expenses which accompany the transfer. Yet the landowners, though they have been masters of the legislation of England, to say the least since 1688, have never made a single move in the direction of law reform, and have been strenuous opponents of some of the improvements of which they would more particularly reap the benefit; especially that great one of a registration of contracts affecting land, which when proposed by a commission of eminent real property lawyers, and introduced into the House of Commons by Lord Campbell, was so offensive to the general body of landlords, and was rejected by so large a majority, as to have long discouraged any repetition of the attempt. This irrational hostility to improvement, in a case in which their own interest would be the most benefited by it, must be ascribed to an intense timidity on the subject of their titles, generated by the defects of the very law which they refuse to alter; and to a conscious ignorance, and incapacity of judgment, on all legal subjects, which makes them helplessly defer to the opinion of their professional advisers, heedless of the fact that every imperfection of the law, in proportion as it is burthensome to them, brings gain to the lawyer.

Insofar as the defects of legal arrangements are a mere burthen on the landowner, they do not much affect the sources of production; but the uncertainty of the title under which land is held must often act as a great discouragement to the expenditure of capital in its improvement; and the expense of making transfers operates to prevent land from coming into the hands of those who would use it to most advantage; often amounting, in the case of small purchases, to more than the price of the land, and tantamount, therefore, to a prohibition of the purchase and sale of land in small portions, unless in exceptional circumstances. Such purchases, however, are almost everywhere extremely desirable, there being hardly any country in which landed property is not either too much or too little subdivided, requiring either that great estates should be broken down, or that small ones should be bought up and consolidated. To make land as easily transferable as stock would be one of the greatest economical improvements which could be bestowed on a country; and has been shown, again and again, to have no insuperable difficulty attending it.

Besides the excellences or defects that belong to the law and judicature of a country as a system of arrangements for attaining direct practical ends, much also depends, even in an economical point of view, upon the moral influences of the law. Enough has been said in a former place on the degree in which both the industrial and all other combined operations of mankind depend for efficiency on their being able to rely on one another for probity and fidelity to engagements; from which we see how greatly even the economical prosperity of a country is liable to be affected by anything in its institutions by which either integrity and trustworthiness, or the contrary qualities, are encouraged. The law everywhere ostensibly favors at least pecuniary honesty and the faith of contracts; but if it affords facilities for evading those obligations, by trick and chicanery, or by the unscrupulous use of riches in instituting unjust or resisting just litigation; if there are ways and means by which persons may attain the ends of roguery, under the apparent sanction of the law; to that extent the law is demoralizing, even in regard to pecuniary integrity. And such cases are, unfortunately, frequent under the English system. If, again, the law, by a misplaced indulgence, protects idleness or prodigality against their natural consequences, or dismisses crime with inadequate penalties, the effect, both on the prudential and on the social virtues, is unfavorable. When the law, by its own dispensations and injunctions, establishes injustice between individual and individual; as all laws do which recognize any form of slavery; as the laws of all countries do, though not all in the same degree, in respect to the family relations; and as the laws of many countries do, though in still more unequal degrees, as between rich and poor; the effect on the moral sentiments of the people is still more disastrous. But these subjects introduce considerations so much larger and deeper than those of political economy that I only advert to them in order not to pass wholly unnoticed, things superior in importance to those of which I treat.

The Grounds and Limits of Laissez-Faire

1

We have now reached the last part of our undertaking—the discussion, so far as suited to this treatise (that is, so far as it is a question of principle, not detail) of the limits of the province of government: the question, to what objects governmental intervention in the affairs of society may or should extend, over and above those which necessarily appertain to it. No subject has been more keenly contested in the present age: the contest, however, has chiefly taken place round certain select points, with only flying excursions into the rest of the field. Those indeed who have discussed any particular question of government interference, such as state education (spiritual or secular), regulation of hours of labor, a public provision for the poor, etc., have often dealt largely in general arguments, far outstretching the special application made of them, and have shown a sufficiently strong bias either in favor of letting things alone, or in favor of meddling; but have seldom declared, or apparently decided in their own minds, how far they would carry either principle. The supporters of interference have been content with asserting a general right and duty on the part of government to intervene, wherever its intervention would be useful: and when those who have been called the laissez-faire school have attempted any definite limitation of the province of government, they have usually restricted it to the protection of person and property against force and fraud; a definition to which neither they nor any one else can deliberately adhere, since it excludes, as has been shown in a preceding chapter, some of the most indispensable and unanimously recognized of the duties of government.

Without professing entirely to supply this deficiency of a general theory, on a question which does not, as I conceive, admit of any universal solution, I shall attempt to afford some little aid toward the resolution of this class of questions as they arise, by examining, in the most general point of view in which the subject can be considered, what are the advantages, and what the evils or inconveniences, of government interference.

We must set out by distinguishing between two kinds of intervention by the government, which, though they may relate to the same subject, differ widely in their nature and effects, and require, for their justification, motives of a very different degree of urgency. The intervention may extend to controlling the free agency of individuals. Government may interdict all persons from doing certain things; or from doing them without its authorization; or may prescribe to them certain things to be done, or a certain manner of doing things which it is left optional with them to do or to abstain from. This is the *authoritative* interference of government. There is another kind of intervention which is not authoritative: when a government, instead of issuing a command and enforcing it by penalties, adopts the course so seldom resorted to by governments, and of which such important use might be made, that of giving advice and promulgating information; or when, leaving individuals free to use their own means of pursuing any object of general interest, the government, not meddling with them, but not trusting the object solely to their care, establishes, side by side with their arrangements, an agency of its own for a like purpose. Thus, it is one thing to maintain a church establishment, and another to refuse toleration to other religions, or to persons professing no religion. It is one thing to provide schools or colleges, and another to require that no person shall act as an instructor of youth without a government licence. There might be a national bank, or a government manufactory, without any monopoly against private banks and manufactories. There might be a post office, without penalties against the conveyance of letters by any other means. There may be a corps of government engineers for civil purposes, while the profession of a civil engineer is free to be adopted by every one. There may be public hospitals, without any restriction upon private medical or surgical practice.

2

It is evident, even at first sight, that the authoritative form of government intervention has a much more limited sphere of legitimate action than the other. It requires a much stronger necessity to justify it in any case; while there are large departments of human life from which it must be unreservedly and imperiously excluded. Whatever theory we adopt respecting the foundation of the social union, and under whatever political institutions we live, there is a circle around every individual human being which no government, be it that of one, of a few, or of the many, ought to be permitted to overstep: there is a part of the life of every person who has come to years of discretion, within which the individuality of that person ought to reign uncontrolled either by any other individual or by the public collectively. That there is, or ought to be, some space in human existence thus entrenched around, and sacred from authoritative intrusion, no one who professes the smallest regard to human freedom or dignity will call in question: the point to be determined is, where the limit should be placed; how large a province of human life this reserved territory should include. I apprehend that it ought to include all that part which concerns only the life, whether inward or outward, of the individual, and does not affect the interests of others, or affects them only through the moral influence of example. With respect to the domain of the inward consciousness, the thoughts and feelings, and as much of external conduct as is personal only, involving no consequences, none at least of a painful or injurious kind, to other people: I hold that it is allowable in all, and in the more thoughtful and cultivated often a duty, to assert and promulgate, with all the force they are capable of, their opinion of what is good or bad, admirable or contemptible, but not to compel others to conform to that opinion; whether the force used is that of extralegal coercion, or exerts itself by means of the law.

Even in those portions of conduct which do affect the interest of others, the onus of making out a case always lies on the defenders of legal prohibitions. It is not a merely constructive or presumptive injury to others, which will justify the interference of law with individual freedom. To be prevented from doing what one is inclined to, from acting according to one's own judgment of what is desirable, is not only always irksome, but always tends, *pro tanto*, to starve the development of some portion of the bodily or mental faculties, either sensitive or active; and unless the conscience of the individual goes freely with the legal restraint, it partakes, either in a great or in a small degree, of the degradation of slavery. Scarcely any degree of utility, short of absolute necessity, will justify a prohibitory regulation, unless it can also be made to recommend itself to the general conscience; unless persons of ordinary good intentions either believe already, or can be induced to believe, that the thing prohibited is a thing which they ought not to wish to do.

It is otherwise with governmental interferences which do not restrain individual free agency. When a government provides means of fulfilling a certain end, leaving individuals free to avail themselves of different means if in their opinion preferable, there is no infringement of liberty, no irksome or degrading restraint. One of the principal objections to government interference is then absent. There is, however, in almost all forms of government agency, one thing which is compulsory: the provision of the pecuniary means. These are derived from taxation; or, if existing in the form of an endowment derived from public property, they are still the cause of as much compulsory taxation as the sale or the annual proceeds of the property would enable to be dispensed with. And the objection necessarily attaching to compulsory contributions, is almost always greatly aggravated by the expensive precautions and onerous restrictions, which are indispensable to prevent evasion of a compulsory tax.

3

A second general objection to government agency, is that every increase of the functions devolving on the government is an increase of its power, both in the form of authority, and still more, in the indirect form of influence. The importance of this consideration, in respect of political freedom, has in general been quite sufficiently recognized, at least in England, but many, in latter times, have been prone to think that limitation of the powers of the government is only essential when the government itself is badly constituted; when it does not represent the people, but is the organ of a class, or coalition of classes: and that a government of sufficiently popular constitution might be trusted with any amount of power over the nation, since its power would be only that of the nation over itself. This might be true, if the nation, in such cases, did not practically mean a mere majority of the nation, and if minorities were only capable of oppressing, but not of being oppressed. Experience, however, proves that the depositaries of power who are mere delegates of the people, that is of a majority, are quite as ready (when they think they can count on popular support) as any organs of oligarchy to assume arbitrary power, and encroach unduly on the liberty of private life. The public collectively is abundantly ready to impose, not only its generally narrow views of its interests, but its abstract opinions, and even its tastes, as laws binding upon individuals. And the present civilization tends so strongly to make the power of persons acting in masses the only substantial power in society, that there never was more necessity for surrounding individual independence of thought, speech, and conduct, with the most powerful defenses, in order to maintain that originality of mind and individuality of character, which are the only source of any real progress, and of most of the qualities which make the human race much superior to any herd of animals. Hence it is no less important in a democratic than in any other government, that all tendency on the part of public authorities to stretch their interference, and assume a power of any sort which can easily be dispensed with, should be regarded with unremitting jealousy. Perhaps this is even more important in a democracy than in any other form of political society; because where public opinion is sovereign, an individual who is oppressed by the sovereign does not, as in most other states of things, find a rival power to which he can appeal for relief, or, at all events, for sympathy.

4

A third general objection to government agency, rests on the principle of the division of labor. Every additional function undertaken by the government is a fresh occupation imposed upon a body already overcharged with duties. A natural consequence is that most things are ill done; much not done at all, because the government is not able to do it without delays which are fatal to its purpose; that the more troublesome and less showy of the functions undertaken are postponed or neglected, and an excuse is always ready for the neglect; while the heads of the administration have their minds so fully taken up with official details, in however perfunctory a manner superintended, that they have no time or thought to spare for the great interests of the state, and the preparation of enlarged measures of social improvement.

But these inconveniences, though real and serious, result much more from the bad organization of governments, than from the extent and variety of the duties undertaken by them. Government is not a name for some one functionary, or definite number of functionaries: there may be almost any amount of division of labor within the administrative body itself. The evil in question is felt in great magnitude under some of the governments of the Continent, where six or eight men, living at the capital and known by the name of ministers, demand that the whole public business of the country shall pass, or be supposed to pass, under their individual eye. But the inconvenience would be reduced to a very manageable compass, in a country in which there was a proper distribution of functions between the central and local officers of government, and in which the central body was divided into a sufficient number of departments. When Parliament thought it expedient to confer on the government an inspecting and partially controlling authority over railways, it did not add railways to the Department of the Home Minister, but created a Railway Board. When it determined to have a central superintending authority for pauper administration, it established the Poor Law Commission. There are few countries in which a greater number of functions are discharged by public officers, than in some states of the American Union, particularly the New England states; but the division of labor in public business is extreme; most of these officers being not even amenable to any common superior, but performing their duties freely, under the double check of election by their townsmen, and civil as well as criminal responsibility to the tribunals.

It is, no doubt, indispensable to good government that the chiefs of the administration, whether permanent or temporary, should extend a commanding, though general, view over the ensemble of all the interests confided, in any degree, to the responsibility of the central power. But with a skillful internal organization of the administrative machine, leaving to subordinates, and as far as possible, to local subordinates, not only the execution, but to a greater degree the control, of details; holding them accountable for the results of their acts rather than for the acts themselves, except where these come within the cognizance of the tribunals; taking the most effectual securities for honest and capable appointments; opening a broad path to promotion from the inferior degrees of the administrative scale to the superior; leaving, at each step, to the functionary, a wider range in the origination of measures, so that, in the highest grade of all, deliberation might be concentrated on the great collective interests of the country in each department; if all this were done, the government would not probably be overburthened by any business, in other respects fit to be undertaken by it; though the overburthening would remain as a serious addition to the inconveniences incurred by its undertaking any which was unfit.

5

But though a better organization of governments would greatly diminish the force of the objection to the mere multiplication of their duties, it would still remain true that in all the more advanced communities, the great majority of things are worse done by the intervention of government, than the individuals most interested in the matter would do them, or cause them to be done, if left to themselves. The grounds of this truth are expressed with tolerable exactness in the popular dictum, that people understand their own business and their own interests better, and care for them more, than the government does, or can be expected to do. This maxim holds true throughout the greatest part of the business of life, and wherever it is true we ought to condemn every kind of government intervention that conflicts with it. The inferiority of government agency, for example, in any of the common operations of industry or commerce, is proved by the fact that it is hardly ever able to maintain itself in equal competition with individual agency, where the individuals possess the requisite degree of industrial enterprise, and can command the necessary assemblage of means. All the facilities which a government enjoys of access to information; all the means which it possesses of remunerating, and therefore of commanding, the best available talent in the market—are not an equivalent for the one great disadvantage of an inferior interest in the result.

It must be remembered, besides, that even if a government were superior in intelligence and knowledge to any single individual in the nation, it must be inferior to all the individuals of the nation taken together. It can neither possess in itself, nor enlist in its service, more than a portion of the acquirements and capacities which the country contains, applicable to any given purpose. There must be many persons equally qualified for the work with those whom the government employs, even if it selects its instruments with no reference to any consideration but their fitness. Now these are the very persons into whose hands, in the cases of most common occurrence, a system of individual agency naturally tends to throw the work, because they are capable of doing it better or on cheaper terms than any other persons. So far as this is the case, it is evident that government, by excluding or even by superceding individual agency, either substitutes a less qualified instrumentality for one better qualified, or at any rate substitutes its own mode of accomplishing the work, for all the variety of modes which would be tried by a number of equally qualified persons aiming at the same end; a competition by many degrees more propitious to the progress of improvement than any uniformity of system.

6

I have reserved for the last place one of the strongest of the reasons against the extension of government agency. Even if the government could comprehend within itself, in each department, all the most eminent intellectual capacity and active talent of the nation, it would not be the less desirable that the conduct of a large portion of the affairs of the society should be left in the hands of the persons immediately interested in them. The business of life is an essential part of the practical education of a people; without which, book and school instruction, though most necessary and salutary, does not suffice to qualify them for conduct, and for the adaptation of means to ends. Instruction is only one of the desiderata of mental improvement; another, almost as indispensable, is a vigorous exercise of the active energies; labor, contrivance, judgment, self-control: and the natural stimulus to these is the difficulties of life. This doctrine is not to be confounded with the complacent optimism, which represents the evils of life as desirable things, because they call forth qualities adapted to combat with evils. It is only because the difficulties exist that the qualities which combat with them are of any value. As practical beings it is our business to free human life from as many as possible of its difficulties, and not to keep up a stock of them as hunters preserve game, for the exercise of pursuing it. But since the need of active talent and practical judgment in the affairs of life can only be diminished, and not, even on the most favorable supposition, done away with, it is important that those endowments should be cultivated not merely in a select few, but in all, and that the cultivation should be more varied and complete than most persons are able to find in the narrow sphere of their merely individual interests. A people among whom there is no habit of spontaneous action for a collective interest—who look habitually to their government to command or prompt them in all matters of joint concern—who expect to have everything done for them, except what can be made an affair of mere habit and routine—have their faculties only half developed; their education is defective in one of its most important branches.

Not only is the cultivation of the active faculties by exercise, diffused through the whole community, in itself one of the most valuable of national possessions: it is rendered, not less, but more necessary, when a high degree of that indispensable culture is systematically kept up in the chiefs and functionaries of the state. There cannot be a combination of circumstances more dangerous to human welfare than that in which intelligence and talent are maintained at a high standard within a governing corporation, but starved and discouraged outside the pale. Such a system, more completely than any other, embodies the idea of despotism, by arming with intellectual superiority as an additional weapon those who have already the legal power. It approaches as nearly as the organic difference between human beings and other animals admits, to the government of sheep by their shepherd, without anything like so strong an interest as the shepherd has in the thriving condition of the flock. The only security against political slavery is the check maintained over governors by the diffusion of intelligence, activity, and public spirit among the governed. Experience proves the extreme difficulty of permanently keeping up a sufficiently high standard of those qualities; a difficulty which increases, as the advance of civilization and security removes one after another of the hardships, embarrassments, and dangers against which individuals had formerly no resource but in their own strength, skill, and courage. It is therefore of supreme importance that all classes of the community, down to the lowest, should have much to do for themselves; that as great a demand should be made upon their intelligence and virtue as it is in any respect equal to; that the government should not only leave as far as possible to their own faculties the conduct of whatever concerns themselves alone, but should suffer them, or rather encourage them, to manage as many as possible of their joint concerns by voluntary cooperation; since this discussion and management of collective interests is the great school of that public spirit, and the great source of that intelligence of public affairs, which are always regarded as the distinctive character of the public of free countries.

A democratic constitution, not supported by democratic institutions in detail, but confined to the central government, not only is not political freedom, but often creates a spirit precisely the reverse, carrying down to the lowest grade in society the desire and ambition of political domination. In some countries the desire of the people is for not being tyrannized over, but in others it is merely for an equal chance to everybody of tyrannizing. Unhappily this last state of the desires is fully as natural to mankind as the former, and in many of the conditions even of civilized humanity is far more largely exemplified. In proportion as the people are accustomed to manage their affairs by their own active intervention, instead of leaving them to the government, their desires will turn to repelling tyranny, rather than to tyrannizing: while in proportion as all real initiative and direction resides in the government, and individuals habitually feel and act as under its perpetual tutelage, popular institutions develop in them not the desire of freedom, but an unmeasured appetite for place and power: diverting the intelligence and activity of the country from its principal business to a wretched competition for the selfish prizes and the petty vanities of office.

7

The preceding are the principal reasons, of a general character, in favor of restricting to the narrowest compass the intervention of a public authority in the business of the community: and few will dispute the more than sufficiency of these reasons, to throw, in every instance, the burthen of making out a strong case, not on those who resist, but on those who recommend, government interference. Laissez faire, in short, should be the general practice: every departure from it, unless required by some great good, is a certain evil.

The degree in which the maxim, even in the cases to which it is most manifestly applicable, has heretofore been infringed by governments, future ages will probably have difficulty in crediting. Some idea may be formed of it from the description of M. Dunoyer of the restraints imposed on the operations of manufacture under the old government of France, by the meddling and regulating spirit of legislation.

> The State exercised over manufacturing industry the most unlimited and arbitrary jurisdiction. It disposed without scruple of the resources of manufacturers: it decided who should be allowed to work, what things it should be permitted to make, what materials should be employed, what processes followed, what forms should be given to productions. It was not enough to do well, to do better; it was necessary to do according to the rules. Everybody knows the regulation of 1670 which prescribed to seize and nail to the pillory, with the names of the makers, goods not conformable to the rules, and which, on a second repetition of the offence, directed that the manufacturers themselves should be attached also. Not the taste of the consumers, but the commands of the law must be attended to. Legions of inspectors, commissioners, controllers, jurymen, guardians, were charged with its execution. Machines were broken, products were burned when not conformable to the rules: improvements were punished; inventors were fined. There were different sets of rules for goods destined for home consumption and for those intended for exportation. An artizan could neither choose the place in which to establish himself, nor work at all seasons, nor work for all customers. There exists a decree of March 30, 1700, which limits to eighteen towns the number of places where stockings might be woven. A decree of June 18, 1723, enjoins the manufacturers at Rouen to suspend their works from the 1st of July to the 15th of September, in order to facilitate the harvest. Louis XIV, when he intended to construct the colonnade of the Louvre, forbade all private persons to employ workmen without his permission, under a penalty of 10,000 livres, and forbade workmen to work for private persons, on pain for the first offence, of imprisonment, and for the second, of the galleys.

That these and similar regulations were not a dead letter, and that the officious and vexatious meddling was prolonged down to the French Revolution, we have the testimony of Roland, the Girondist minister. "I have seen," says he, "eighty, ninety, a hundred pieces of cotton or woollen stuff cut up, and completely destroyed. I have witnessed similar scenes

every week for a number of years. I have seen manufactured goods con-
fiscated; heavy fines laid on the manufacturers; some pieces of fabric were
burnt in public places, and at the hours of market: others were fixed to
the pillory, with the name of the manufacturer inscribed upon them, and
he himself was threatened with the pillory, in case of a second offence.
All this was done under my eyes, at Rouen, in conformity with existing
regulations, or ministerial orders. What crime deserved so cruel a punishment? Some defects in the materials employed, or in the texture of the
fabric, or even in some of the threads of the warp.

> I have frequently seen manufacturers visited by a band of satellites
> who put all in confusion in their establishments, spread terror in
> their families, cut the stuffs from the frames, tore off the warp
> from the looms, and carried them away as proofs of infringement;
> the manufacturers were summoned, tried, and condemned: their
> goods confiscated; copies of their judgment of confiscation posted
> up in every public place; fortune, reputation, credit, all was lost
> and destroyed. And for what offence? Because they had made of
> worsted, a kind of cloth called shag, such as the English used to
> manufacture, and even sell in France, while the French regula-
> tions stated that that kind of cloth should be made with mohair.
> I have seen other manufacturers treated in the same way, because
> they had made camlets of a particular width, used in England
> and Germany, for which there was a great demand from Spain,
> Portugal, and other countries, and from several parts of France,
> while the French regulations prescribed other widths for camlets.

The time is gone by, when such applications as these of the principle
of "paternal government" would be attempted, in even the least enlightened country of the European commonwealth of nations. In such cases as
those cited, all the general objections to government interference are valid,
and several of them in nearly their highest degree. But we must now turn
to the second part of our task, and direct our attention to cases, in which
some of those general objections are altogether absent, while those which
can never be got rid of entirely, are overruled by counter-considerations
of still greater importance.

We have observed that, as a general rule, the business of life is better
performed when those who have an immediate interest in it are left to take
their own course, uncontrolled either by the mandate of the law or by the
meddling of any public functionary. The persons, or some of the persons,
who do the work, are likely to be better judges than the government, of
the means of attaining the particular end at which they aim. Were we to
suppose, what is not very probable, that the government has possessed
itself of the best knowledge which had been acquired up to a given time

by the persons most skilled in the occupation; even then, the individual agents have so much stronger and more direct an interest in the result, that the means are far more likely to be improved and perfected if left to their uncontrolled choice. But if the workman is generally the best selector of means, can it be affirmed with the same universality that the consumer, or person served, is the most competent judge of the end? Is the buyer always qualified to judge of the commodity? If not, the presumption in favor of the competition of the market does not apply to the case; and if the commodity be one, in the quality of which society has much at stake, the balance of advantages may be in favor of some mode and degree of intervention, by the authorized representatives of the collective interest of the state.

8

Now, the proposition that the consumer is a competent judge of the commodity can be admitted only with numerous abatements and exceptions. He is generally the best judge (though even this is not true universally) of the material objects produced for his use. These are destined to supply some physical want, or gratify some taste or inclination, respecting which wants or inclinations there is no appeal from the person who feels them; or they are the means and appliances of some occupation, for the use of the persons engaged in it, who may be presumed to be judges of the things required in their own habitual employment. But there are other things, of the worth of which the demand of the market is by no means a test; things of which the utility does not consist in ministering to inclinations, nor in serving the daily uses of life, and the want of which is least felt where the need is greatest. This is peculiarly true of those things which are chiefly useful as tending to raise the character of human beings. The uncultivated cannot be competent judges of cultivation. Those who most need to be made wiser and better, usually desire it least, and if they desired it, would be incapable of finding the way to it by their own lights. It will continually happen, on the voluntary system, that, the end not being desired, the means will not be provided at all, or that, the persons requiring improvement having an imperfect or altogether erroneous conception of what they want, the supply called forth by the demand of the market will be anything but what is really required. Now any well-intentioned and tolerably civilized government may think, without presumption, that it does or ought to possess a degree of cultivation above the average of the community which it rules, and that it should therefore be capable of offering better education and better instruction to the people, than the greater number of them would spontaneously demand. Education, therefore, is one of those things which it is admissible in principle that a government should provide for the people. The case is one to which the reasons of the noninteference principle do not necessarily or universally extend.

With regard to elementary education, the exception to ordinary rules may, I conceive, justifiably be carried still further. There are certain primary elements and means of knowledge which it is in the highest degree desirable that all human beings born into the community should acquire during childhood. If their parents, or those on whom they depend, have the power of obtaining for them this instruction, and fail to do it, they commit a double breach of duty, toward the children themselves, and toward the members of the community generally, who are all liable to suffer seriously from the consequences of ignorance and want of education in their fellow citizens. It is therefore an allowable exercise of the powers of government to impose on parents the legal obligation of giving elementary instruction to children. This, however, cannot fairly be done, without taking measures to insure that such instruction shall be always accessible to them, either gratuitously or at a trifling expense.

It may indeed be objected that the education of children is one of those expenses which parents, even of the laboring class, ought to defray; that it is desirable that they should feel it incumbent on them to provide by their own means for the fulfillment of their duties, and that by giving education at the cost of others, just as much by giving subsistence, the standard of necessary wages is proportionally lowered, and the springs of exertion and self-restraint is so much relaxed. This argument could, at best, be only valid if the question were that of substituting a public provision for what individuals would otherwise do for themselves; if all parents in the laboring class recognized and practiced the duty of giving instruction to their children at their own expense. But inasmuch as parents do not practice this duty, and do not include education among those necessary expenses which their wages must provide for, therefore the general rate of wages is not high enough to bear those expenses, and they must be borne from some other source. And this is not one of the cases in which the tender of help perpetuates the state of things which renders help necessary. Instruction, when it is really such, does not enervate, but strengthens as well as enlarges the active faculties: in whatever manner acquired, its effect on the mind is favorable to the spirit of independence: and when, unless had gratuitously, it would not be had at all, help in this form has the opposite tendency to that which in so many other cases makes it objectionable; it is help toward doing without help.

In England, and most European countries, elementary instruction cannot be paid for, at its full cost, from the common wages of unskilled labor, and would not if it could. The alternative, therefore, is not between government and private speculation, but between a government provision and voluntary charity: between interference by government, and interference by associations of individuals, subscribing their own money for the purpose, like the two great School Societies. It is, of course, not desirable that anything should be done by funds derived from compulsory taxation, which is already sufficiently well done by individual liberality. How far this is the case with school instruction, is, in each particular instance, a question of fact. The education provided in this country on the voluntary principle has of late been so much discussed, that it is needless in this place to criticize it minutely, and I shall merely express my conviction, that even in quantity it is, and is likely to remain, altogether insufficient, while in quality, though with some slight tendency to improvement, it is never good except by some rare accident, and generally so bad as to be little more than nominal. I hold it therefore the duty of the government to supply the defect, by giving pecuniary support to elementary schools, such as to render them accessible to all the children of the poor, either freely, or for a payment too inconsiderable to be sensibly felt.

One thing must be strenuously insisted on: that the government must claim no monopoly for its education, either in the lower or in the higher branches; must exert neither authority nor influence to induce the people to resort to its teachers in preference to others, and must confer no peculiar advantages on those who have been instructed by them. Though the government teachers will probably be superior to the average of private instructors, they will not embody all the knowledge and sagacity to be found in all instructors taken together, and it is desirable to leave open as many roads as possible to the desired end. It is not endurable that a government should, either de jure or de facto, have a complete control over the education of the people. To possess such a control, and actually exert it, is to be despotic. A government which can mold the opinions and sentiments of the people from their youth upward can do with them whatever it pleases. Though a government, therefore, may, and in many cases, ought to, establish schools and colleges, it must neither compel nor bribe any person to come to them; nor ought the power of individuals to set up rival establishments, to depend in any degree upon its authorization. It would be justified in requiring from all the people that they shall possess instruction in certain things, but not in prescribing to them how or from whom they shall obtain it.

9

In the matter of education, the intervention of government is justifiable, because the case is not one in which the interest and judgment of the consumer are a sufficient security for the goodness of the commodity. Let us now consider another class of cases, where there is no person in the situation of a consumer, and where the interest and judgment to be relied on are those of the agent himself; as in the conduct of any business in which he is exclusively interested, or in entering into any contract or engagement by which he himself is to be bound.

The ground of the practical principle of noninterference must here be that most persons take a juster and more intelligent view of their own interest, and of the means of promoting it, than can either be prescribed to them by a general enactment of the legislature, or pointed out in the particular case by a public functionary. The maxim is unquestionably sound as a general rule; but there is no difficulty in perceiving some very large and conspicuous exceptions to it. These may be classed under several heads.

First: the individual who is presumed to be the best judge of his own interests may be incapable of judging or acting for himself; may be a lunatic, an idiot, an infant: or though not wholly incapable, may be of immature years and judgment. In this case the foundation of the laissez-faire principle breaks down entirely. The person most interested is not the best judge of the matter, nor a competent judge at all. Insane persons are everywhere regarded as proper objects of the care of the state. In the case of children and young persons, it is common to say, that though they cannot judge for themselves, they have their parents or other relatives to judge for them. But this removes the question into a different category; making it no longer a question whether the government should interfere with individuals in the direction of their own conduct and interests, but whether it should leave absolutely in their power the conduct and interests of somebody else. Parental power is as susceptible of abuse as any other power, and is, as a matter of fact, constantly abused. If laws do not succeed in preventing parents from brutally ill-treating, and even from murdering their children, far less ought it to be presumed that the interests of children will never be sacrificed, in more commonplace and less revolting ways, to the selfishness or the ignorance of their parents. Whatever it can be clearly seen that parents ought to do or forbear for the interest of children, the law is warranted, if it is able, in compelling to be done or forborne, and is generally bound to do so. To take an example from the peculiar province of political economy; it is right that children, and young persons not yet arrived at maturity, should be protected so far as the eye and hand of the state can reach, from being overworked. Laboring for too many hours in the day, or on work beyond their strength, should not be permitted to them, for if permitted it may always be compelled. Freedom of contract, in the case of children, is but another word for freedom of coercion. Education also, the best which circumstances admit of their receiving, is not a thing which parents or relatives, from indifference, jealousy, or avarice, should have it in their power to withhold.

The reasons for legal intervention in favor of children, apply not less strongly to the case of those unfortunate slaves and victims of the most brutal part of mankind, the lower animals. It is by the grossest misunderstanding of the principles of liberty, that the infliction of exemplary punishment on ruffianism practiced toward these defenseless creatures has been treated as a meddling by government with things beyond its province; an interference with domestic life. The domestic life of domestic tyrants is one of the things which it is the most imperative on the law to interfere with; and it is to be regretted that metaphysical scruples respecting the nature and source of the authority of government, should induce many warm supporters of laws against cruelty to animals, to seek for a justification of such laws in the incidental consequences of the indulgence of ferocious habits to the interests of human beings, rather than in the intrinsic merits of the case itself. What it would be the duty of a human being, possessed of the requisite physical strength, to prevent by force if attempted in his presence, it cannot be less incumbent on society generally to repress. The existing laws of England on the subject are chiefly defective in the trifling, often almost nominal, maximum, to which the penalty even in the worst cases is limited.

Among those members of the community whose freedom of contract ought to be controlled by the legislature for their own protection, on account (it is said) of their dependent position, it is frequently proposed to include women: and in the existing Factory Acts, their labor, in common with that of young persons, has been placed under peculiar restrictions. But the classing together, for this and other purposes, of women and children, appears to me both indefensible in principle and mischievous in practice. Children below a certain age *cannot* judge or act for themselves; up to a considerably greater age they are inevitably more or less disqualified for doing so; but women are as capable as men of appreciating and managing their own concerns, and the only hindrance to their doing so arises from the injustice of their present social position. So long as the law makes everything which the wife acquires the property of the husband, while by compelling her to live with him it forces her to submit to almost any amount of moral and even physical tyranny which he may choose to inflict, there is some ground for regarding every act done by her as done under coercion: but it is the great error of reformers and philanthropists in our time, to nibble at the consequences of unjust power, instead of redressing the injustice itself. If women had as absolute a control as men have, over their own persons and their own patrimony or acquisitions, there would be no plea for limiting their hours of laboring for themselves, in order that they might have time to labor for the husband, in what is called, by the advocates of restriction, *his* home. Women employed in factories are the only women in the laboring rank of life whose position is not that of slaves and drudges; precisely because they cannot easily be compelled to work and earn wages in factories against their will. For improving the condition of women, it should, in the contrary, be an object to give them the readiest access to independent industrial employment, instead of closing, either entirely or partially, that which is already open to them.

10

A second exception to the doctrine that individuals are the best judges of their own interest, is when an individual attempts to decide irrevocably now, what will be best for his interest at some future and distant time. The presumption in favor of individual judgment is only legitimate where the judgment is grounded on actual, and especially on present, personal experience; not where it is formed antecedently to experience, and not suffered to be reversed even after experience has condemned it. When persons have bound themselves by a contract, not simply to do some one thing, but to continue doing something forever or for a prolonged period, without any power of revoking the engagement, the presumption which their perseverance in that course of conduct would otherwise raise in favor of its being advantageous to them, does not exist; and any such presumption which can be grounded on their having voluntarily entered into the contract, perhaps at an early age, and without any real knowledge of what they undertook, is commonly next to null. The practical maxim of leaving contracts free is not applicable without great limitations in case of engagement in perpetuity; and the law should be extremely jealous of such engagements; should refuse its sanction to them, when the obligations they impose are such as the contracting party cannot be a competent judge of; if it ever does sanction them, it should take every possible security for their being contracted with foresight and deliberation; and in compensation for not permitting the parties themselves to revoke their engagement, should grant them a release from it, on a sufficient case being made out before an impartial authority. These considerations are eminently applicable to marriage, the most important of all cases of engagement for life.

11

The third exception which I shall notice, to the doctrine that government cannot manage the affairs of individuals as well as the individuals themselves, has reference to the great class of cases in which the individuals can only manage the concern by delegated agency, and in which the so-called private management is, in point of fact, hardly better entitled to be called management by the persons interested, than administration by a public officer. Whatever, if left to spontaneous agency, can only be done by joint-stock associations, will often be as well, and sometimes better done, as far as the actual work is concerned, by the state. Government management is, indeed, proverbially jobbing, careless, and ineffective, but so likewise has generally been joint-stock management. The directors of a joint-stock company, it is true, are always shareholders; but also the members of a government are invariably taxpayers; and in the case of directors, no more than in that of governments, is their proportional share of the benefits of good management equal to the interest they may possibly have in mismanagement, even without reckoning the interest of their case. It may be objected that the shareholders, in their collective character, exercise a certain control over the directors, and have almost always full power to remove them from office. Practically, however, the difficulty of exercising this power is found to be so great, that it is hardly ever exercised except in cases of such flagrantly unskillful, or, at least, unsuccessful management, as would generally produce the ejection from office of managers appointed by the government. Against the very ineffectual security afforded by meetings of shareholders, and by their individual inspection and inquiries, may be placed the greater publicity and more active discussion and comment, to be expected in free countries with regard to affairs in which the general government takes part. The defects, therefore, of government management, do not seem to be necessarily much greater, if necessarily greater at all, than those of management by joint-stock.

The true reasons in favor of leaving to voluntary associations all such things as they are competent to perform, would exist in equal strength if it were certain that the work itself would be as well or better done by public officers. These reasons have been already pointed out: the mischief of overloading the chief functionaries of government with demands on their attention, and diverting them from duties which they alone can discharge, to objects which can be sufficiently well attained without them; the danger of unnecessarily swelling the direct power and indirect influence of government, and multiplying occasions of collision between its agents and private citizens; and the inexpediency of concentrating in a dominant bureaucracy all the skill and experience in the management of large interests, and all the power of organized action, existing in the community; a practice which keeps the citizens in a relation to the government like that of children to their guardians, and is a main cause of the inferior capacity for political life which has hitherto characterized the overgoverned countries of the Continent, whether with or without the forms of representative government.

But although, for these reasons, most things which are likely to be even tolerably done by voluntary associations, should, generally speaking, be left to them; it does not follow that the manner in which those associations perform their work should be entirely uncontrolled by the government.

There are many cases in which the agency, of whatever nature, by which a service is performed, is certain, from the nature of the case, to be virtually single; in which a practical monopoly, with all the power it confers of taxing the community, cannot be prevented from existing. I have already more than once adverted to the case of the gas and water companies, among which, though perfect freedom is allowed to competition, none really takes place, and practically they are found to be even more irresponsible, and unapproachable by individual complaints, than the government. There are the expenses without the advantages of plurality of agency; and the charge made for services which cannot be dispensed with, is, in substance, quite as much compulsory taxation as if imposed by law; there are few householders who make any distinction between their "water rate" and other local taxes. In the case of these particular services, the reasons preponderate in favor of their being performed, like the paving and cleansing of the streets, not certainly by the general government of the state, but by the municipal authorities of the town, and the expense defrayed, as even now it in fact is, by a local rate. But in the many analogous cases which it is best to resign to voluntary agency, the community needs some other security for the fit performance of the service than the interest of the managers; and it is the part of the government, either to subject the business to reasonable conditions for the general advantage, or to retain such power over it, that the profits of the monopoly may at least be obtained for the public. This applies to the case of a road, a canal, or a railway. These are always, in a great degree, practical monopolies; and a government which concedes such monopoly unreservedly to a private company does much the same thing as if it allowed an individual or an association to levy any tax they chose, for their own benefit, on all the malt produced in the country, or on all the cotton imported into it. To make the concession for a limited time is generally justifiable, on the principle which justifies patents for invention: but the state should either reserve to itself a reversionary property in such public works, or should retain, and freely exercise, the right of fixing a maximum of fares and charges, and, from time to time, varying that maximum. It is perhaps necessary to remark that the state may be the proprietor of canals or railways without itself working them; and that they will almost always be better worked by means of a company renting the railway or canal for a limited period from the state.

12

To a fourth case of exception I must request particular attention, it being one to which as it appears to me, the attention of political economists has not yet been sufficiently drawn. There are matters in which the interference of law is required, not to overrule the judgment of individuals respecting their own interest, but to give the effect to that judgment: they being unable to give effect to it except by concert, which concert again cannot be effectual unless it receives validity and sanction from the law. For illustration, and without prejudging the particular point, I may advert to the question of diminishing the hours of labor. Let us suppose, what is at least supposable, whether it be the fact or not, that a general reduction of the hours of factory labor, say from ten to nine, would be for the advantage of the workpeople: that they would receive as high wages, or nearly as high, for nine hours' labor as they receive for ten. If this would be the result, and if the operatives generally are convinced that it would, the limitation, some may say, will be adopted spontaneously. I answer, that it will not be adopted unless the body of operatives bind themselves to one another to abide by it. A workman who refused to work more than nine hours while there were others who worked ten, would either not be employed at all, or if employed, must submit to lose one-tenth of his wages. However convinced, therefore, he may be that it is the interest of the class to work short time, it is contrary to his own interest to set the example, unless he is well assured that all or most others will follow it. But suppose a general agreement of the whole class: might not this be effectual without the sanction of law? Not unless enforced by opinion with a rigor practically equal to that of law. For however beneficial the observance of the regulation might be to the class collectively, the immediate interest of every individual would lie in violating it: and the more numerous those were who adhered to the rule, the more would individuals gain by departing from it. If nearly all restricted themselves to nine hours, those who chose to work for ten would gain all the advantages of the restriction, together with the profit from infringing it; they would get ten hours' wages for nine hours' work, and an hour's wages besides. I grant that if a large majority adhered to the nine hours, there would be no harm done; the benefit would be, in the main, secured to the class, while those individuals who preferred to work harder and earn more, would have an opportunity of doing so. This certainly would be the state of things to be wished for; and assuming that a reduction of hours without any diminution of wages could take place without expelling the commodity from some of its markets—which is in every particular instance a question of fact, not of principle—the manner in which it would be most desirable that this effect should be brought about, would be by a quiet change in the general custom of the trade; short hours becoming, by spontaneous choice, the general practice, but those who chose to deviate from it having the fullest liberty to do so. Probably, however, so many would prefer the ten hours' work on the improved terms, that the limitation could not be maintained as a general practice: what some did from choice, others would soon be obliged to do from necessity, and those who had chosen long hours for the sake of increased wages would be forced in the end to work long hours for no greater wages than before. Assuming then that it really would be the interest of each to work only nine hours if he could be assured that all others would do the same, there might be no means of attaining this object but by converting their supposed mutual agreement into an engagement under penalty, by consenting to have it enforced by law. I am not expressing any opinion in favor of such an enactment, which has never in this country been demanded, and which I certainly should not, in present circumstances, recommend: but it serves to exemplify the manner in which classes of persons may need the assistance of law, to give effect to their deliberate collective opinion of their own interest, by affording to every individual a guarantee that his competitors will pursue the same course, without which he cannot safely adopt it himself.

Another exemplification of the same principle is afforded by what is known as the Wakefield system of colonization. This system is grounded on the important principle that the degree of productiveness of land and labor depends on their being in a due proportion to one another; that if a few persons in a newly settled country attempt to occupy and appropriate a large district, or if each laborer becomes too soon an occupier and cultivator of land, there is a loss of productive power, and a great retardation of the progress of the colony in wealth and civilization: that nevertheless the instinct (as it may almost be called) of appropriation, and the feelings associated in old countries with landed proprietorship, induce almost every emigrant to take possession of as much land as he has the means of acquiring, and every laborer to become at once a proprietor, cultivating his own land with no other aid than that of his family. If this propensity to the immediate possession of land could be in some degree restrained, and each laborer induced to work a certain number of years on hire before he become a landed proprietor, a perpetual stock of hired laborers could be maintained, available for roads, canals, works of irrigation, etc., and for the establishment and carrying on of the different branches of town industry; whereby the laborer, when he did at last become a landed proprietor, would find his land much more valuable, through access to markets, and facility of obtaining hired labor. Mr. Wakefield therefore proposed to check the premature occupation of land, and dispersion of the people, by putting upon all unappropriated lands a rather high price, the proceeds of which were to be expended in conveying emigrant laborers from the mother country.

This salutary provision, however, has been objected to, in the name and on the authority of what was represented as the great principle of political economy, that individuals are the best judges of their own interest. It was said that when things are left to themselves, land is appropriated and occupied by the spontaneous choice of individuals, in the quantities and at the times most advantageous to each person, and therefore to the community generally; and that to interpose artificial obstacles to their obtaining land is to prevent them from adopting the course which in their own judgment is most beneficial to them, from a self-conceited notion of the legislator, that he knows what is most for their interest, better than they do themselves. Now this is a complete misunderstanding, either of the system itself, or of the principle with which it is alleged to conflict. The oversight is similar to that which we have just seen exemplified on the subject of hours of labor. However beneficial it might be to the colony in the aggregate, and to each individual composing it, that no one should occupy more land than he can properly cultivate, nor become a proprietor until there are other laborers ready to take his place in working for hire; it can never be the interest of an individual to exercise this forbearance, unless he is assured that others will do so too. Surrounded by settlers who have each their thousand acres, how is he benefited by restricting himself to fifty? Or what does a laborer gain by deferring the acquisition altogether for a few years, if all other laborers rush to convert their first earnings into estates in the wilderness, several miles apart from one another? If they, by seizing on land, prevent the formation of a class of laborers for wages, he will not, by postponing the time of his becoming a proprietor, be enabled to employ the land with any greater advantage when he does obtain it; to what end therefore should he place himself in what will appear to him and others a position of inferiority, by remaining a hired laborer, when all around him are proprietors? It is the interest of each to do what is good for all, but only if others will do likewise.

The principle that each is the best judge of his own interest, understood as these objectors understand it, would prove that governments ought not to fulfill any of their acknowledged duties—ought not, in fact, to exist at all. It is greatly the interest of the community, collectively and individually, not to rob or defraud one another; but there is not the less necessity for laws to punish robbery and fraud; because, though it is the interest of each that nobody should rob or cheat, it is not any one's interest to refrain from robbing and cheating others when all others are permitted to rob and cheat him. Penal laws exist at all, chiefly for this reason—because even an unanimous opinion that a certain line of conduct is for the general interest, does not always make it people's individual interest to adhere to that line of conduct.

13

Fifthly, the argument against government interference grounded on the maxim that individuals are the best judges of their own interest, cannot apply to the very large class of cases, in which those acts of individuals with which the government claims to interfere, are not done by those individuals for their own interest, but for the interest of other people. This includes, among other things, the important and much agitated subject of public charity. Though individuals should, in general, be left to do for themselves whatever it can reasonably be expected that they should be capable of doing, yet when they are at any rate not to be left to themselves, but to be helped by other people, the question arises whether it is better that they should receive this help exclusively from individuals, and therefore uncertainly and casually, or by systematic arrangements, in which society acts through its organ, the state.

This brings us to the subject of Poor Laws; a subject which would be of very minor importance if the habits of all classes of the people were temperate and prudent, and the diffusion of property satisfactory; but of the greatest moment in a state of things so much the reverse of this, in both points, as that which the British islands present.

Apart from any metaphysical considerations respecting the foundation of morals or of the social union, it will be admitted to be right that human beings should help one another; and the more so, in proportion to the urgency of the need: and none needs help so urgently as one who is starving. The claim to help, therefore, created by destitution, is one of the strongest which can exist; and there is prima facie the amplest reason for making the relief of so extreme an exigency as certain to those who require it, as by any arrangements of society it can be made.

On the other hand, in all cases of helping, there are two sets of consequences to be considered: the consequences of the assistance itself, and the consequences of relying on the assistance. The former are generally beneficial, but the latter, for the most part, injurious; so much so, in many cases, as greatly to outweigh the value of the benefit. And this is never more likely to happen than in the very cases where the need of help is the most intense. There are few things for which it is more mischievous that people should rely on the habitual aid of others, than for the means of subsistence, and unhappily there is no lesson which they more easily learn. The problem to be solved is therefore one of peculiar nicety as well as importance; how to give the greatest amount of needful help, with the smallest encouragement to undue reliance on it.

Energy and self-dependence are, however, liable to be impaired by the absence of help, as well as by its excess. It is even more fatal to exertion to have no hope of succeeding by it, than to be assured of succeeding without it. When the condition of any one is so disastrous that his energies are paralyzed by discouragement, assistance is a tonic, not a sedative: it braces instead of deadening the active faculties: always provided that the assistance is not such as to dispense with self-help, by substituting itself for the person's own labor, skill, and prudence, but is limited to affording him a better hope of attaining success by those legitimate means. This accordingly is a test to which all plans of philanthropy and benevolence should be brought, whether intended for the benefit of individuals or of classes, and whether conducted on the voluntary or on the government principle.

Insofar as the subject admits of any general doctrine or maxim, it would appear to be this—that if assistance is given in such a manner that the condition of the person helped is as desirable as that of the person who succeeds in doing the same thing without help, the assistance, if capable of being previously calculated on, is mischievous: but if, while available to everybody, it leaves to every one a strong motive to do without it if he can, it is then for the most part beneficial. This principle, applied to a system of public charity, is that of the Poor Law of 1834. If the condition of a person receiving relief is made as eligible as that of the laborer who supports himself by his own exertions, the system strikes at the root of all individual industry and self-government; and, if fully acted up to, would require as its supplement an organized system of compulsion, for governing and setting to work like cattle, those who had been removed from the influence of the motives that act on human beings. But if, consistently with guaranteeing all persons against absolute want, the condition of those who are supported by legal charity can be kept considerably less desirable than the condition of those who find support for themselves, none but beneficial consequences can arise from a law which renders it impossible for any person, except by his own choice, to die from insufficiency of food. That in England at least this supposition can be realized, is proved by the experience of a long period preceding the close of the last century, as well as by that of many highly pauperized districts in more recent times, which have been dispauperized by adopting strict rules of Poor Law administration, to the great and permanent benefit of the whole laboring class. There is probably no country in which, by varying the means suitably to the character of the people, a legal provision for the destitute might not be made compatible with the observance of the conditions necessary to its being innocuous.

Subject to these conditions, I conceive it to be highly desirable that the certainty of subsistence should be held out by law to the destitute able-bodied, rather than that their relief should depend on voluntary charity. In the first place, charity almost always does too much or too little: it lavishes its bounty in one place, and leaves people to starve in another. Secondly, since the state must necessarily provide subsistence for the criminal poor while undergoing punishment, not to do the same for the poor who have not offended is to give a premium on crime. And lastly, if the poor are left to individual charity, a vast amount of mendacity is inevitable. What the state may and should abandon to private charity, is the task of distinguishing between one case of real necessity and another. Private charity can give more to the more deserving. The state must act by general rules. It cannot undertake to discriminate between the deserving and the undeserving indigent. It owes no more than subsistence to the first, and can give no less to the last. What is said about the injustice of a law which has no better treatment for the merely unfortunate poor than for the ill-conducted, is founded on a misconception of the province of law and public authority. The dispensers of public relief have no business to be inquisitors. Guardians and overseers are not fit to be trusted to give or withhold other people's money according to their verdict on the morality of the person soliciting it; and it would show much ignorance of the ways of mankind to suppose that such persons, even in the almost impossible case of their being qualified, will take the trouble of ascertaining and sifting the past conduct of a person in distress, so as to form a rational judgment on it. Private charity can make these distinctions; and in bestowing its own money, is entitled to do so according to its own judgment. It should understand that this is its peculiar and appropriate province, and that it is commendable or the contrary, as it exercises the function with more or less discernment. But the administrators of a public fund ought not to be required to do more for anybody, than that minimum which is due even to the worst. If they are, the indulgence very speedily becomes the rule, and refusal the more or less capricious or tyrannical exception.

14

Another class of cases which fall within the same general principle as the case of public charity are those in which the acts done by individuals, though intended solely for their own benefit, involve consequences extending indefinitely beyond them, to interests of the nation or of posterity, for which society in its collective capacity is alone able, and alone bound, to provide. One of these cases is that of colonization. If it is desirable, as no one will deny it to be, that the planting of colonies should be conducted, not with an exclusive view to the private interests of the first founders, but with a deliberate regard to the permanent welfare of the nations afterwards to arise from these small beginnings; such regard can only be secured by placing the enterprise, from its commencement, under regulations constructed with the foresight and enlarged views of philosophical legislators; and the government alone has power either to frame such regulations, or to enforce their observance.

The question of government intervention in the work of colonization involves the future and permanent interests of civilization itself, and far outstretches the comparatively narrow limits of purely economical considerations. But even with a view to those considerations alone, the removal of population from the overcrowded to the unoccupied parts of the earth's surface is one of those works of eminent social usefulness, which most require, and which at the same time best repay, the intervention of government.

To appreciate the benefits of colonization, it should be considered in its relation, not to a single country, but to the collective economical interests of the human race. The question is in general treated too exclusively as one of distribution; of relieving one labor market and supplying another. It is this, but it is also a question of production, and of the most efficient employment of the productive resources of the world. Much has been said of the good economy of importing commodities from the place where they can be bought cheapest; while the good economy of producing them where they can be produced cheapest is comparatively little thought of. If to carry consumable goods from the places where they are superabundant to those where they are scarce is a good pecuniary speculation, is it not an equally good speculation to do the same thing with regard to labor and instruments? The exportation of laborers and capital from old to new countries, from a place where their productive power is less to a place where it is greater, increases by so much the aggregate produce of the labor and capital of the world. It adds to the joint wealth of the old and the new country, what amounts in a short period to many times the mere cost of effecting the transport. There needs be no hesitation in affirming that colonization, in the present state of the world, is the best affair of business, in which the capital of an old and wealthy country can engage.

It is equally obvious, however, that colonization on a great scale can be undertaken, as an affair of business, only by the government, or by some combination of individuals in complete understanding with the government; except under such very peculiar circumstances as those which succeeded the Irish famine. Emigration on the voluntary principle rarely has any material influence in lightening the pressure of population in the old country, though as far as it goes it is doubtless a benefit to the colony. Those laboring persons who voluntarily emigrate are seldom the very poor; they are small farmers with some little capital, or laborers who have saved something, and who, in removing only their own labor from the crowded labor market, withdraw from the capital of the country a fund which maintained and employed more laborers than themselves. Besides, this portion of the community is so limited in number that it might be removed entirely, without making any sensible impression upon the numbers of the population, or even upon the annual increase. Any considerable emigration of labor is only practicable when its cost is defrayed, or at least advanced, by others than the emigrants themselves. Who then is to advance it? Naturally, it may be said, the capitalists of the colony, who require the labor, and who intend to employ it. But to this there is the obstacle, that a capitalist, after going to the expense of carrying out laborers, has no security that he shall be the person to derive any benefit from them. If all the capitalists of the colony were to combine, and bear the expense by subscription, they would still have no security that the laborers, when there, would continue to work for them. After working for a short time and earning a few pounds, they always, unless prevented by the government, squat on unoccupied land, and work only for themselves. The experiment has been repeatedly tried whether it was possible to enforce contracts for labor, or the repayment of the passage money of emigrants to those who advanced it, and the trouble and expense have always exceeded the advantage. The only other resource is the voluntary contributions of parishes or individuals, to rid themselves of surplus laborers who are already, or who are likely to become, locally chargeable on the poor-rate. Were this speculation to become general, it might produce a sufficient amount of emigration to clear off the existing unemployed population, but not to raise the wages of the employed: and the same thing would require to be done over again in less than another generation.

One of the principal reasons why colonization should be a national undertaking is that in this manner alone, save in highly exceptional cases, can emigration be self-supporting. The exportation of capital and labor to a new country being, as before observed, one of the best of all affairs of business, it is absurd that it should not, like other affairs of business, repay its own expenses. Of the great addition which it makes to the produce of the world, there can be no reason why a sufficient portion should not be intercepted, and employed in reimbursing the outlay incurred in effecting it. For reasons already given, no individual, or body of individuals, can reimburse themselves for the expense; the government, however, can. It can take from the annual increase of wealth, caused by the emigration, the fraction which suffices to repay with interest what the emigration has cost. The expenses of emigration to a colony ought to be borne by the colony; and this, in general, is only possible when they are borne by the colonial government.

Of the modes in which a fund for the support of colonization can be raised in the colony, none is comparable in advantage to that which was first suggested, and so ably and perseveringly advocated, by Mr. Wakefield: the plan of putting a price on all unoccupied land, and devoting the proceeds to emigration. The unfounded and pedantic objections to this plan have been answered in a former part of this chapter: we have now to speak of its advantages. First, it avoids the difficulties and discontents incident to raising a large annual amount by taxation; a thing which is almost useless to attempt with a scattered population of settlers in the wilderness, who, as experience proves, can seldom be compelled to pay direct taxes, except at a cost exceeding their amount; while in an infant community indirect taxation soon reaches its limit. The sale of lands is thus by far the easiest mode of raising the requisite funds. But it has other and still greater recommendations. It is a beneficial check upon the tendency of a population of colonists to adopt the tastes and inclinations of savage life, and to disperse so widely as to lose all the advantages of commerce, of markets, of separation of employments, and combination of labor. By making it necessary for those who emigrate at the expense of the fund, to earn a considerable sum before they can become landed proprietors, it keeps up a perpetual succession of laborers for hire, who in every country are a most important auxiliary even to peasant proprietors: and by diminishing the eagerness of agricultural speculators to add to their domain, it keeps the settlers within reach of each other for purposes of cooperation, arranges a numerous body of them within easy distance of each center of foreign commerce and nonagricultural industry, and insures the formation and rapid growth of towns and town products. This concentration, compared with the dispersion which uniformly occurs when unoccupied land can be had for nothing, greatly accelerates the attainment of prosperity, and enlarges the fund which may be drawn upon for further emigration. Before the adoption of the Wakefield system, the early years of all new colonies were full of hardship and difficulty: the last colony founded on the old principle, the Swan River settlement, being one of the most characteristic instances. In all subsequent colonization, the Wakefield principle has been acted upon, though imperfectly, a part only of the proceeds of the sale of land being devoted to emigration: yet wherever it has been introduced at all, as in South Australia, Victoria, and New Zealand, the restraint put upon the dispersion of the settlers, and the influx of capital caused by the assurance of being able to obtain hired labor has, in spite of many difficulties and much mismanagement, produced a suddenness and rapidity of prosperity more like fable than reality.

The self-supporting system of colonization, once established, would increase in efficiency every year; its effect would tend to increase in geometrical progression: for since every able-bodied emigrant, until the country is fully peopled, adds in a very short time to its wealth, over and above his own consumption, as much as would defray the expense of bringing out another emigrant, it follows that the greater the number already sent, the greater number might continue to be sent, each emigrant laying the foundation of a succession of other emigrants at short intervals without fresh expense, until the colony is filled up. It would therefore be worthwhile to the mother country to accelerate the early stages of this progression, by loans to the colonies for the purpose of emigration, repayable from the fund formed by the sales of land. In thus advancing the means of accomplishing a large immediate emigration, it would be investing that amount of capital in the mode, of all others, most beneficial to the colony; and the labor and savings of these emigrants would hasten the period at which a large sum would be available from sales of land. It would be necessary, in order not to overstock the labor market, to act in concert with the persons disposed to remove their own capital to the colony. The knowledge that a large amount of hired labor would be available, in so productive a field of employment, would insure a large emigration of capital from a country, like England, of low profits and rapid accumulation: and it would only be necessary not to send out a greater number of laborers at one time, than this capital could absorb and employ at high wages.

Inasmuch as, on this system, any given amount of expenditure, once incurred, would provide not merely a single emigration, but a perpetually flowing stream of emigrants, which would increase in breadth and depth as it flowed on; this mode of relieving overpopulation has a recommendation, not possessed by any other plan ever proposed for making head against the consequences of increase without restraining the increase itself: there is an element of indefiniteness in it; no one can perfectly foresee how far its influence, as a vent for surplus population, might possibly reach. There is hence the strongest obligation on the government of a country like our own, with a crowded population, and unoccupied continents under its command, to build, as it were, and keep open, in concert with the colonial governments, a bridge from the mother country to those continents, by establishing the self-supporting system of colonization on such a scale, that as great an amount of emigration as the colonies can at the time accommodate, may at all times be able to take place without cost to the emigrants themselves.

The importance of these considerations, as regards the British islands, has been of late considerably diminished by the unparalleled amount of spontaneous emigration from Ireland; an emigration not solely of small farmers, but of the poorest class of agricultural laborers, and which is at once voluntary and self-supporting, the succession of emigrants being kept up by funds contributed from the earnings of their relatives and connexions who had gone before. To this has been added a large amount of voluntary emigration to the seats of the gold discoveries, which has partly supplied the wants of our most distant colonies, where, both for local and national interests, it was most of all required. But the stream of both these emigrations has already considerably slackened, and though that from Ireland has since partially revived, it is not certain that the aid of government in a systematic form, and on the self-supporting principle, will not again become necessary to keep the communication open between the hands needing work in England, and the work which needs hands elsewhere.

15

The same principle which points out colonization, and the relief of the indigent, as cases to which the principal objection to government interference does not apply, extends also to a variety of cases, in which important public services are to be performed, while yet there is no individual specially interested in performing them, nor would any adequate remuneration naturally or spontaneously attend their performance. Take for instance a voyage of geographical or scientific exploration. The information sought may be of great public value, yet no individual would derive any benefit from it which would repay the expense of fitting out the expedition; and there is no mode of intercepting the benefit on its way to those who profit by it, in order to levy a toll for the remuneration of its authors. Such voyages are, or might be, undertaken by private subscription; but this is a rare and precarious resource. Instances are more frequent in which the expense has been borne by public companies or philanthropic associations; but in general such enterprises have been conducted at the expense of government, which is thus enabled to entrust them to the persons in its judgment best qualified for the task. Again, it is a proper office of government to build and maintain lighthouses, establish buoys, etc., for the security of navigation: for since it is impossible that the ships at sea which are benefited by a lighthouse, should be made to pay a toll on the occasion of its use, no one would build lighthouses from motives of personal interest, unless indemnified and rewarded from a compulsory levy made by the state. There are many scientific researches, of great value to a nation and to mankind, requiring assiduous devotion of time and labor, and not unfrequently great expense, by persons who can obtain a high price for their services in other ways. If the government had no power to grant indemnity for expense, and remuneration for time and labor thus employed, such researches could only be undertaken by the very few persons who, with an independent fortune, unite technical knowledge, laborious habits, and either great public spirit, or an ardent desire of scientific celebrity.

Connected with this subject is the question of providing by means of endowments or salaries, for the maintenance of what has been called a learned class. The cultivation of speculative knowledge, though one of the most useful of all employments, is a service rendered to a community collectively, not individually, and one consequently for which is it, prima facie, reasonable that the community collectively should pay; since it gives no claim on any individual for a pecuniary remuneration; and unless a provision is made for such services from some public fund, there is not only no encouragement to them, but there is as much discouragement as is implied in the impossibility of gaining a living by such pursuits, and the necessity consequently imposed on most of those who would be capable of them, to employ the greatest part of their time in gaining a subsistence. The evil, however, is greater in appearance than in reality. The greatest things, it has been said, have generally been done by those who had the least time at their disposal; and the occupation of some hours every day in a routine employment, has often been found compatible with the most brilliant achievements in literature and philosophy. Yet there are investigations and experiments which require not only a long but a continuous devotion of time and attention: there are also occupations which so engross and fatigue the mental faculties, as to be inconsistent with any vigorous employment of them upon other subjects, even in any intervals of leisure. It is highly desirable, therefore, that there should be a mode of insuring to a public the services of scientific discoverers, and perhaps of some other classes of savants, by affording them the means of support consistently with devoting a sufficient portion of time to their peculiar pursuits. The fellowships of the universities are an institution excellently adapted for such a purpose; but are hardly ever applied to it, being bestowed, at the best, as a reward for past proficiency, in committing to memory what has been done by others, and not as the salary of future labors in the advancement of knowledge. In some countries, academies of science, antiquities, history, etc., have been formed with emoluments annexed. The most effectual plan, and at the same time least liable to abuse, seems to be that of conferring professorships, with duties of instruction attached to them. The occupation of teaching a branch of knowledge, at least in its higher departments, is a help rather than an impediment to the systematic cultivation of the subject itself. The duties of a professorship almost always leave much time for original researches; and the greatest advances which have been made in the various sciences, both moral and physical, have originated with those who were public teachers of them; from Plato and Aristotle to the great names of the Scotch, French, and German universities. I do not mention the English, because until very lately their professorships have been, as is well known, little more than nominal. In the case, too, of a lecturer in a great institution of education, the public at large has the means of judging, if not the quality of the teaching, at least the talents and industry of the teacher; and is more difficult to misemploy the power of appointment to such an office, than to job in pensions and salaries to persons not so directly before the public eye.

It may be said generally, that anything which it is desirable should be done for the general interests of mankind or of future generations, or for the present interests of those members of the community who require external aid, but which is not of a nature to remunerate individuals or associations for undertaking it, is in itself a suitable thing to be undertaken by government: though, before making the work their own, governments ought always to consider if there be any rational probability of its being done on what is called the voluntary principle, and if so, whether it is likely to be done in a better or more effectual manner by government agency, than by the zeal and liberality of individuals.

16

The preceding heads comprise, to the best of my judgment, the whole of the exceptions to the practical maxim, that the business of society can be best performed by private and voluntary agency. It is, however, necessary to add that the intervention of government cannot always practically stop short at the limit which defines the cases intrinsically suitable for it. In the particular circumstances of a given age or nation, there is scarcely anything really important to the general interest, which it may not be desirable, or even necessary, that the government should take upon itself, not because private individuals cannot effectually perform it, but because they will not. At some times and places there will be no roads, docks, harbors, canals, works of irrigation, hospitals, schools, colleges, printing presses, unless the government establishes them; the public being either too poor to command the necessary resources, or too little advanced in intelligence to appreciate the ends, or not sufficiently practiced in joint action to be capable of the means. This is true, more or less, of all countries inured to despotism, and particularly of those in which there is a very wide distance in civilization between the people and the government: as in those which have been conquered and are retained in subjection by a more energetic and more cultivated people. In many parts of the world, the people can do nothing for themselves which requires large means and combined action: all such things are left undone, unless done by the state. In these cases, the mode in which the government can most surely demonstrate the sincerity with which it intends the greatest good of its subjects, is by doing the things which are made incumbent on it by the helplessness of the public, in such a manner as shall tend not to increase and perpetuate, but to correct that helplessness. A good government will give all its aid in such a shape as to encourage and nurture any rudiments it may find of a spirit of individual exertion. It will be assiduous in removing obstacles and discouragements to voluntary enterprise, and in giving whatever facilities and whatever direction and guidance may be necessary: its pecuniary means will be applied, when practicable, in aid of private efforts rather than in supersession of them, and it will call into play its machinery of rewards and honors to elicit such efforts. Government aid, when given merely in default of private enterprise, should be so given as to be as far as possible a course of education for the people in the art of accomplishing great objects by individual energy and voluntary cooperation.

I have not thought it necessary here to insist on that part of the functions of government which all admit to be indispensable, the function of prohibiting and punishing such conduct on the part of individuals in the exercise of their freedom as is clearly injurious to other persons, whether the case be one of force, fraud, or negligence. Even in the best state which society has yet reached, it is lamentable to think how great a proportion of all the efforts and talents in the world are employed in merely neutralizing one another. It is the proper end of government to reduce this wretched waste to the smallest possible amount, by taking such measures as shall cause the energies now spent by mankind in injuring one another, or in protecting themselves against injury, to be turned to the legitimate employment of the human faculties, that of compelling the powers of nature to be more and more subservient to physical and moral good.

Economy

ment in a laissez-faire economy?

sts "who think no state of
is not a rapid increase of

ritative" and "not authoritative"

ion?

omic principles in his agreement
rstand their own business and
n more, than the government

does, or can be expected to do"? (122)

FOR FURTHER DISCUSSION

1. How should a democracy avoid "diverting the intelligence and activity of the country from its principal business to a wretched competition for the selfish prizes and the petty vanities of office"?

2. Under what conditions would a laissez-faire policy be beneficial to an economy? When would it be harmful?

3. Is Mill correct in asserting, "There cannot be a combination of circumstances more dangerous to human welfare than that in which intelligence and talent are maintained at a high standard within a governing corporation, but starved and discouraged outside the pale"?

K arl Marx (1818–1883) was one of the most controversial and influential thinkers of all time, inspiring an extraordinary level of devotion and disparagement among his many millions of disciples and detractors. Although the majority of his voluminous writings dealt with political economy, his main historical impact was not on economics as an academic discipline. Rather, his historical significance chiefly lies in the inspiration he provided—both in his writings and in his person—to the revolutionary socialist movement in Europe in the nineteenth century, out of which grew the various Communist regimes of the twentieth. Even today, Marxist-inspired regimes govern a large portion of the world's population.

Marx was born in Trier, Prussia (now Germany), the son of an affluent lawyer. He entered the University of Berlin in 1836, where he studied law and philosophy, and fell in with the Young Hegelians, who used G. W. F. Hegel's dialectical theory of world history as a basis for criticizing contemporary society. Marx was also deeply influenced by Ludwig Feuerbach's critique of religion, and became a lifelong atheist. After receiving his doctorate in 1841, Marx turned his hand to journalism and became editor of a radical journal; however, he soon became embroiled in controversy, and the authorities suspended its publication. In 1843 the newly married Marx moved to Paris, where he met Friedrich Engels, the radical son of a wealthy industrialist who became Marx's lifelong collaborator. During the next several years, Marx was expelled from various countries, and he had to relocate his young family more than once. Finally, in 1849, he settled in London, where he remained for the rest of his life.

In the revolutionary year of 1848, Marx and Engels issued their *Communist Manifesto*, which fired the imaginations of radicals across Europe. In 1867 Marx published the first volume of *Das Kapital*, in which he recast the Hegelian theory of historical development as a struggle of social classes, provided a profound and detailed analysis of capitalism, and predicted the inevitable ascendance of communism. The following selection from *Das Kapital* represents one of the most persistently influential aspects of Marx's work, which is his critique of all things produced by human culture from the perspective of his economic theory.

The Fetishism of Commodities and the Secret Thereof

A commodity appears, at first sight, a very trivial thing, and easily understood. Its analysis shows that it is, in reality, a very queer thing, abounding in metaphysical subtleties and theological niceties. So far as it is a value in use, there is nothing mysterious about it, whether we consider it from the point of view that by its properties it is capable of satisfying human wants, or from the point that those properties are the product of human labor. It is as clear as noonday, that man, by his industry, changes the forms of the materials furnished by nature, in such a way as to make them useful to him. The form of wood, for instance, is altered by making a table out of it. Yet, for all that the table continues to be that common, everyday thing, wood. But, so soon as it steps forth as a commodity, it is changed into something transcendent. It not only stands with its feet on the ground, but, in relation to all other commodities, it stands on its head, and evolves out of its wooden brain grotesque ideas, far more wonderful than "table-turning" ever was.

The mystical character of commodities does not originate, therefore, in their use-value. Just as little does it proceed from the nature of the determining factors of value. For, in the first place, however varied the useful kinds of labor, or productive activities, may be, it is a physiological fact, that they are functions of the human organism, and that each such function, whatever may be its nature or form, is essentially the expenditure of human brain, nerves, muscles, etc. Secondly, with regard to that which forms the groundwork for the quantitative determination of value, namely, the duration of that expenditure, or the quantity of labor, it is quite clear that there is a palpable difference between its quantity and quality. In all states of society, the labor-time that it costs to produce the means of subsistence must necessarily be an object of interest to mankind,

This selection is taken from part 1, chapter 1 of Capital: A Critique of Political Economy, *vol. 1.*

though not of equal interest in different stages of development. And lastly, from the moment that men in any way work for one another, their labor assumes a social form.

Whence, then, arises the enigmatical character of the product of labor, so soon as it assumes the form of commodities? Clearly from this form itself. The equality of all sorts of human labor is expressed objectively by their products all being equally values; the measure of the expenditure of labor-power by the duration of that expenditure, takes the form of the quantity of value of the products of labor; and finally, the mutual relations of the producers, within which the social character of their labor affirms itself, take the form of a social relation between the products.

A commodity is therefore a mysterious thing, simply because in it the social character of men's labor appears to them as an objective character stamped upon the product of that labor; because the relation of the producers to the sum total of their own labor is presented to them as a social relation, existing not between themselves, but between the products of their labor. This is the reason why the products of labor become commodities, social things whose qualities are at the same time perceptible and imperceptible by the senses. In the same way the light from an object is perceived by us not as the subjective excitation of our optic nerve, but as the objective form of something outside the eye itself. But, in the act of seeing, there is at all events an actual passage of light from one thing to another, from the external object to the eye. There is a physical relation between physical things. But it is different with commodities. There, the existence of the things qua commodities, and the value relation between the products of labor which stamps them as commodities, have absolutely no connection with their physical properties and with the material relations arising therefrom. There is a definite social relation between men, that assumes, in their eyes, the fantastic form of a relation between things. In order, therefore, to find an analogy, we must have recourse to the mist-enveloped regions of the religious world. In that world the productions of the human brain appear as independent beings endowed with life, and entering into relation both with one another and the human race. So it is in the world of commodities with the products of men's hands. This I call the *fetishism* which attaches itself to the products of labor, so soon as they are produced as commodities, and which is therefore inseparable from the production of commodities.

This fetishism of commodities has its origin, as the foregoing analysis has already shown, in the peculiar social character of the labor that produces them.

As a general rule, articles of utility become commodities, only because they are products of the labor of private individuals or groups of individuals who carry on their work independently of one another. The sum total of the labor of all these private individuals forms the aggregate labor of society. Since the producers do not come into social contact with each other until they exchange their products, the specific social character of each producer's labor does not show itself except in the act of exchange. In other words, the labor of the individual asserts itself as a part of the labor of society, only by means of the relations which the act of exchange establishes directly between the products, and indirectly, through them, between the producers. To the latter, therefore, the relations connecting the labor of the individual with that of the rest appear, not as direct social relations between individuals at work, but as what they really are, material relations between persons and social relations between things. It is only by being exchanged that the products of labor acquire, as values, one uniform social status, distinct from their varied forms of existence as objects of utility. This division of a product into a useful thing and a value becomes practically important, only when exchange has acquired such an extension that useful articles are produced for the purpose of being exchanged, and their character as values has therefore to be taken into account, before-hand, during production. From this moment the labor of the individual producer acquires socially a twofold character. On the one hand, it must, as a definite useful kind of labor, satisfy a definite social want, and thus hold its place as part and parcel of the collective labor of all, as a branch of a social division of labor that has sprung up spontaneously. On the other hand, it can satisfy the manifold wants of the individual producer himself, only insofar as the mutual exchangeability of all kinds of useful private labor is an established social fact, and therefore the private useful labor of each producer ranks on an equality with that of all others. The equalization of the most different kinds of labor can be the result only of an abstraction from their inequalities, or of reducing them to their common denominator, viz., expenditure of human labor power or human labor in the abstract. The twofold social character of the labor of the individual appears to him, when reflected in his brain, only under those forms which are impressed upon that labor in everyday practice by the exchange of products. In this way, the character that his own labor possesses of being socially useful takes the form of the condition, that the product must be not only useful, but useful for others, and the social character that his particular labor has of being the equal of all other particular kinds of labor, takes the form that all the physically different articles that are the products of labor, have one common quality, viz., that of having value.

Hence, when we bring the products of our labor into relation with one another as values, it is not because we see in these articles the material receptacles of homogeneous human labor. Quite the contrary; whenever, by an exchange, we equate as values our different products, by that very act, we also equate, as human labor, the different kinds of labor expended upon them. We are not aware of this, nevertheless we do it. Value, therefore, does not stalk about with a label describing what it is. It is value, rather, that converts every product into a social hieroglyphic. Later on, we try to decipher the hieroglyphic, to get behind the secret of our own social products; for to stamp an object of utility as a value, is just as much a social product as language. The recent scientific discovery that the products of labor, so far as they are values, are but material expressions of the human labor spent in their production, marks, indeed, an epoch in the history of the development of the human race, but by no means dissipates the mist through which the social character of labor appears to us to be an objective character of the products themselves. The fact that in the particular form of production with which we are dealing, viz., the production of commodities, the specific social character of private labor carried on independently, consists in the equality of every kind of the labor, by virtue of its being human labor, which character, therefore, assumes in the product the form of value—this fact appears to the producers, notwithstanding the discovery above referred to, to be just as real and final, as the fact, that, after the discovery by science of the component gases of air, the atmosphere itself remained unaltered.

What, first of all, practically concerns producers when they make an exchange, is the question, how much of some other product they get for their own? In what proportions the products are exchangeable? When these proportions have, by custom, attained a certain stability, they appear to result from the nature of the products, so that, for instance, one ton of iron and two ounces of gold appear as naturally to be of equal value as a pound of gold and a pound of iron in spite of their different physical and chemical qualities appear to be of equal weight. The character of having value, when once impressed upon products, obtains fixity only by reason of their acting and reacting upon each other as quantities of value. These quantities vary continually, independently of the will, foresight, and action of the producers. To them, their own social action takes the form of the action of objects, which rule the producers instead of being ruled by them. It requires a fully developed production of commodities before, from accumulated experience alone, the scientific conviction springs up, that all the different kinds of private labor, which are carried on independently of each other, and yet as spontaneously developed branches of the social division of labor, are continually being reduced to the quantitive proportions in which society requires them. And why? Because, in the midst of all the accidental and ever fluctuating exchange-relations between the products, the labor-time socially necessary for their production forcibly asserts itself like an overriding law of nature. The law of gravity thus asserts itself when a house falls about our ears. The determination of the magnitude of value by labor-time is therefore a secret, hidden under the apparent fluctuations in the relative values of commodities. Its discovery, while removing all appearance of mere accidentality from the determination of the magnitude of the values of products, yet in no way alters the mode in which that determination takes place.

Man's reflections on the forms of social life, and consequently, also, his scientific analysis of those forms, have taken a course directly opposite to that of their actual historical development. He begins, *post festum*, with the results of the process of development ready to hand before him. The characters that stamp products as commodities, and whose establishment is a necessary preliminary to the circulation of commodities, have already acquired the stability of natural, self-understood forms of social life, before man seeks to decipher, not their historical character, for in his eyes they are immutable, but their meaning. Consequently it was the analysis of the prices of commodities that alone led to the determination of the magnitude of value, and it was the common expression of all commodities in money that alone led to the establishment of their characters as values. It is, however, just this ultimate money form of the world of commodities that actually conceals, instead of disclosing, the social character of private labor, and the social relations between the individual producers. When I state that coats or boots stand in a relation to linen, because it is the universal incarnation of abstract human labor, the absurdity of the statement is self-evident. Nevertheless, when the producers of coats and boots compare those articles with linen, or, what is the same thing with gold or silver, as the universal equivalent, they express the relation between their own private labor and the collective labor of society in the same absurd form.

The categories of bourgeois economy consist of such like forms. They are forms of thought expressing with social validity the conditions and relations of a definite, historically determined mode of production, viz., the production of commodities. The whole mystery of commodities, all the magic and necromancy that surrounds the products of labor as long as they take the form of commodities, vanishes therefore, so soon as we come to other forms of production.

Since Robinson Crusoe's experiences are a favorite theme with political economists, let us take a look at him on his island. Moderate though he be, yet some few wants he has to satisfy, and must therefore do a little useful work of various sorts, such as making tools and furniture, taming goats, fishing and hunting. Of his prayers and the like we take no account, since they are a source of pleasure to him, and he looks upon them as so much recreation. In spite of the variety of his work, he knows that his labor, whatever its form, is but the activity of one and the same Robinson, and consequently, that it consists of nothing but different modes of human labor. Necessity itself compels him to apportion his time accurately between his different kinds of work. Whether one kind occupies a greater space in his general activity than another depends on the difficulties, greater or less as the case may be, to be overcome in attaining the useful effect aimed at. This our friend Robinson soon learns by experience, and having rescued a watch, ledger, and pen and ink from the wreck, commences, like a true-born Briton, to keep a set of books. His stock-book contains a list of the objects of utility that belong to him, of the operations necessary for their production; and lastly; of the labor time that definite quantities of those objects have, on an average, cost him. All the relations between Robinson and the objects that form this wealth of his own creation, are here so simple and clear as to be intelligible without exertion, even to Mr. Sedley Taylor. And yet those relations contain all that is essential to the determination of value.

Let us now transport ourselves from Robinson's island bathed in light to the European Middle Ages shrouded in darkness. Here, instead of the independent man, we find everyone dependent, serfs and lords, vassals and suzerains, laymen and clergy. Personal dependence here characterizes the social relations of production just as much as it does the other spheres of life organized on the basis of that production. But for the very reason that personal dependence forms the groundwork of society, there is no necessity for labor and its products to assume a fantastic form different from their reality. They take the shape, in the transactions of society, of services in kind and payments in kind. Here the particular and natural form of labor, and not, as in a society based on production of commodities, its general abstract form is the immediate social form of labor. Compulsory labor is just as properly measured by time, as commodity-producing labor; but every serf knows that what he expends in the service of his lord, is a definite quantity of his own personal labor-power. The tithe to be rendered to the priest is more matter of fact than his blessing. No matter, then, what we may think of the parts played by the different classes of people themselves in this society, the social relations between individuals in the performance of their labor, appear at all events as their own mutual personal relations, and are not disguised under the shape of social relations between the products of labor.

For an example of labor in common or directly associated labor, we have no occasion to go back to that spontaneously developed form which we find on the threshold of the history of all civilized races. We have one close at hand in the patriarchal industries of a peasant family, that produces corn, cattle, yarn, linen, and clothing for home use. These different articles are, as regards the family, so many products of its labor, but as between themselves, they are not commodities. The different kinds of labor, such as tillage, cattle tending, spinning, weaving, and making clothes, which result in the various products, are in themselves, and such as they are, direct social functions, because functions of the family, which just as much as a society based on the production of commodities, possesses a spontaneously developed system of division of labor. The distribution of the work within the family, and the regulation of the labor-time of the several members, depend as well upon differences of age and sex as upon natural conditions varying with the seasons. The labor-power of each individual, by its very nature, operates in this case merely as a definite portion of the whole labor-power of the family, and therefore, the measure of the expenditure of individual labor-power by its duration, appears here by its very nature as a social character of their labor.

Let us now picture to ourselves, by way of change, a community of free individuals, carrying on their work with the means of production in common, in which the labor-power of all the different individuals is consciously applied as the combined labor-power of the community. All the characteristics of Robinson's labor are here repeated, but with this difference, that they are social, instead of individual. Everything produced by him was exclusively the result of his own personal labor, and therefore simply an object of use for himself. The total product of our community is a social product. One portion serves as fresh means of production and remains social. But another portion is consumed by the members as means of subsistence. A distribution of this portion amongst them is consequently necessary. The mode of this distribution will vary with the productive organization of the community, and the degree of historical development attained by the producers. We will assume, but merely for the sake of a parallel with the production of commodities, that the share of each individual producer in the means of subsistence is determined by his labor-time. Labor-time would, in that case, play a double part. Its apportionment in accordance with a definite social plan maintains the proper proportion between the different kinds of work to be done and the various wants of the community. On the other hand, it also serves as a measure of the portion of the common labor borne by each individual and of his share in the part of the total product destined for individual consumption. The social relations of the individual producers, with regard both to their labor and to its products, are in this case perfectly simple and intelligible, and that with regard not only to production but also to distribution.

The religious world is but the reflex of the real world. And for a society based upon the production of commodities, in which the producers in general enter into social relations with one another by treating their products as commodities and values, whereby they reduce their individual private labor to the standard of homogeneous human labor—for such a society, Christianity with its cultus of abstract man, more especially in its bourgeois developments, Protestantism, Deism, etc., is the most fitting form of religion. In the ancient Asiatic and other ancient modes of production, we find that the conversion of products into commodities, and therefore the conversion of men into producers of commodities, holds a subordinate place, which, however, increases in importance as the primitive communities approach nearer and nearer to their dissolution. Trading nations, properly so called, exist in the ancient world only in its interstices, like the gods of Epicurus in the Intermundia, or like Jews in the pores of Polish society. Those ancient social organisms of production are, as compared with bourgeois society, extremely simple and transparent. But they are founded either on the immature development of man individually, who has not yet severed the umbilical cord that unites him with his fellow men in a primitive tribal community, or upon direct relations of subjection. They can arise and exist only when the development of the productive power of labor has not risen beyond a low stage, and when, therefore, the social relations within the sphere of material life, between man and man, and between man and Nature, are correspondingly narrow. This narrowness is reflected in the ancient worship of Nature, and in the other elements of the popular religions. The religious reflex of the real world can, in any case, only then finally vanish, when the practical relations of everyday life offer to man none but perfectly intelligible and reasonable relations with regard to his fellowmen and to nature.

The life-process of society, which is based on the process of material production, does not strip off its mystical veil until it is treated as production by freely associated men, and is consciously regulated by them in accordance with a settled plan. This, however, demands for society a certain material groundwork or set of conditions of existence which in their turn are the spontaneous product of a long and painful process of development.

Political economy has indeed analyzed, however incompletely, value and its magnitude, and has discovered what lies beneath these forms. But it has never once asked the question why labor is represented by the value of its product and labor time by the magnitude of that value. These formulas, which bear stamped upon them in unmistakeable letters that they belong to a state of society in which the process of production has the mastery over man, instead of being controlled by him—such formulas appear to the bourgeois intellect to be as much a self-evident necessity imposed by nature as productive labor itself. Hence forms of social production that preceded the bourgeois form are treated by the bourgeoisie in much the same way as the Fathers of the Church treated pre-Christian religions.

To what extent some economists are misled by the fetishism inherent in commodities, or by the objective appearance of the social characteristics of labor, is shown, amongst other ways, by the dull and tedious quarrel over the part played by Nature in the formation of exchange-value. Since exchange-value is a definite social manner of expressing the amount of labor bestowed upon an object, Nature has no more to do with it, than it has in fixing the course of exchange.

The mode of production in which the product takes the form of a commodity, or is produced directly for exchange, is the most general and most embryonic form of bourgeois production. It therefore makes its appearance at an early date in history, though not in the same predominating and characteristic manner as nowadays. Hence its fetish character is comparatively easy to be seen through. But when we come to more concrete forms, even this appearance of simplicity vanishes. Whence arose the illusions of the monetary system? To it gold and silver, when serving as money, did not represent a social relation between producers, but were natural objects with strange social properties. And modern economy, which looks down with such disdain on the monetary system, does not its superstition come out as clear as noonday, whenever it treats of capital? How long is it since economy discarded the physiocratic illusion, that rents grow out of the soil and not out of society?

But not to anticipate, we will content ourselves with yet another example relating to the commodity form. Could commodities themselves speak, they would say: Our use-value may be a thing that interests men. It is no part of us as objects. What, however, does belong to us as objects, is our value. Our natural intercourse as commodities proves it. In the eyes of each other we are nothing but exchange values. Now listen how those commodities speak through the mouth of the economist. "Value"—(i.e., exchange-value) "is a property of things, riches"—(i.e., use-value) "of man. Value, in this sense, necessarily implies exchanges, riches do not." "Riches" (use-value) "are the attribute of men, value is the attribute of commodities. A man or a community is rich, a pearl or a diamond is valuable. . . . A pearl or a diamond is valuable" as a pearl or diamond. So far no chemist has ever discovered exchange-value either in a pearl or a diamond. The economical discoverers of this chemical element, who by the bye lay special claim to critical acumen, find however that the use-value of objects belongs to them independently of their material properties, while their value, on the other hand, forms a part of them as objects. What confirms them in this view is the peculiar circumstances that the use-value of objects is realized without exchange by means of a direct relation between the objects and man, while, on the other hand, their value is realized only by exchange, that is, by means of a social process. Who fails here to call to mind our good friend, Dogberry, who informs neighbor Seacoal, that "to be a well-favored man is the gift of fortune; but reading and writing comes by nature."

QUESTIONS

1. According to Marx, why are commodities "social things whose qualities are at the same time perceptible and imperceptible by the senses"? (153)

2. What does Marx mean by the term *fetishism*? Why is it "inseparable from the production of commodities"? (153)

3. According to Marx, how does money conceal rather than reveal "the social character of private labor, and the social relations between the individual producers"? (156)

4. For a society that treats the products of labor as commodities and values, why does Marx say that Christianity is "the most fitting form of religion"? (158–159)

5. Why does Marx distinguish between the "value" and "use-value" of a commodity? (160)

FOR FURTHER REFLECTION

1. Is the term *fetishism* an appropriate one to apply to our relationship to commodities in our own society?

2. What commodities in our own society typically have a high "value" compared to their "use-value"? How is that "value" determined?

3. Do you agree with Marx's view that the life-process of society "is based on the process of material production"?

WALTER BAGEHOT

Walter Bagehot (1826–1877) was not only a successful banker and accomplished economist, but also an eminent journalist and political commentator. His popularity was due in part to his brilliant writing style, and although he is best known today for *The English Constitution* (1867), an analysis of the British system of government, his most lasting contributions to economics appear in *Lombard Street* (1873), a pioneering study of banking and finance.

Bagehot was born in Somerset, England, and was descended from bankers and businessmen on both sides of his family. He received a solid early education, showing special aptitude for philosophy and classics. Bagehot attended University College, London, and after graduating with honors in moral and intellectual philosophy, he studied law for three years. However, he decided to join his family's bank—one of the largest in the west of England—where he eventually managed the Bristol office. Finding himself in Paris during Louis Napoleon's seizure of power in 1851, Bagehot was inspired to write a series of letters defending the coup, which were published and which established Bagehot's reputation as a writer. Over the next several years he published numerous essays on political, economic, and literary subjects. In 1858 he married the daughter of the founder of the *Economist* magazine. Upon his father-in-law's death two years later, Bagehot took over as editor of the magazine and turned it into the preeminent British economic and political periodical, which it remains to this day.

Lombard Street, the source of the following selection, was one of the first attempts to provide a serious analysis of modern banking and finance. In this excerpt, Bagehot argues that one of the consequences of prosperity is the creation of the modern bubble-and-recession business cycle and proposes a way to mitigate its adverse effects. In doing so, he sets the tone for our contemporary debates of similar issues.

Why Lombard Street Is Often Very Dull, and Sometimes Extremely Excited

Any sudden event which creates a great demand for actual cash may cause, and will tend to cause, a panic in a country where cash is much economized, and where debts payable on demand are large. In such a country an immense credit rests on a small cash reserve, and an unexpected and large diminution of that reserve may easily break up and shatter very much, if not the whole, of that credit. Such accidental events are of the most various nature: a bad harvest, an apprehension of foreign invasion, the sudden failure of a great firm which everybody trusted, and many other similar events, have all caused a sudden demand for cash. And some writers have endeavored to classify panics according to the nature of the particular accidents producing them. But little, however, is, I believe, to be gained by such classifications. There is little difference in the effect of one accident and another upon our credit system. We must be prepared for all of them, and we must prepare for all of them in the same way—by keeping a large cash reserve.

But it is of great importance to point out that our industrial organization is liable not only to irregular external accidents, but likewise to regular internal changes; that these changes make our credit system much more delicate at some times than at others; and that it is the recurrence of these periodical seasons of delicacy which has given rise to the notion that panics come according to a fixed rule—that every ten years or so we must have one of them.

Most persons who begin to think of the subject are puzzled on the threshold. They hear much of "good times" and "bad times," meaning by "good" times in which nearly everyone is very well off, and by "bad" times

This selection is taken from chapter 6 of Lombard Street.

in which nearly everyone is comparatively ill off. And at first it is natural to ask why should everybody, or almost everybody, be well off together? Why should there be any great tides of industry, with large diffused profit by way of flow, and large diffused want of profit, or loss, by way of ebb? The main answer is hardly given distinctly in our common books of political economy. These books do not tell you what is the fund out of which large general profits are paid in good times, nor do they explain why that fund is not available for the same purpose in bad times.

Our current political economy does not sufficiently take account of *time* as an element in trade operations; but as soon as the division of labor has once established itself in a community, two principles at once begin to be important, of which time is the very essence. These are:

1. That as goods are produced to be exchanged, it is good that they should be exchanged as quickly as possible.

2. That as every producer is mainly occupied in producing what others want, and not what he wants himself, it is desirable that he should always be able to find, without effort, without delay, and without uncertainty, others who want what he can produce.

In themselves these principles are self-evident. Everyone will admit it to be expedient that all goods wanting to be sold should be sold as soon as they are ready; that every man who wants to work should find employment as soon as he is ready for it. Obviously also, as soon as the "division of labor" is really established, there is a difficulty about both of these principles. A produces what he thinks B wants, but it may be a mistake, and B may not want it. A may be able and willing to produce what B wants, but he may not be able to find B—he may not know of his existence.

The general truth of these principles is obvious, but what is not obvious is the extreme greatness of their effects. Taken together, they make the whole difference between times of brisk trade and great prosperity, and times of stagnant trade and great adversity, so far as that prosperity and that adversity are real and not illusory. If they are satisfied, everyone knows whom to work for, and what to make, and he can get immediately in exchange what he wants himself. There is no idle labor and no sluggish capital in the whole community, and, in consequence, all which can be produced is produced, the effectiveness of human industry is augmented, and both kinds of producers—both capitalists and laborers—are much richer than usual, because the amount to be divided between them is also much greater than usual.

And there is a partnership in industries. No single large industry can be depressed without injury to other industries; still less can any great group of industries. Each industry when prosperous buys and consumes the produce probably of most (certainly of very many) other industries, and if industry A fail and is in difficulty, industries B, and C, and D, which used to sell to it, will not be able to sell that which they had produced in reliance on A's demand, and in [the] future they will stand idle till industry A recovers, because in default of A there will be no one to buy the commodities which they create. Then as industry B buys of C, D, etc., the adversity of B tells on C, D, etc., and as these buy of E, F, etc., the effect is propagated through the whole alphabet. And in a certain sense it rebounds. Z feels the want caused by the diminished custom of A, B, and C, and so it does not earn so much; in consequence, it cannot lay out as much on the produce of A, B, and C, and so these do not earn as much either. In all this money is but an instrument. The same thing would happen equally well in a trade of barter, if a state of barter on a very large scale were not practically impossible, on account of the time and trouble which it would necessarily require. As has been explained, the fundamental cause is that under a system in which everyone is dependent on the labor of everyone else, the loss of one spreads and multiplies through all, and spreads and multiplies the faster the higher the previous perfection of the system of divided labor, and the more nice and effectual the mode of interchange. And the entire effect of a depression in any single large trade requires a considerable *time* before it can be produced. It has to be propagated, and to be returned through a variety of industries, before it is complete. Short depressions, in consequence, have scarcely any discernible consequences; they are over before we think of their effects. It is only in the case of continuous and considerable depressions that the cause is in action long enough to produce discernible effects.

The most common, and by far the most important, case where the depression in one trade causes depression in all others, is that of depressed agriculture. When the agriculture of the world is ill off, food is dear. And as the amount of absolute necessaries which a people consumes cannot be much diminished, the additional amount which has to be spent on them is so much subtracted from what used to be spent on other things. All the industries, A, B, C, D, up to Z, are somewhat affected by an augmentation in the price of corn, and the most affected are the large ones, which produce the objects in ordinary times most consumed by the working classes. The clothing trades feel the difference at once, and in this country the liquor trade (a great source of English revenue) feels it almost equally soon. Especially when for two or three years harvests have been bad, and corn has long been dear, every industry is impoverished, and almost every one, by becoming poorer, makes every other poorer too. All trades are slack from diminished custom, and the consequence is a vast stagnant capital, much idle labor, and a greatly retarded production.

It takes two or three years to produce this full calamity, and the recovery from it takes two or three years also. If corn should long be cheap, the laboring classes have much to spend on what they like besides. The producers of those things become prosperous, and have a greater purchasing power. They exercise it, and that creates in the class they deal with another purchasing power, and so all through society. The whole machine of industry is stimulated to its maximum of energy, just as before much of it was slackened almost to its minimum.

A great calamity to any great industry will tend to produce the same effect, but the fortunes of the industries on which the wages of labor are expended are much more important than those of all others, because they act much more quickly upon a larger mass of purchasers. On principle, if there was a perfect division of labor, every industry would have to be perfectly prosperous in order that any one might be so. So far, therefore, from its being at all natural that trade should develop constantly, steadily, and equably, it is plain, without going farther, from theory as well as from experience, that there are inevitably periods of rapid dilatation, and as inevitably periods of contraction and of stagnation.

Nor is this the only changeable element in modern industrial societies. Credit—the disposition of one man to trust another—is singularly varying. In England, after a great calamity, everybody is suspicious of everybody; as soon as that calamity is forgotten, everybody again confides in everybody. On the Continent there has been a stiff controversy as to whether credit should or should not be called capital: in England, even the little attention once paid to abstract economics is now diverted, and no one cares in the least for refined questions of this kind: the material practical point is that, in M. Chevalier's language, credit is "additive," or additional—that is, in times when credit is good productive power is more efficient, and in times when credit is bad productive power is less efficient. And the state of credit is thus influential, because of the two principles which have just been explained. In a good state of credit, goods lie on hand a much less time than when credit is bad; sales are quicker; intermediate dealers borrow easily to augment their trade, and so more and more goods are more quickly and more easily transmitted from the producer to the consumer.

These two variable causes are causes of real prosperity. They augment trade and production, and so are plainly beneficial, except where by mistake the wrong things are produced, or where also by mistake misplaced credit is given, and a man who cannot produce anything which is wanted gets the produce of other people's labor upon a false idea that he will produce it. But there is another variable cause which produces far more of apparent than of real prosperity and of which the effect is in actual life mostly confused with those of the others.

In our common speculations we do not enough remember that interest on money is a refined idea, and not a universal one. So far indeed is it from being universal, that the majority of saving persons in most countries would reject it. Most savings in most countries are held in hoarded specie. In Asia, in Africa, in South America, largely even in Europe, they are thus held, and it would frighten most of the owners to let them out of their keeping. An Englishman—a modern Englishman at least—assumes as a first principle that he ought to be able to "put his money into something safe that will yield five percent;" but most saving persons in most countries are afraid to "put their money" into anything. Nothing is safe to their minds; indeed, in most countries, owing to a bad government and a backward industry, no investment, or hardly any, really is safe. In most countries most men are content to forego interest; but in more advanced countries, at some times there are more savings seeking investment than there are known investments for; at other times there is no such superabundance. Lord Macaulay has graphically described one of the periods of excess. He says—

> During the interval between the Restoration and the Revolution the riches of the nation had been rapidly increasing. Thousands of busy men found every Christmas that, after the expenses of the year's housekeeping had been defrayed out of the year's income, a surplus remained; and how that surplus was to be employed was a question of some difficulty. In our time, to invest such a surplus, at something more than three percent, on the best security that has ever been known in the world, is the work of a few minutes. But in the seventeenth century, a lawyer, a physician, a retired merchant, who had saved some thousands, and who wished to place them safely and profitably, was often greatly embarrassed. Three generations earlier, a man who had accumulated wealth in a profession generally purchased real property, or lent his savings on mortgage. But the number of acres in the kingdom had remained the same; and the value of those acres, though it had greatly increased, had by no means increased so fast as the quantity of capital which was seeking for employment. Many too wished to put their money where they could find it at an hour's notice, and looked about for some species of property which could be more readily transferred than a house or a field. A capitalist might lend on bottomry or on personal security; but, if he did so, he ran a great risk of losing interest and principal. There were a few joint stock companies, among which the East India Company held the foremost place; but the demand for the stock of such companies was far greater than the supply. Indeed the cry for a new East India Company was chiefly raised by persons who had found difficulty in placing their savings at interest on good security. So great was that difficulty that the practice of hoarding was common. We are told

that the father of Pope, the poet, who retired from business in the City about the time of the Revolution, carried to a retreat in the country a strong box containing near twenty thousand pounds, and took out from time to time what was required for household expenses; and it is highly probable that this was not a solitary case. At present the quantity of coin which is hoarded by private persons is so small, that it would, if brought forth, make no perceptible addition to the circulation. But, in the earlier part of the reign of William the Third, all the greatest writers on currency were of opinion that a very considerable mass of gold and silver was hidden in secret drawers and behind wainscots.

The natural effect of this state of things was that a crowd of projectors, ingenious and absurd, honest and knavish, employed themselves in devising new schemes for the employment of redundant capital. It was about the year 1688 that the word stockjobber was first heard in London. In the short space of four years a crowd of companies, every one of which confidently held out to subscribers the hope of immense gains, sprang into existence— the Insurance Company, the Paper Company, the Lutestring Company, the Pearl Fishery Company, the Glass Bottle Company, the Alum Company, the Blythe Coal Company, the Swordblade Company. There was a Tapestry Company, which would soon furnish pretty hangings for all the parlors of the middle class, and for all the bedchambers of the higher. There was a Copper Company, which proposed to explore the mines of England, and held out a hope that they would prove not less valuable than those of Potosi. There was a Diving Company, which undertook to bring up precious effects from shipwrecked vessels, and which announced that it had laid in a stock of wonderful machines resembling complete suits of armor. In front of the helmet was a huge glass eye like that of a Cyclops; and out of the crest went a pipe through which the air was to be admitted. The whole process was exhibited on the Thames. Fine gentlemen and fine ladies were invited to the show, were hospitably regaled, and were delighted by seeing the divers in their panoply descend into the river and return laden with old iron and ship's tackle. There was a Greenland Fishing Company, which could not fail to drive the Dutch whalers and herring busses out of the Northern Ocean. There was a Tanning Company, which promised to furnish leather superior to the best that was brought from Turkey or Russia. There was a society which undertook the office of giving gentlemen a liberal education on low terms, and which assumed the sounding name of the Royal Academies

Company. In a pompous advertisement it was announced that the directors of the Royal Academies Company had engaged the best masters in every branch of knowledge, and were about to issue twenty thousand tickets at twenty shillings each. There was to be a lottery—two thousand prizes were to be drawn; and the fortunate holders of the prizes were to be taught, at the charge of the Company, Latin, Greek, Hebrew, French, Spanish, conic sections, trigonometry, heraldry, japaning, fortification, bookkeeping, and the art of playing the theorbo.

The panic was forgotten till Lord Macaulay revived the memory of it. But, in fact, in the South Sea Bubble, which has always been remembered, the form was the same, only a little more extravagant; the companies in that mania were for objects such as these: " 'Wrecks to be fished for on the Irish Coast—Insurance of Horses and other Cattle (two millions)—Insurance of Losses by Servants—To make Salt Water Fresh—For building of Hospitals for Bastard Children—For building of Ships against Pirates—For making of Oil from Sun-flower Seeds—For improving of Malt Liquors—For recovery of Seamen's Wages—For extracting of Silver from Lead—For the transmuting of Quicksilver into a malleable and fine Metal—For making of Iron with Pit-coal—For importing a Number of large Jack Asses from Spain—For trading in Human Hair—For fatting of Hogs—For a Wheel of Perpetual Motion.' But the most strange of all, perhaps, was 'For an Undertaking which shall in due time be revealed.' Each subscriber was to pay down two guineas, and hereafter to receive a share of one hundred, with a disclosure of the object; and so tempting was the offer, that one thousand of these subscriptions were paid the same morning, with which the projector went off in the afternoon." In 1825 there were speculations in companies nearly as wild, and just before 1866 there were some of a like nature, though not equally extravagant. The fact is, that the owners of savings not finding, in adequate quantities, their usual kind of investments, rush into anything that promises speciously, and when they find that these specious investments can be disposed of at a high profit, they rush into them more and more. The first taste is for high interest, but that taste soon becomes secondary. There is a second appetite for large gains to be made by selling the principal which is to yield the interest. So long as such sales can be effected the mania continues; when it ceases to be possible to effect them, ruin begins.

So long as the savings remain in possession of their owners, these hazardous gamblings in speculative undertakings are almost the whole effect of an excess of accumulation over tested investment. Little effect is produced on the general trade of the country. The owners of the savings are too scattered and far from the market to change the majority of mercantile transactions. But when these savings come to be lodged in the hands of bankers, a much wider result is produced. Bankers are close to mercantile life; they are always ready to lend on good mercantile securities; they wish to lend on such securities a large part of the money entrusted to them. When, therefore, the money so entrusted is unusually large, and when it long continues so, the general trade of the country is, in the course of time, changed. Bankers are daily more and more ready to lend money to mercantile men; more is lent to such men; more bargains are made in consequence; commodities are more sought after; and, in consequence, prices rise more and more.

The rise of prices is quickest in an improving state of credit. Prices in general are mostly determined by wholesale transactions. The retail dealer adds a percentage to the wholesale prices, not, of course, always the same percentage, but still mostly the same. Given the wholesale price of most articles, you can commonly tell their retail price. Now wholesale transactions are commonly not cash transactions, but bill transactions. The duration of the bill varies with the custom of the trade; it may be two, three months, or six weeks, but there is always a bill. Times of credit mean times in which the bills of many people are taken readily; times of bad credit, times when the bills of much fewer people are taken, and even of those suspiciously. In times of good credit there are a great number of strong purchasers, and in times of bad credit only a smaller number of weak ones; and, therefore, years of improving credit, if there be no disturbing cause, are years of rising price, and years of decaying credit, years of falling price.

This is the meaning of the saying "John Bull can stand many things, but he cannot stand two percent": it means that the greatest effect of the three great causes is nearly peculiar to England; here, and here almost alone, the excess of savings over investments is deposited in banks; here, and here only, is it made use of so as to affect trade at large; here, and here only, are prices gravely affected. In these circumstances, a low rate of interest, long protracted, is equivalent to a total depreciation of the precious metals. In his book on the effect of the great gold discoveries, Professor Jevons showed, and so far as I know, was the first to show, the necessity of eliminating these temporary changes of value in gold before you could judge properly of the permanent depreciation. He proved, that in the years preceding both 1847 and 1857 there was a general rise of prices; and in the years succeeding these years, a great fall. The same might be shown of the years before and after 1866, mutatis mutandis. . . .

. . . The surplus of loanable capital which lies in the hands of bankers is not employed by them in any original way; it is almost always lent to a trade already growing and already improving. The use of it develops that trade yet farther, and this again augments and stimulates other trades. Capital may long lie idle in a stagnant condition of industry; the mercantile securities which experienced bankers know to be good do not augment, and they will not invent other securities, or take bad ones.

In most great periods of expanding industry, the three great causes— much loanable capital, good credit, and the increased profits derived from better-used labor and better-used capital—have acted simultaneously; and though either may act by itself, there is a permanent reason why mostly they will act together. They both tend to grow together, if you begin from a period of depression. In such periods credit is bad, and industry unemployed; very generally provisions are high in price, and their dearness was one of the causes which made the times bad. Whether there was or was not too much loanable capital when that period begins, there soon comes to be too much. Quiet people continue to save part of their incomes in bad times as well as in good; indeed, of the two, people of slightly varying and fixed incomes have better means of saving in bad times because prices are lower. Quiescent trade affords no new securities in which the new saving can be invested, and therefore there comes soon to be an excess of loanable capital. In a year or two after a crisis credit usually improves, as the remembrance of the disasters which at the crisis impaired credit is becoming fainter and fainter. Provisions get back to their usual price, or some great industry makes, from some temporary cause, a quick step forward. At these moments, therefore, the three agencies which, as has been explained, greatly develop trade, combine to develop it simultaneously.

The certain result is a bound of national prosperity; the country leaps forward as if by magic. But only part of that prosperity has a solid reason. As far as prosperity is based on a greater quantity of production, and that of the right articles—as far as it is based on the increased rapidity with which commodities of every kind reach those who want them—its basis is good. Human industry is more efficient, and therefore there is more to be divided among mankind. But insofar as that prosperity is based on a general rise of prices, it is only imaginary. A general rise of prices is a rise only in name; whatever anyone gains on the article which he has to sell he loses on the articles which he has to buy, and so he is just where he was. The only real effects of a general rise of prices are these: First, it straightens people of fixed incomes, who suffer as purchasers, but who have no gain to correspond; and secondly, it gives an extra profit to fixed capital created before the rise happened. Here the sellers gain, but without any equivalent loss as buyers. Thirdly, this gain on fixed capital is greatest in what may be called the industrial "implements," such as coal and iron. These are wanted in all industries, and in any general increase of prices, they are sure to rise much more than other things. Everybody wants them; the supply of them cannot be rapidly augmented, and therefore their price rises very quickly. But to the country as a whole, the general rise of prices is no benefit at all; it is simply a change of nomenclature for an identical relative value in the same commodities. Nevertheless, most people are happier for it; they think they are getting richer, though they are not. And as the rise does not happen on all articles at the same moment, but is propagated gradually through society, those to whom it first comes gain really; and as at first everyone believes that he will gain when his own article is rising, a buoyant cheerfulness overflows the mercantile world.

This prosperity is precarious as far as it is real, and transitory insofar as it is fictitious. The augmented production, which is the reason of the real prosperity, depends on the full working of the whole industrial organization—of all capitalists and laborers—that prosperity was caused by that full working, and will cease with it. But that full working is liable to be destroyed by the occurrence of any great misfortune to any considerable industry. This would cause misfortune to the industries dependent on that one, and, as has been explained, all through society and *back again*. But every such industry is liable to grave fluctuations, and the most important—the provision industries—to the gravest and the suddenest. They are dependent on the casualties of the seasons. A single bad harvest diffused over the world, a succession of two or three bad harvests, even in England only, will raise the price of corn exceedingly, and will keep it high. And a great and protracted rise in the price of corn will at once destroy all the real part of the unusual prosperity of previous good times. It will change the full working of the industrial machine into an imperfect working; it will make the produce of that machine less than usual instead of more than usual; instead of there being more than the average of general dividend to be distributed between the producers, there will immediately be less than the average.

And insofar as the apparent prosperity is caused by an unusual plentifulness of loanable capital and a consequent rise in prices, that prosperity is not only liable to reaction, but *certain* to be exposed to reaction. The same causes which generate this prosperity will, after they have been acting a little longer, generate an equivalent adversity. The process is this: the plentifulness of loanable capital causes a rise of prices; that rise of prices makes it necessary to have more loanable capital to carry on the same trade. One hundred thousand pounds will not buy as much when prices are high as it will when prices are low, it will not be so effectual for carrying on business; more money is necessary in dear times than in cheap times to produce the same changes in the same commodities. Even supposing trade to have remained stationary, a greater capital would be required to carry it on after such a rise of prices as has been described than was necessary before that rise. But in this case the trade will *not* have remained stationary; it will have increased—certainly to some extent, probably to a great extent. The "loanable capital," the lending of which caused the rise of prices, was lent to enable it to augment. The loanable capital lay idle in the banks till some trade started into prosperity, and then was lent in order to develop that trade; that trade caused other secondary developments; those secondary developments enabled more loanable capital to be lent; and that lending caused a tertiary development of trade; and so on through society.

In consequence, a long-continued low rate of interest is almost always followed by a rapid rise in that rate. Till the available trade is found it lies idle, and can scarcely be lent at all; some of it is not lent. But the moment the available trade is discovered—the moment that prices have risen—the demand for loanable capital becomes keen. For the most part, men of business must carry on their regular trade; if it cannot be carried on without borrowing ten percent more capital, ten percent more capital they must borrow. Very often they have incurred obligations which must be met; and if that is so the rate of interest which they pay is comparatively indifferent. What is necessary to meet their acceptances they will borrow, pay for it what they may; they had better pay any price than permit those acceptances to be dishonoured. And in less extreme cases men of business have a fixed capital, which cannot lie idle except at a great loss; a set of laborers which must be, if possible, kept together; a steady connection of customers, which they would very unwillingly lose. To keep all these, they borrow; and in a period of high prices many merchants are peculiarly anxious to borrow, because the augmentation of the price of the article in which they deal makes them really see, or imagine that they see, peculiar opportunities of profit. An immense new borrowing soon follows upon the new and great trade, and the rate of interest rises at once, and generally rises rapidly.

This is the surer to happen that Lombard Street is, as has been shown before, a very delicate market. A large amount of money is held there by bankers and by bill brokers at interest: this they must employ, or they will be ruined. It is better for them to reduce the rate they charge, and compensate themselves by reducing the rate they pay, rather than to keep up the rate of charge, if by so doing they cannot employ all their money. It is vital to them to employ all the money on which they pay interest. A little excess therefore forces down the rate of interest very much. But if that low rate of interest should cause, or should aid in causing, a great growth of trade, the rise is sure to be quick, and is apt to be violent. The figures of trade are reckoned by hundreds of millions, where those of loanable capital count only by millions. A great increase in the borrowing demands of English commerce almost always changes an excess of loanable capital above the demand to a greater deficiency below the demand. That deficiency causes adversity, or apparent adversity, in trade, just as, and in the same manner, that the previous excess caused prosperity, or apparent prosperity. It causes a fall of price that runs through society; that fall causes a decline of activity and a diminution of profits—a painful contraction instead of the previous pleasant expansion.

The change is generally quicker because some check to credit happens at an early stage of it. The mercantile community will have been unusually fortunate if during the period of rising prices it has not made great mistakes. Such a period naturally excites the sanguine and the ardent; they fancy that the prosperity they see will last always, that it is only the beginning of a greater prosperity. They altogether overestimate the demand for the article they deal in, or the work they do. They all in their degree—and the ablest and the cleverest the most—work much more than they should, and trade far above their means. Every great crisis reveals the excessive speculations of many houses which no one before suspected, and which commonly indeed had not begun or had not carried very far those speculations, till they were tempted by the daily rise of price and the surrounding fever.

The case is worse, because at most periods of great commercial excitement there is some mixture of the older and simpler kind of investing mania. Though the money of saving persons is in the hands of banks, and though, by offering interest, banks retain the command of much of it, yet they do not retain the command of the whole, or anything near the whole; all of it can be used, and much of it is used, by its owners. They speculate with it in bubble companies and in worthless shares, just as they did in the time of the South Sea mania, when there were no banks, and as they would again in England supposing that banks ceased to exist. The mania of 1825 and the mania of 1866 were striking examples of this; in their case to a great extent, as in most similar modern periods to a less extent, the delirium of ancient gambling cooperated with the milder madness of modern overtrading. At the very beginning of adversity, the counters in the gambling mania, the shares in the companies created to feed the mania, are discovered to be worthless; down they all go, and with them much of credit.

The good times too of high price almost always engender much fraud. All people are most credulous when they are most happy; and when much money has just been made, when some people are really making it, when most people think they are making it, there is a happy opportunity for ingenious mendacity. Almost everything will be believed for a little while, and long before discovery the worst and most adroit deceivers are geographically or legally beyond the reach of punishment. But the harm they have done diffuses harm, for it weakens credit still farther.

When we understand that Lombard Street is subject to severe alternations of opposite causes, we should cease to be surprised at its seeming cycles. We should cease too to be surprised at the sudden panics. During the period of reaction and adversity, just even at the last instant of prosperity, the whole structure is delicate. The peculiar essence of our banking system is an unprecedented trust between man and man: and when that trust is much weakened by hidden causes, a small accident may greatly hurt it, and a great accident for a moment may almost destroy it.

Now too that we comprehend the inevitable vicissitudes of Lombard Street, we can also thoroughly comprehend the cardinal importance of always retaining a great banking reserve. Whether the times of adversity are well met or ill met depends far more on this than on any other single circumstance. If the reserve be large, its magnitude sustains credit; and if it be small, its diminution stimulates the gravest apprehensions. And the better we comprehend the importance of the banking reserve, the higher we shall estimate the responsibility of those who keep it.

QUESTIONS

1. Why does Bagehot argue that the political economy must "take account of *time* as an element in trade operations"? (165)

2. Why does Bagehot believe that periods of rapid expansion, contraction, and stagnation are inevitable?

3. What does Bagehot believe to be the principal cause of economic cycles of expansion and contraction?

4. For Bagehot, what role does the availability of credit play in economic expansions and contractions?

5. Why does Bagehot say that prosperity based on rising prices is "only imaginary"? (172) Why does he believe that such prosperity is "*certain* to be exposed to reaction"? (173)

FOR FURTHER REFLECTION

1. How are Bagehot's explanations of the causes of economic expansion and contraction during the latter half of the nineteenth century applicable to the global economic situation at the beginning of the twenty-first century?

2. Should governments attempt to intervene to mitigate the worst effects of excessive economic expansion and contraction?

3. If cycles of boom and bust are inevitable, how should we prepare for them?

FLEEMING JENKIN

Fleeming Jenkin (1833–1885) was an engineer deeply involved in the development of the transoceanic telegraph, and he held numerous patents for his inventions. He also wrote, was an accomplished draftsman, spoke several languages fluently, and acted in amateur theaters. Charles Darwin considered him his most penetrating critic. Among Jenkin's original contributions to political economy was the supply and demand curve, still widely reproduced in introductory economics textbooks.

Jenkin was born in Kent, England. His father was a captain in the Royal Navy and his mother, a novelist, closely supervised her gifted son's early education. Jenkin received his secondary schooling at Edinburgh Academy, in Scotland, where he established a lifelong friendship with the future physicist James Clerk Maxwell. After Jenkin's father retired, the family spent several years residing in Europe, first in Frankfurt, then in Paris, and finally in Genoa, where Jenkin attended the university and completed a degree after studying natural philosophy and specializing in electromagnetism. He also attended an art school in Genoa. In 1851, the family returned to England, settling in Manchester, where Jenkin became apprenticed as a mechanical engineer. Eventually, he came to specialize in the design, production, and deployment of underwater telegraph cables. Beginning in the 1850s, he made numerous voyages to oversee the laying of cables. In this connection, he became friends, and later business partners, with William Thomson. In 1866 Jenkin was appointed professor of engineering at University College, London. Two years later, he received an endowed chair at the University of Edinburgh where he remained until his death.

Jenkin published "The Graphic Representation of the Laws of Supply and Demand and Their Application to Labour," the source of the following selection, in 1870. In it he introduced the supply and demand curve which has been called the most famous graphic in all of economics. In the same paper, he also continued the break with the classical theory of the value of commodities, which held that labor is the main determinant of prices, and pioneered the idea that the price of a commodity is determined by the utility—or subjective value—it has in the minds of buyers.

FLEEMING JENKIN

Application of the Laws of Demand and Supply to the Special Problem of Wages

T he rate of wages paid to a certain class of workmen is simply the market price of their labor, and this price will be determined by the same laws as determine the price of other commodities. This truism is often interpreted as though it meant that no efforts on the part of the masters could lower wages, and no action on the part of men raise wages, the price of labor being, as is supposed, fixed by some natural law depending for its action in no wise on the will of men, but solely on the number of laborers and the amount of capital which is ready to be spent on labor. The natural deduction from this hypothesis is, that whatever wages happen to be paid are the right wages, and that men should thankfully accept them, abandoning all attempt to bargain as a useless waste of time and trouble in contending against the inevitable law of nature.

What is true of wages is true of other commodities, and it would be just as difficult to persuade the holders of any merchandise to desist from bargaining about the price of goods, as to persuade laborers to refrain from bargaining about wages. Nevertheless, it is certainly true that by competition among buyers, a market price would be settled both for wages and other commodities, as at an auction with unreserved price even if the sellers did not bargain at all; and this is precisely what the more reasonable opponents of trade unions mean when they assert that wages are fixed by the laws of supply and demand. It is unnecessary now to refute the other absurd form of the doctrine by which it was assumed that, the wages fund being fixed, and the number of laborers fixed, you had only to compute the mean wages by a simple sum in division—it being clearly understood that the wages fund is a fluctuating quantity, altered by every

This selection is taken from chapter 2 of "The Graphic Representation of the Laws of Supply and Demand and Their Application to Labour."

circumstance which affects the minds of capitalists. In an article in the *North British Review*, the writer dwelt at much length on this fallacy, and nearly the same arguments, subsequently used by Mr. Thornton, have been acknowledged as just by Mr. John Stuart Mill. The theory of wages, therefore, presents two questions only:

1. Does the power of bargaining give the laborer any advantage?
2. What is the cost of production of a laborer in a given trade?

If we can settle these two questions, we may feel certain of being able to answer all contingent questions, for we have found that the cost of production ultimately regulates the average of all prices, and therefore the average rate of wages; and in a given market we have found how the fluctuations in the average price are determined. The one question which has not been touched being the effect on the market of the power of bargaining on the part of sellers, leaving the competition to buyers only.

I will first discuss this special case, which is that of the laborer who does not bargain as to his wages; it is also the case of a forced sale, as at a bankruptcy, and of any other sale by auction without a reserved price. . . . The power of bargaining, or, in other words, of reserving some of the goods for sale, may lower the supply curve below the straight line, and thus raise the price, diminishing the quantity bought; but it must be remembered that the demand curve is no fixed line depending on some numerical quantity or material weight, but represents a certain mental state. Now, it is observed that the knowledge that goods must be sold, that in fact there is no reserved price, does tend to diminish the desire for these goods quite independently of the knowledge of the mere material quantity in the market. The knowledge that the bankruptcy of some firm will necessitate the immediate sale of a stock, at once lowers the demand curve while it raises the supply, and by a double action lowers the price. This is often described as the effect of a sudden increase of supply; so it is, but the words, *at a price*, should be added, and whenever we take away the power of bargaining, or of fixing a reserved price, we virtually increase the supply at a price, putting the sellers into the position of bankrupts whose effects must be realised.

Now the legitimate action of trade unions is to enable the laborer to set a reserved price on his merchandise, precisely as any other dealer in goods can, and to deprive him of this power is to put him to the same disadvantage as the bankrupt salesman. Each laborer who has a reserve fund may bargain for himself, and concerted action is not theoretically necessary to allow of bargaining; practically the individual laborer seldom bargains, but, acting in concert with others, he can and does set a reserved price on his labor, and gets precisely the advantage that any other salesman would. Probably the quantity of labor or any other material bought under these circumstances will be less than when no reserved price is fixed; but this need not be so and even if it be, it may be more advantageous to the salesman to sell a moderate quantity at a good price than a large quantity at a bad price. It may be more advantageous to laborers that a moderate number should be employed at good wages than a large number at bad wages.

It is said that when men have this power they abuse it, and will set so high a reserved price on their labor, as ultimately to stop the purchase of it altogether, or at least diminish it so far as to injure both themselves and capitalists. Self-interest is the natural remedy for this. We do not object to fishmongers setting a reserved price on fish, although they may so diminish the consumption as materially to injure both themselves and the community. The only motive by which the demands of a fishmonger are kept within reason is that of self-interest, and precisely the same motive may be trusted to in the case of a combination of laborers, unless they are so foolish as to be unable to perceive the consequences of their own actions—a case which is quite possible, though rarer than is imagined.

Thus we find that the power of bargaining given to the laborer does tend to raise wages; but that it may diminish the number of laborers employed, and often does so.

It will be very rationally asked: how is this statement consistent with the doctrine that price, and consequently wages, depend ultimately on the cost of production? The explanation of the apparent inconsistency is to be found in the fact that the cost of production is itself not a fixed material thing, but depends on men's desires and will in a great measure. The cost of production is the cost at which a man thinks it worth his while to produce the article; this depends on his desires and opinions, and is affected by a vast number of circumstances. If he has a reserve fund, so that he need not perish should he cease to produce, the immediate motive to produce is very much weakened, and he will not think it worth his while to produce except at a higher profit to himself; and when it is said that the cost of production regulates the price, in that cost must be included the profit to the producer. Indeed, if we analyze the cost of production, it will be found to consist solely of the sum of a succession of profits reaped by the producers of food, of raw materials, and of tools—each of these profits depending solely on the desires or fancied necessities of each class of laborers. Thus the power of bargaining actually tends to increase the cost of production, and thus the apparent paradox is justified.

While, however, we find that, both in a given market and on an average of years, the power of bargaining will enable a seller to obtain higher prices, this does not assist us in determining what those prices shall be. The first law of demand and supply gives no help, since it requires for its operation that men's minds shall be already determined; the second law, when applied to labor, brings us to the Malthusian doctrine, and when misunderstood, to the erroneous wages-fund theory. It is true that if the number of laborers be increased, without a corresponding increase in the demand at a price, probably wages will fall; it is also true that if the maximum of available capital be not increased, probably the demand at a price will not increase, and therefore it is true that if the population of a country increases faster than at a certain rate, determined by the increase of wealth, probably wages will fall. But all these truths help us little. Certainly, we cannot a priori determine the fit proportion between land and population. Many countries are poor, and afford bad wages, when thinly populated or semi-savage: and are rich, giving good wages, when thickly populated. Nor can we fix a ratio between increase of population and increase of wealth. If the population be a productive one, the more it increases the better, until the limit to food production in the world be reached. Only the laborer who, by want of education or natural gifts, is able to produce less than he requires, impoverishes a country; and I see no reason to suppose that as yet any man, born in the most thickly populated country, need be in this condition. It is often said that to produce is useless if there be no demand, but it is no real production of wealth if the thing made be not wealth, that is, if it is not wanted; the producer, falsely so called, is producing a wrong thing; demand is limited by production as much as production by demand. The demander can only demand in virtue of his possessing or having produced what others want, and hence if all were truly skilled, demand and the power of production would keep pace. Demand falls short of production from two reasons: the thing produced is a thing not wanted, or those who want it can produce nothing in return. If labor were wisely applied, the only limit to the increase of a well-to-do population is the difficulty of producing food. To say that the wealth of a country depends on its powers of production, is as true as to say that its powers of profitable production depend on its wealth; no doubt, the two things are dependent on one another, but there is no *fixed* ratio between them, such that knowing one you may calculate the other. Capital is produced by labor; the relative amounts of these two elements which can be employed in production *at a given moment* is approximately fixed, but fixed only by the customs and desires of that particular country at that particular time, when capital expects such-and-such profit, and laborers expect such-and-such comforts. Change these feelings, and the fixed ratio between capital and labor vanishes, so that the Malthusian law, true as it is, gives no help in determining the rate of wages, because it gives no help in determining what profit a capitalist will expect or what comfort a laborer will expect; because, in fact, it gives no help in determining the cost of production either of labor or of anything else.

The action of the increase of population depends on the second law of demand and supply, showing the probable direction of the change in wages under given circumstances, but not helping to determine what wages must be at any time, nor what they will be in future.

To determine ultimately the rate of wages, we are therefore driven, as in all other cases, to the third law, that price is determined by cost of production. But before applying this law to labor, let us run over the mental machinery by which the price of any article is brought to coincide with the cost of production.

The value which buyers and sellers set on any article depends on different motives. The demand in the buyers' minds corresponds to the utility which, in their opinion, attaches to the article; and the causes which help to form that opinion are too numerous for classification. If their desire be slight, they can force no one to produce; if it be strong, they will tempt so many to produce that competition will bring down the price to the cost of production; so that their opinion of the utility of the article does not ultimately affect the price. Applying this to labor, the capitalist, if willing only to pay low wages, can neither force men to enter his workshop, nor to marry and produce children; and if willing to pay high wages, he will attract crowds, and produce such welfare as results in many marriages. The competition among laborers will bring down the wages to something which is equivalent to the cost of production. So far the parallels run on all fours.

The value set on any article by the mind of the seller, who only holds it with the object of obtaining money for it, depends on simple motives as compared with those which may actuate the buyer. The seller does not think of the utility of the article, but he will remember the past, guess at the present, and estimate the future demand, and he will compare these with the cost of production which he has borne. He will be loathe to sell below the cost price, reckoning in that a given profit to himself. Nevertheless, if he thinks that the future demand will be less than the present he will sell: but if he estimates that the demand will presently rise, he will hold back his ware. The different estimates of the present and future demand determine the differences in the supplies at various prices in any given market; but if the market price be below cost price, he will refrain from producing the article in future; and thus supply will be diminished until the market price rise up to or above cost price, then production will continue at a diminished rate. If the market price is much above cost price, more will be produced, until cost price and market price again agree.

Now, how far do similar motives affect the production of labor? The laborer is precisely in the position of the seller who attaches no value to his goods in themselves. The cost of production of his labor may be defined as the cost of maintaining the laborer from his birth to his death; and if our law is to hold good, his average wages must simply be such as will enable him so to maintain himself; but in what style? Goods will not be produced unless they pay the producer, besides his outlay, such a profit as makes it in his opinion worth while to produce them. Similarly, laborers do not produce and keep a family until their wages equal the cost of maintenance, including such enjoyment or comfort as in their opinion make life tolerable. The producer of other goods, when dissatisfied with his profit, ceases to produce. The laborer, if dissatisfied with his comforts, does not cumber himself with a wife and family—he even emigrates, or, in last resort, goes on the parish, and dies. A man being alive will generally sell himself day by day, even below the rate at which he can be said to care for life, just as in a temporary depression of the market the producer of cotton goods sells below cost price rather than not sell at all; but he will not commence the production or rearing of a family unless satisfied with his wages; and thus the wages of each class depend on the standard of comfort at which they think it worth while to marry and beget children. This action does not, indeed, take place with the view of producing goods for sale; but it does produce goods for sale, and it only occurs when existing goods (i.e., labor) meet with a sale satisfying the producers. The case of labor is here again analogous to that of any other goods produced for profit.

We can now answer the question whether men, by any action of theirs, can raise wages. How can they? Not by emigration, unless at the same time the cost of production of labor vary. Such emigration will simply increase the production of human beings, representing, as it does, one form of increased demand for them, and we have seen that, in the long run, demand has nothing to do with price. Not by increasing the capital employed productively. This again will only increase the number of human beings employed, not the wages they receive. Not by limiting the number of children to be born in a given area and time; this will limit trade, but will not permanently raise wages, though the diminution in the number of workmen of a given class at any moment will temporarily raise wages, which will gradually fall, unless the standard of comfort be permanently raised. Not by the limitation of the number of apprentices to a given trade; this will have but the same effect as limiting the number of children. If not all these, what then? Simply by creating an increased standard of comfort among the laborers. Do this, and our young laborer will claim higher wages, and failing to obtain them, will not marry, or will emigrate. Our young apprentice will not enter those trades which do not offer him that profit which he expects. The cost of production of labor will have risen—the price or wages must rise—the quantity supplied will have fallen, unless the demand have risen. A new state of equilibrium between capital and labor will have been reached, and although production of wealth may have been checked for a while, it will afterward progress as before.

It is futile to preach Malthusian doctrines of self-restraint to a laborer. The upper classes may grasp at those doctrines as an excuse for selfishness, and precisely that class which by education and wealth is fitted to produce valuable members of society may be induced to refrain from so doing; but it is useless to expect that the mass of mankind, having once married, or feeling sufficiently comfortable to think of marrying, will ever refrain from self-indulgence for the sake of humanity at large. It is only by appealing to self-interest that the desired end can be attained, and this end is attained in the middle and upper classes by means of self-interest. Educated men and women will not, as a rule, marry until they see their way to live in such a style as suits them, and the production of the educated class is thus limited probably as much as is desirable; the fear here being, rather that the standard of comfort should be chosen falsely with reference to imaginary luxuries, wholly unnecessary to a really refined and cultivated existence. The learned professions maintain their fees on no other principle than that of maintaining a high standard of comfort. Men fitted to exercise them will not enter them or remain in them unless they see their way to live in the style they have chosen; should this fail them, they change their occupation, they emigrate, or at least remain single, just as in the case of a laborer. The average remuneration of a doctor or of an architect depends on the cost of his production, being mainly the cost of his living in the style which men who have received that degree of education expect. The number of doctors employed at this rate depends on the number of people willing to pay the fees asked. It is frequently supposed to be the limitation produced by the cost of education which enables the professional man to earn higher wages than the mechanic, limiting as it does the supply of educated men. It does this to some extent, but if there were openings for a thousand more doctors tomorrow the funds for their education would be found next day; and again, if the social position of doctors were to fall so that much smaller fees were expected, the profession would be far more numerous than at present.

It appears, then, that our third law, rigid as it is, only brings us to a point at which once more the feelings of men are the true arbiters of price. The cost of production of labor determines wages, but is itself determined by men's expectation of comfort.

Are we then to conclude that by simply asking for higher pay men can always obtain it? By no means.

The alternative presented to each man is, or might be, work at the present rate or starve. However serious his discontent at his present pay, he may well falter at the alternative; but if his dissatisfaction be real, he will, at least, refrain from producing more labor, and thus his discontent will tend to raise the wages as he wished. This is not the old doctrine of simply limiting the number of human beings in order to raise wages, but contains the truth partly taught by the old doctrine. The ultimate effect of the limitation of labor can only be to limit the production of wealth, and the bargain between labor and capital will always, in time, result in driving the laborer back to the lowest standard of comfort at which he will marry; but if we begin by raising the standard of comfort which our laborer desires, we shall both limit the population and raise the wages. The limitation of population is the intermediate machinery by which the desired end is to be effected, but the motive power must be sought in individual self-interest or discontent.

Every action which tends to make the laborer put up with less comfort, or less security, tends to lower his wages. Teach him nothing, so that he wants no books nor other pleasures of the mind. Abolish bodily amusements, so that he expects no pleasures of the body. Accustom him to live like a beast in a hovel; remove all fear of absolute starvation by a poor-law; use the same machinery to persuade him that he may, with a good conscience, desert helpless children or old parents; give him little doles at every pinch, lest he be tempted to rebel—do all this, and your dull aimless wretch will plod from day to day, expecting nothing more, and spawning swarms of wretched beings to succeed him in his hopeless contentment with a pittance. All this has been too much done, undo it; teach him, in order that he may desire knowledge; let him know that the world has pleasure in it, so that he may long for pleasure; show him what comfort is, so that he may learn to want, not live as a savage without wants; and when he has learned how good a thing it is to enjoy life, let him fear poverty and starvation, as that man does fear them who must subdue them or perish; teach him to trust himself; teach him that his wife, his little ones, should trust him and him alone; let him look on miscalled charity as a temptation of the devil; and add to all this the greatest want of all, the longing that he may be that excellent thing, the man who walks in the ways of God; and never fear that this being will grovel out a life of hardship, or fail to learn how to win that which he so much desires.

Discontent with that which is vile is the mainspring by which the world is to be moved to good. Contentment with degradation is a vice—a vice only too difficult to eradicate. The action of these truths is everywhere to be seen. There is hardly a grain of truth in the doctrine that men's wages are in proportion to the pleasantness of their occupations. On the contrary, all loathsome occupations are undertaken by apathetic beings for a miserable hire. The plodding agricultural laborer has small wages; the discontented mechanic lives in comfort; the professional man, who never ceases struggling for more, wins luxuries—yet the best paid is the most pleasant life. Now the common explanation of this is that there are few capable of fulfilling the higher and pleasanter functions, and many capable of performing the baser work; but why are there few fit for the higher lot?

Simply because of the high standard obtaining among those who rejoice in it. A doctor with half a dozen sons will not make all doctors; he could afford to do this very well. It is not the expense of the education which deters; he knows he could not find openings for all in the one path—he means by this, not in the style to which he is accustomed, and in which he expects his sons to live. It is the standard of comfort held by the present doctors which limits the number entering the profession, not the expense of education: again, a young doctor says that he cannot marry on £300 a year, although he knows that a mechanic on £100 lives in real comfort, and brings up a well-to-do family. Again, it is the young doctor's standard of comfort which limits the number of the well-to-do class, and so keeps up their pay. But, it may be said, if it is not the expense of education which limits the number of doctors, why do not the well-to-do of the lower class make their sons professional men, and so lower the standard of refinement and culture? They actually do so to a limited extent, but no sooner has the lad received the professional education, and learnt the wants of the new and higher class, than he adopts these; and while his father married on £100 a year, he refuses to be contented with less than £500.

Now, there is nothing which so much helps a man to keep up the standard of his desires as the possession of some wealth. A man who has something can hold out. If he cannot enjoy large profits he can enjoy idleness; but the pauper must work or starve. Thus those who have money make the larger incomes, and the poor in a profession make small profits. Money makes money, because money produces a high standard of ease. Trade unions are one of the most powerful agents for raising wages, because they enable the community of workmen to acquire wealth. They are more powerful than savings banks or building societies, by which individuals obtain reserve funds. The individual workman knows that his reserve fund will be nearly useless unless his neighbor has a reserve fund also. If each workman in a strike trusted to his own funds only, the poorer ones must give in first; and these would secure work while the richer, after spending a part of their reserve, would find themselves supplanted by the poorer competitors, and the sacrifice made uselessly. A combined reserve fund gives great power by insuring that all suffer alike. The trade union, therefore, has a permanent action in raising wages, because it enables men to accumulate a common fund, with which they can sustain their resolution not to work unless they obtain such pay as will give increased comfort. The common reserve fund plays just the same part in raising their wages, as is played by the small patrimony or sustenance given by a doctor to his son, which enables him, without risk of starvation, to refrain from taking unprofessional fees.

Strange, therefore, as the doctrine may sound, it is the wants of men which regulate their wages: and this is a simple deduction from the principle that the cost of production ultimately determines the prices. Where wants are few and simple, there wages are low; where wants are numerous, wages are high; and it is the wants which raise the wages, not the wages which have created the wants: pay a savage more than he is accustomed to, and he simply squanders the money. But while the wants of men determine their pay, it is the demand for men of that class which determines how many shall be employed at that pay. This is the corrective to discontent. If their wants are great, few or no men of the given class may get any pay at all. It is the seller of labor who determines the price, but it is the buyer who determines the number of transactions. Capital settles how many men are wanted at given wages, but labor settles what wages the man shall have.

Surely we may be well satisfied with this conclusion. The laws of demand and supply, rigid as they are, point to no necessary impoverishment and degradation of the laborer as men and means multiply; they require for his improvement no superhuman exercise of prudence on his part; they ask for no bounty from the men of great wealth. Well might men exclaim that the law was a law of death, when they so misread it as to believe that unless an ignorant and brutish population could be taught for the sake of unborn men to restrain their strongest passion, poverty must be perpetuated in an ever-increasing ratio. I do not so read the law; but say, convince these paupers of their own misery. Teach them what comfort is, and a rational self-interest will lead them to independence, which the more wealthy have reached by the same path. Rational self-interest has done most things in this world, the great duty of the teacher being to distinguish rational from irrational self-interest. Whatever school of religion or philosophy we belong to, we cannot deny that each man, acting rationally for his own advantage, will conduce to the good of all; and if the motive be not the highest, it is one which at least can always be counted on. It were a poor world if higher motives were banished; but in looking to the improvement of the pauper it is well that we may count on a motive which is at least effectual. And, looking to this motive alone, I say that the laws of demand and supply are so far from being antagonistic to improvement, that we need only teach men what they should desire, and excite in their minds a real disgust at their miserable condition, in order, by the very laws of price, to create the utopia of labor where all men shall get a fair day's wages for a fair day's work, by which vague phrase the workman means that the pay for his labor shall buy him enjoyment as well as bread.

QUESTIONS

1. Why does Jenkin believe the laws of supply and demand are inadequate to properly determine the rate of wages?

2. According the Jenkin, why are "the feelings of men . . . the true arbiters of price"? (186)

3. If "the bargain between labor and capital will always, in time, result in driving the laborer back to the lowest standard of comfort," why does Jenkin believe in a "utopia of labor"? (187, 189)

4. What does Jenkin mean when he says that "it is the wants which raise the wages, not the wages which have created the wants"? (189)

5. According to Jenkin, how does "rational self-interest" lead to higher wages for labor? (189)

FOR FURTHER REFLECTION

1. Should governments set a minimum wage for labor?

2. Do you agree with Jenkin when he says, "Discontent with that which is vile is the mainspring by which the world is to be moved to good"?

3. Is Jenkin correct that for labor to receive a fair wage "we need only teach men what they should desire, and excite in their minds a real disgust at their miserable condition"?

ALFRED MARSHALL

Alfred Marshall (1842–1924) was one of the principal founders of the modern academic discipline of economics. His *Principles of Economics* (1890) was immensely influential in the transformation of the field from a liberal art into a scientific discipline, and became the standard textbook for several decades. In it, Marshall achieved a systematic synthesis of the classical economics of Adam Smith and David Ricardo with the marginalist revolution initiated by W. S. Jevons, Carl Menger, and Léon Walras. The latter approach to economics is based on the idea that values are determined by the utility conferred on goods and services by consumers. Marshall also brought scientific methods in economics to a new level of sophistication. In addition, Marshall established an important institutional base for the new scientific economics at Cambridge University, where he numbered John Maynard Keynes and A. C. Pigou among his students.

Marshall was born in a poor district of London. His family rose to middle-class respectability and raised Alfred to join the clergy. But he was drawn to study physics, philosophy, and political economy, eventually securing a scholarship to study at Cambridge. His mathematical and scientific training had a profound impact on his work in economics. Marshall spent much of his career as a professor, first at Balliol College, Oxford, then at Cambridge, where he taught from 1885 until his retirement in 1908.

Principles of Economics expands upon the formal graphical methods of representing relations between economic variables such as supply and demand that were pioneered by A. A. Cournot and Fleeming Jenkin. It also introduces several important new concepts, notably price elasticity of demand and consumer surplus; it lays stress upon the importance of short, medium, and long timescales for understanding economic phenomena; and it makes significant use of statistical data. In the following excerpt, Marshall carefully distinguishes between the benefits and the limitations of a scientific approach to the study of human behavior.

ALFRED MARSHALL

The Substance of Economics

1

Economics is a study of men as they live and move and think in the
ordinary business of life. But it concerns itself chiefly with those motives
which affect, most powerfully and most steadily, man's conduct in the
business part of his life. Everyone who is worth anything carries his higher
nature with him into business; and, there as elsewhere, he is influenced by
his personal affections, by his conceptions of duty and his reverence for
high ideals. And it is true that the best energies of the ablest inventors and
organizers of improved methods and appliances are stimulated by a noble
emulation more than by any love of wealth for its own sake. But, for all
that, the steadiest motive to ordinary business work is the desire for the
pay which is the material reward of work. The pay may be on its way to be
spent selfishly or unselfishly, for noble or base ends; and here the variety
of human nature comes into play. But the motive is supplied by a definite
amount of money: and it is this definite and exact money measurement
of the steadiest motives in business life which has enabled economics far
to outrun every other branch of the study of man. Just as the chemist's
fine balance has made chemistry more exact than most other physical
sciences; so this economist's balance, rough and imperfect as it is, has
made economics more exact than any other branch of social science. But
of course economics cannot be compared with the exact physical sciences:
for it deals with the ever changing and subtle forces of human nature.

The advantage which economics has over other branches of social science appears then to arise from the fact that its special field of work gives
rather larger opportunities for exact methods than any other branch. It
concerns itself chiefly with those desires, aspirations, and other affections

This selection is taken from book 1, chapter 2 of Principles of Economics.

of human nature, the outward manifestations of which appear as incentives to action in such a form that the force or quantity of the incentives can be estimated and measured with some approach to accuracy; and which therefore are in some degree amenable to treatment by scientific machinery. An opening is made for the methods and the tests of science as soon as the force of a person's motives—*not* the motives themselves—can be approximately measured by the sum of money which he will just give up in order to secure a desired satisfaction; or again by the sum which is just required to induce him to undergo a certain fatigue.

It is essential to note that the economist does not claim to measure any affection of the mind in itself, or directly; but only indirectly through its effect. No one can compare and measure accurately against one another even his own mental states at different times: and no one can measure the mental states of another at all except indirectly and conjecturally by their effects. Of course various affections belong to man's higher nature and others to his lower, and are thus different in kind. But, even if we confine our attention to mere physical pleasures and pains of the same kind, we find that they can only be compared indirectly by their effects. In fact, even this comparison is necessarily to some extent conjectural, unless they occur to the same person at the same time.

For instance the pleasures which two persons derive from smoking cannot be directly compared: nor can even those which the same person derives from it at different times. But if we find a man in doubt whether to spend a few pence on a cigar, or a cup of tea, or on riding home instead of walking home, then we may follow ordinary usage, and say that he expects from them equal pleasures.

If then we wish to compare even physical gratifications, we must do it not directly, but indirectly by the incentives which they afford to action. If the desires to secure either of two pleasures will induce people in similar circumstances each to do just an hour's extra work, or will induce men in the same rank of life and with the same means each to pay a shilling for it—we then may say that those pleasures are equal for our purposes, because the desires for them are equally strong incentives to action for persons under similar conditions.

Thus measuring a mental state, as men do in ordinary life, by its motor force or the incentive which it affords to action, no new difficulty is introduced by the fact that some of the motives of which we have to take account belong to man's higher nature, and others to his lower.

For suppose that the person, whom we saw doubting between several little gratifications for himself, had thought after a while of a poor invalid whom he would pass on his way home; and had spent some time in making up his mind whether he would choose a physical gratification for himself, or would do a kindly act and rejoice in another's joy. As his desires turned now toward the one, now the other, there would be change in the quality of his mental states; and the philosopher is bound to study the nature of the change.

But the economist studies mental states rather through their manifestations than in themselves; and if he finds they afford evenly balanced incentives to action, he treats them prima facie as for his purpose equal. He follows indeed in a more patient and thoughtful way, and with greater precautions, what everybody is always doing every day in ordinary life. He does not attempt to weigh the real value of the higher affections of our nature against those of our lower: he does not balance the love for virtue against the desire for agreeable food. He estimates the incentives to action by their effects just in the same way as people do in common life. He follows the course of ordinary conversation, differing from it only in taking more precautions to make clear the limits of his knowledge as he goes. He reaches his provisional conclusions by observations of men in general under given conditions without attempting to fathom the mental and spiritual characteristics of individuals. But he does not ignore the mental and spiritual side of life. On the contrary, even for the narrower uses of economic studies, it is important to know whether the desires which prevail are such as will help to build up a strong and righteous character. And in the broader uses of those studies, when they are being applied to practical problems, the economist, like everyone else, must concern himself with the ultimate aims of man, and take account of differences in real value between gratifications that are equally powerful incentives to action and have therefore equal economic measures. A study of these measures is only the starting point of economics: but it is the starting point.

2

There are several other limitations of the measurement of motive by money to be discussed. The first of these arises from the necessity of taking account of the variations in the amount of pleasure, or other satisfaction, represented by the same sum of money to different persons and under different circumstances.

A shilling may measure a greater pleasure (or other satisfaction) at one time than at another even for the same person; because money may be more plentiful with him, or because his sensibility may vary. And persons whose antecedents are similar, and who are outwardly like one another, are often affected in very different ways by similar events. When, for instance, a band of city schoolchildren are sent out for a day's holiday in the country, it is probable that no two of them derive from it enjoyment exactly the same in kind, or equal in intensity. The same surgical operation causes different amounts of pain to different people. Of two parents who are, so far as we can tell, equally affectionate, one will suffer much more than the other from the loss of a favorite son. Some who are not very sensitive generally are yet specially susceptible to particular kinds of pleasure and pain; while differences in nature and education make one man's total capacity for pleasure or pain much greater than another's.

It would therefore not be safe to say that any two men with the same income derive equal benefit from its use; or that they would suffer equal pain from the same diminution of it. Although when a tax of £1 is taken from each of two persons having an income of £300 a year, each will give up that £1 worth of pleasure (or other satisfaction) which he can most easily part with, i.e., each will give up what is measured to him by just £1; yet the intensities of the satisfaction given up may not be nearly equal.

Nevertheless, if we take averages sufficiently broad to cause the personal peculiarities of individuals to counterbalance one another, the money which people of equal incomes will give to obtain a benefit or avoid an injury is a good measure of the benefit or injury. If there are a thousand persons living in Sheffield, and another thousand in Leeds, each with about £100 a year, and a tax of £1 is levied on all of them—we may be sure that the loss of pleasure or other injury which the tax will cause in Sheffield is of about equal importance with that which it will cause in Leeds: and anything that increased all the incomes by £1 would give command over equivalent pleasures and other benefits in the two towns. This probability becomes greater still if all of them are adult males engaged in the same trade; and therefore presumably somewhat similar in sensibility and temperament, in taste and education. Nor is the probability much diminished, if we take the family as our unit, and compare the loss of pleasure that results from diminishing by £1 the income of each of a thousand families with incomes of £100 a year in the two places.

Next we must take account of the fact that a stronger incentive will be required to induce a person to pay a given price for anything if he is poor than if he is rich. A shilling is the measure of less pleasure, or satisfaction of any kind, to a rich man than to a poor one. A rich man in doubt whether to spend a shilling on a single cigar, is weighing against one another smaller pleasures than a poor man, who is doubting whether to spend a shilling on a supply of tobacco that will last him for a month. The clerk with £100 a year will walk to business in a much heavier rain than the clerk with £300 a year; for the cost of a ride by tram or omnibus measures a greater benefit to the poorer man than to the richer. If the poorer man spends the money, he will suffer more from the want of it afterward than the richer would. The benefit that is measured in the poorer man's mind by the cost is greater than that measured by it in the richer man's mind.

But this source of error also is lessened when we are able to consider the actions and the motives of large groups of people. If we know, for instance, that a bank failure has taken £200,000 from the people of Leeds and £100,000 from those of Sheffield, we may fairly assume that the suffering caused in Leeds has been about twice as great as in Sheffield; unless indeed we have some special reason for believing that the shareholders of the bank in the one town were a richer class than those in the other; or that the loss of employment caused by it pressed in uneven proportions on the working classes in the two towns.

By far the greater number of the events with which economics deals affect in about equal proportions all the different classes of society; so that if the money measures of the happiness caused by two events are equal, it is reasonable and in accordance with common usage to regard the amounts of the happiness in the two cases as equivalent. And, further, as money is likely to be turned to the higher uses of life in about equal proportions, by any two large groups of people taken without special bias from any two parts of the Western world, there is even some prima facie probability that equal additions to their material resources will make about equal additions to the fullness of life, and the true progress of the human race.

3

To pass to another point. When we speak of the measurement of desire by the action to which it forms the incentive, it is not to be supposed that we assume every action to be deliberate, and the outcome of calculation. For in this, as in every other respect, economics takes man just as he is in ordinary life: and in ordinary life people do not weigh beforehand the results of every action, whether the impulses to it come from their higher nature or their lower.

Now the side of life with which economics is specially concerned is that in which man's conduct is most deliberate, and in which he most often reckons up the advantages and disadvantages of any particular action before he enters on it. And further it is that side of his life in which, when he does follow habit and custom, and proceeds for the moment without calculation, the habits and customs themselves are most nearly sure to have arisen from a close and careful watching of the advantages and disadvantages of different courses of conduct. There will not in general have been any formal reckoning up of two sides of a balance sheet: but men going home from their day's work, or in their social meetings, will have said to one another, "It did not answer to do this, it would have been better to do that," and so on. What makes one course answer better than another will not necessarily be a selfish gain, nor any material gain; and it will often have been argued that "though this or that plan saved a little trouble or a little money, yet it was not fair to others," and "it made one look mean," or "it made one feel mean."

It is true that when a habit or a custom, which has grown up under one set of conditions, influences action under other conditions, there is so far no exact relation between the effort and the end which is attained by it. In backward countries there are still many habits and customs similar to those that lead a beaver in confinement to build himself a dam; they are full of suggestiveness to the historian, and must be reckoned with by the legislator. But in business matters in the modern world such habits quickly die away.

Thus then the most systematic part of people's lives is generally that by which they earn their living. The work of all those engaged in any one occupation can be carefully observed; general statements can be made about it, and tested by comparison with the results of other observations; and numerical estimates can be framed as to the amount of money or general purchasing power that is required to supply a sufficient motive for them.

The unwillingness to postpone enjoyment, and thus to save for future use, is measured by the interest on accumulated wealth which just affords a sufficient incentive to save for the future. This measurement presents however some special difficulties, the study of which must be postponed.

4

Here, as elsewhere, we must bear in mind that the desire to make money does not itself necessarily proceed from motives of a low order, even when it is to be spent on oneself. Money is a means toward ends, and if the ends are noble, the desire for the means is not ignoble. The lad who works hard and saves all he can, in order to be able to pay his way afterward at a university, is eager for money; but his eagerness is not ignoble. In short, money is general purchasing power, and is sought as a means to all kinds of ends, high as well as low, spiritual as well as material.

Thus though it is true that "money" or "general purchasing power" or "command over material wealth" is the center around which economic science clusters—this is so, not because money or material wealth is regarded as the main aim of human effort, nor even as affording the main subject matter for the study of the economist, but because in this world of ours it is the one convenient means of measuring human motive on a large scale. If the older economists had made this clear, they would have escaped many grievous misrepresentations; and the splendid teachings of Carlyle and Ruskin as to the right aims of human endeavor and the right uses of wealth would not then have been marred by bitter attacks on economics, based on the mistaken belief that that science had no concern with any motive except the selfish desire for wealth, or even that it inculcated a policy of sordid selfishness.

Again, when the motive to a man's action is spoken of as supplied by the money which he will earn, it is not meant that his mind is closed to all other considerations save those of gain. For even the most purely business relations of life assume honesty and good faith; while many of them take for granted, if not generosity, yet at least the absence of meanness, and the pride which every honest man takes in acquitting himself well. Again, much of the work by which people earn their living is pleasurable in itself; and there is truth in the contention of socialists that more of it might be made so. Indeed even business work that seems at first sight unattractive often yields a great pleasure by offering scope for the exercise of men's faculties, and for their instincts of emulation and of power. For just as a racehorse or an athlete strains every nerve to get in advance of his competitors, and delights in the strain—so a manufacturer or a trader is often stimulated much more by the hope of victory over his rivals than by the desire to add something to his fortune.

5

It has indeed always been the practice of economists to take careful account of all the advantages which attract people generally toward an occupation, whether they appear in a money form or not. Other things being equal, people will prefer an occupation in which they do not need to soil their hands, in which they enjoy a good social position, and so on; and since these advantages affect, not indeed everyone exactly in the same way, but most people in nearly the same way, their attractive force can be estimated and measured by the money wages to which they are regarded as equivalent.

Again, the desire to earn the approval, to avoid the contempt of those around one is a stimulus to action which often works with some sort of uniformity in any class of persons at a given time and place; though local and temporary conditions influence greatly not only the intensity of the desire for approval, but also the range of persons whose approval is desired. A professional man, for instance, or an artisan will be very sensitive to the approval or disapproval of those in the same occupation, and care little for that of other people; and there are many economic problems, the discussion of which would be altogether unreal, if care were not taken to watch the direction and to estimate pretty closely the force of motives such as these.

As there may be a taint of selfishness in a man's desire to do what seems likely to benefit his fellow workers, so there may be an element of personal pride in his desire that his family should prosper during his life and after it. But still the family affections generally are so pure a form of altruism that their action might have shown little semblance of regularity, had it not been for the uniformity in the family relations themselves. As it is, their action is fairly regular; and it has always been fully reckoned with by economists, especially in relation to the distribution of the family income between its various members, the expenses of preparing children for their future career, and the accumulation of wealth to be enjoyed after the death of him by whom it has been earned.

It is then not the want of will but the want of power that prevents economists from reckoning in the action of motives such as these; and they welcome the fact that some kinds of philanthropic action can be described in statistical returns, and can to a certain extent be reduced to law, if sufficiently broad averages are taken. For indeed there is scarcely any motive so fitful and irregular, but that some law with regard to it can be detected by the aid of wide and patient observation. It would perhaps be possible even now to predict with tolerable closeness the subscriptions that a population of a hundred thousand Englishmen of average wealth will give to support hospitals and chapels and missions; and, insofar as this can be done, there is a basis for an economic discussion of supply and demand with reference to the services of hospital nurses, missionaries, and other religious ministers. It will however probably be always true that the greater part of those actions, which are due to a feeling of duty and love of one's neighbor, cannot be classed, reduced to law, and measured; and it is for this reason, and not because they are not based on self-interest, that the machinery of economics cannot be brought to bear on them.

6

Perhaps the earlier English economists confined their attention too much to the motives of individual action. But in fact economists, like all other students of social science, are concerned with individuals chiefly as members of the social organism. As a cathedral is something more than the stones of which it is made, as a person is something more than a series of thoughts and feelings, so the life of society is something more than the sum of the lives of its individual members. It is true that the action of the whole is made up of that of its constituent parts; and that in most economic problems the best starting point is to be found in the motives that affect the individual, regarded not indeed as an isolated atom, but as a member of some particular trade or industrial group; but it is also true, as German writers have well urged, that economics has a great and an increasing concern in motives connected with the collective ownership of property, and the collective pursuit of important aims. The growing earnestness of the age, the growing intelligence of the mass of the people, and the growing power of the telegraph, the press, and other means of communication are ever widening the scope of collective action for the public good; and these changes, together with the spread of the cooperative movement and other kinds of voluntary association, are growing up under the influence of various motives besides that of pecuniary gain: they are ever opening to the economist new opportunities of measuring motives whose action it had seemed impossible to reduce to any sort of law.

But in fact the variety of motives, the difficulties of measuring them, and the manner of overcoming those difficulties are among the chief subjects with which we shall be occupied in this treatise. Almost every point touched in the present chapter will need to be discussed in fuller detail with reference to some one or more of the leading problems of economics.

7

To conclude provisionally: economists study the actions of individuals, but study them in relation to social rather than individual life; and therefore concern themselves but little with personal peculiarities of temper and character. They watch carefully the conduct of a whole class of people, sometimes the whole of a nation, sometimes only those living in a certain district, more often those engaged in some particular trade at some time and place: and by the aid of statistics, or in other ways, they ascertain how much money on the average the members of the particular group they are watching are just willing to pay as the price of a certain thing which they desire, or how much must be offered to them to induce them to undergo a certain effort or abstinence that they dislike. The measurement of motive thus obtained is not indeed perfectly accurate; for if it were, economics would rank with the most advanced of the physical sciences; and not, as it actually does, with the least advanced.

But yet the measurement is accurate enough to enable experienced persons to forecast fairly well the extent of the results that will follow from changes in which motives of this kind are chiefly concerned. Thus, for instance, they can estimate very closely the payment that will be required to produce an adequate supply of labor of any grade, from the lowest to the highest, for a new trade which it is proposed to start in any place. When they visit a factory of a kind that they have never seen before, they can tell within a shilling or two a week what any particular worker is earning, by merely observing how far his is a skilled occupation and what strain it involves on his physical, mental, and moral faculties. And they can predict with tolerable certainty what rise of price will result from a given diminution of the supply of a certain thing, and how that increased price will react on the supply.

And, starting from simple considerations of this kind, economists go on to analyze the causes which govern the local distribution of different kinds of industry, the terms on which people living in distant places exchange their goods with one another, and so on: and they can explain and predict the ways in which fluctuations of credit will affect foreign trade; or again the extent to which the burden of a tax will be shifted from those on whom it is levied, onto those for whose wants they cater; and so on.

In all this they deal with man as he is: not with an abstract or "economic" man; but a man of flesh and blood. They deal with a man who is largely influenced by egoistic motives in his business life to a great extent with reference to them; but who is also neither above vanity and recklessness, nor below delight in doing his work well for its own sake, or in sacrificing himself for the good of his family, his neighbors, or his country; a man who is not below the love of a virtuous life for its own sake. They deal with man as he is: but being concerned chiefly with those aspects of life in which the action of motive is so regular that it can be predicted, and the estimate of the motor forces can be verified by results, they have established their work on a scientific basis.

For in the first place, they deal with facts which can be observed, and quantities which can be measured and recorded; so that when differences of opinion arise with regard to them, the differences can be brought to the test of public and well-established records; and thus science obtains a solid basis on which to work. In the second place, the problems, which are grouped as economic, because they relate specially to man's conduct under the influence of motives that are measurable by a money price, are found to make a fairly homogeneous group. Of course they have a great deal of subject matter in common: that is obvious from the nature of the case. But, though not so obvious a priori, it will also be found to be true that there is a fundamental unity of form underlying all the chief of them; and that in consequence, by studying them together, the same kind of economy is gained, as by sending a single postman to deliver all the letters in a certain street, instead of each one entrusting his letters to a separate messenger. For the analyses and organized processes of reasoning that are wanted for any one group of them will be found generally useful for other groups.

The less we trouble ourselves with scholastic inquiries as to whether a certain consideration comes within the scope of economics, the better. If the matter is important let us take account of it as far as we can. If it is one as to which there exist divergent opinions, such as cannot be brought to the test of exact and well-ascertained knowledge; if it is one on which the general machinery of economic analysis and reasoning cannot get any grip, then let us leave it aside in our purely economic studies. But let us do so simply because the attempt to include it would lessen the certainty and the exactness of our economic knowledge without any commensurate gain; and remembering always that some sort of account of it must be taken by our ethical instincts and our common sense, when they as ultimate arbiters come to apply to practical issues the knowledge obtained and arranged by economics and other sciences.

QUESTIONS

1. What distinction does Marshall make between human incentive and motive? Why does he believe that incentives can be measured more accurately than motives?

2. Why does Marshall claim that economics is "more exact than any other branch of social science"? (192)

3. What distinction does Marshall draw between the philosopher and the economist?

4. Why does Marshall rank economics with the "least advanced" of the physical sciences? (200)

5. What does Marshall mean when he says economists "deal with man as he is"? (201)

6. According to Marshall, what enables economists to make valid predictions?

FOR FURTHER REFLECTION

1. In what respects can economics claim to be a science?

2. In your view, is Marshall arguing more as a philosopher or as a scientist?

3. Do you agree with Marshall when he says, "The less we trouble ourselves with scholastic inquiries as to whether a certain consideration comes within the scope of economics, the better"?

THORSTEIN VEBLEN

Thorstein Veblen (1857–1929) is difficult to categorize. As an analyst of the economic dimensions of human society, he often touches on ethical and moral questions. At the same time, he frequently adopts the detailed descriptive mode of a cultural anthropologist and the shrewd tone of a literary satirist and has been appreciated by readers as much for his literary style as for his incisive ideas.

The son of a Norwegian-born Wisconsin farmer, Veblen attended Carleton College with the intention of entering the Lutheran ministry. Instead, his interest in philosophy led him to graduate school at Johns Hopkins and Yale Universities. Unable to find an academic job upon earning his PhD in 1884, he returned to the family farm for several years before enrolling as a student at Cornell in 1891. There he obtained a fellowship and, one year later, went to the University of Chicago where he taught for more than a decade and wrote his best-known work, *The Theory of the Leisure Class* (1899), one of the most astute studies of capitalist consumer culture ever written. Veblen later taught at Stanford University, the University of Missouri, and the New School for Social Research in New York City, and published several more books including *Imperial Germany and the Industrial Revolution* (1915) and *The Higher Learning in America* (1918). Though Veblen enjoyed a brief period of public recognition in the early 1920s, his iconoclastic outlook put him at odds with the booming economic optimism of the decade. He died just a month before the stock market crash of 1929.

In *The Theory of the Leisure Class*, from which the following selection is taken, Veblen argues that the leisure class in all societies establishes the forms of wasteful behavior likely to be emulated by the rest of society, and he suggests how conspicuous consumption becomes associated with other values perceived as being of a higher, even spiritual, nature. As in his other works, Veblen seldom limits his observations to what can be understood in terms of economic laws, but rather expands the domain of economic theory by taking into consideration rational and irrational decision making in the context of human psychology.

THORSTEIN VEBLEN

Industrial Exemption
and Conservatism

he life of man in society, just like the life of other species, is a struggle
for existence, and therefore it is a process of selective adaptation. The
evolution of social structure has been a process of natural selection
of institutions. The progress which has been and is being made in human
institutions and in human character may be set down, broadly, to a natural
selection of the fittest habits of thought and to a process of enforced adaptation of individuals to an environment which has progressively changed
with the growth of the community and with the changing institutions
under which men have lived. Institutions are not only themselves the
result of a selective and adaptive process which shapes the prevailing or
dominant types of spiritual attitude and aptitudes; they are at the same
time special methods of life and of human relations, and are therefore in
their turn efficient factors of selection. So that the changing institutions
in their turn make for a further selection of individuals endowed with the
fittest temperament, and a further adaptation of individual temperament
and habits to the changing environment through the formation of new
institutions.

The forces which have shaped the development of human life and of
social structure are no doubt ultimately reducible to terms of living tissue
and material environment; but proximately, for the purpose in hand, these
forces may best be stated in terms of an environment, partly human, partly
nonhuman, and a human subject with a more or less definite physical and
intellectual constitution. Taken in the aggregate or average, this human
subject is more or less variable; chiefly, no doubt, under a rule of selective
conservation of favorable variations. The selection of favorable variations
is perhaps in great measure a selective conservation of ethnic types. In the
life history of any community whose population is made up of a mixture

This selection is taken from chapter 8 of The Theory of the Leisure Class.

of diverse ethnic elements, one or another of several persistent and relatively stable types of body and of temperament rises into dominance at any given point. The situation, including the institutions in force at any given time, will favor the survival and dominance of one type of character in preference to another; and the type of man so selected to continue and to further elaborate the institutions handed down from the past will in some considerable measure shape these institutions in his own likeness. But apart from selection as between relatively stable types of character and habits of mind, there is no doubt simultaneously going on a process of selective adaptation of habits of thought within the general range of aptitudes which is characteristic of the dominant ethnic type or types. There may be a variation in the fundamental character of any population by selection between relatively stable types; but there is also a variation due to adaptation in detail within the range of the type, and to selection between specific habitual views regarding any given social relation or group of relations.

For the present purpose, however, the question as to the nature of the adaptive process—whether it is chiefly a selection between stable types of temperament and character, or chiefly an adaptation of men's habits of thought to changing circumstances—is of less importance than the fact that, by one method or another, institutions change and develop. Institutions must change with changing circumstances, since they are of the nature of a habitual method of responding to the stimuli which these changing circumstances afford. The development of these institutions is the development of society. The institutions are, in substance, prevalent habits of thought with respect to particular relations and particular functions of the individual and of the community; and the scheme of life, which is made up of the aggregate of institutions in force at a given time or at a given point in the development of any society, may, on the psychological side, be broadly characterized as a prevalent spiritual attitude or a prevalent theory of life. As regards its generic features, this spiritual attitude or theory of life is in the last analysis reducible to terms of a prevalent type of character.

The situation of today shapes the institutions of tomorrow through a selective, coercive process, by acting upon men's habitual view of things, and so altering or fortifying a point of view or a mental attitude handed down from the past. The institutions—that is to say the habits of thought—under the guidance of which men live are in this way received from an earlier time; more or less remotely earlier, but in any event they have been elaborated in and received from the past. Institutions are products of the past process, are adapted to past circumstances, and are therefore never in full accord with the requirements of the present. In the nature of the case, this process of selective adaptation can never catch up with the progressively changing situation in which the community finds itself at any given time; for the environment, the situation, the exigencies of life which enforce the adaptation and exercise the selection, change from day to day; and each successive situation of the community in its turn tends to obsolescence as soon as it has been established. When a step in the development has been taken, this step itself constitutes a change of situation which requires a new adaptation; it becomes the point of departure for a new step in the adjustment, and so on interminably.

It is to be noted then, although it may be a tedious truism, that the institutions of today—the present accepted scheme of life—do not entirely fit the situation of today. At the same time, men's present habits of thought tend to persist indefinitely, except as circumstances enforce a change. These institutions which have so been handed down, these habits of thought, points of view, mental attitudes and aptitudes, or whatnot are therefore themselves a conservative factor. This is the factor of social inertia, psychological inertia, conservatism.

Social structure changes, develops, adapts itself to an altered situation, only through a change in the habits of thought of the several classes of the community; or in the last analysis, through a change in the habits of thought of the individuals which make up the community. The evolution of society is substantially a process of mental adaptation on the part of individuals under the stress of circumstances which will no longer tolerate habits of thought formed under and conforming to a different set of circumstances in the past. For the immediate purpose it need not be a question of serious importance whether this adaptive process is a process of selection and survival of persistent ethnic types or a process of individual adaptation and an inheritance of acquired traits.

Social advance, especially as seen from the point of view of economic theory, consists in a continued progressive approach to an approximately exact "adjustment of inner relations to outer relations"; but this adjustment is never definitively established, since the "outer relations" are subject to constant change as a consequence of the progressive change going on in the "inner relations." But the degree of approximation may be greater or less, depending on the facility with which an adjustment is made. A readjustment of men's habits of thought to conform with the exigencies of an altered situation is in any case made only tardily and reluctantly, and only under the coercion exercised by a situation which has made the accredited views untenable. The readjustment of institutions and habitual views to an altered environment is made in response to pressure from without; it is of the nature of a response to stimulus. Freedom and facility of readjustment, that is to say capacity for growth in social structure, therefore depends in great measure on the degree of freedom with which the situation at any given time acts on the individual members of the community—the degree of exposure of the individual members to the constraining forces of the environment. If any portion or class of society is sheltered from the action of the environment in any essential respect, that portion of the community, or that class, will adapt its views and its scheme of life more tardily to the altered general situation; it will insofar tend to retard the process of social transformation. The wealthy leisure class is in such a sheltered position with respect to the economic forces that make for change and readjustment. And it may be said that the forces which make for a readjustment of institutions, especially in the case of a modern industrial community, are, in the last analysis, almost entirely of an economic nature.

Any community may be viewed as an industrial or economic mechanism, the structure of which is made up of what is called its economic institutions. These institutions are habitual methods of carrying on the life process of the community in contact with the material environment in which it lives. When given methods of unfolding human activity in this given environment have been elaborated in this way, the life of the community will express itself with some facility in these habitual directions. The community will make use of the forces of the environment for the purposes of its life according to methods learned in the past and embodied in these institutions. But as population increases, and as men's knowledge and skill in directing the forces of nature widen, the habitual methods of relation between the members of the group, and the habitual method of carrying on the life process of the group as a whole, no longer give the same result as before; nor are the resulting conditions of life distributed and apportioned in the same manner or with the same effect among the various members as before. If the scheme according to which the life process of the group was carried on under the earlier conditions gave approximately the highest attainable result—under the circumstances—in the way of efficiency or facility of the life process of the group; then the same scheme of life unaltered will not yield the highest result attainable in this respect under the altered conditions. Under the altered conditions of population, skill, and knowledge, the facility of life as carried on according to the traditional scheme may not be lower than under the earlier conditions; but the chances are always that it is less than might be if the scheme were altered to suit the altered conditions.

The group is made up of individuals, and the group's life is the life of individuals carried on in at least ostensible severalty. The group's accepted scheme of life is the consensus of views held by the body of these individuals as to what is right, good, expedient, and beautiful in the way of human life. In the redistribution of the conditions of life that comes of the altered method of dealing with the environment, the outcome is not an equable change in the facility of life throughout the group. The altered conditions may increase the facility of life for the group as a whole, but the redistribution will usually result in a decrease of facility or fullness of life for some members of the group. An advance in technical methods, in population, or in industrial organization will require at least some of the members of the community to change their habits of life, if they are to enter with facility and effect into the altered industrial methods; and in doing so they will be unable to live up to the received notions as to what are the right and beautiful habits of life.

Anyone who is required to change his habits of life and his habitual relations to his fellowmen will feel the discrepancy between the method of life required of him by the newly arisen exigencies, and the traditional scheme of life to which he is accustomed. It is the individuals placed in this position who have the liveliest incentive to reconstruct the received scheme of life and are most readily persuaded to accept new standards; and it is through the need of the means of livelihood that men are placed in such a position. The pressure exerted by the environment upon the group, and making for a readjustment of the group's scheme of life, impinges upon the members of the group in the form of pecuniary exigencies; and it is owing to this fact—that external forces are in great part translated into the form of pecuniary or economic exigencies—it is owing to this fact that we can say that the forces which count toward a readjustment of institutions in any modern industrial community are chiefly economic forces; or more specifically, these forces take the form of pecuniary pressure. Such a readjustment as is here contemplated is substantially a change in men's views as to what is good and right, and the means through which a change is wrought in men's apprehension of what is good and right is in large part the pressure of pecuniary exigencies.

Any change in men's views as to what is good and right in human life makes its way but tardily at the best. Especially is this true of any change in the direction of what is called progress; that is to say, in the direction of divergence from the archaic position—from the position which may be accounted the point of departure at any step in the social evolution of the community. Retrogression, reapproach to a standpoint to which the race has been long habituated in the past, is easier. This is especially true in case the development away from this past standpoint has not been due chiefly to a substitution of an ethnic type whose temperament is alien to the earlier standpoint.

The cultural stage which lies immediately back of the present in the life history of Western civilization is what has here been called the *quasi-peaceable stage*. At this quasi-peaceable stage the law of status is the dominant feature in the scheme of life. There is no need of pointing out how prone the men of today are to revert to the spiritual attitude of mastery and of personal subservience which characterizes that stage. It may rather be said to be held in an uncertain abeyance by the economic exigencies of today, than to have been definitively supplanted by a habit of mind that is in full accord with these later-developed exigencies. The predatory and quasi-peaceable stages of economic evolution seem to have been of long duration in the life history of all the chief ethnic elements which go to make up the populations of the Western culture. The temperament and the propensities proper to those cultural stages have, therefore, attained such a persistence as to make a speedy reversion to the broad features of the corresponding psychological constitution inevitable in the case of any class or community which is removed from the action of those forces that make for a maintenance of the later-developed habits of thought.

It is a matter of common notoriety that when individuals, or even considerable groups of men, are segregated from a higher industrial culture and exposed to a lower cultural environment, or to an economic situation of a more primitive character, they quickly show evidence of reversion toward the spiritual features which characterize the predatory type; and it seems probable that the dolicho-blond type of European man is possessed of a greater facility for such reversion to barbarism than the other ethnic elements with which that type is associated in the Western culture. Examples of such a reversion on a small scale abound in the later history of migration and colonization. Except for the fear of offending that chauvinistic patriotism which is so characteristic a feature of the predatory culture, and the presence of which is frequently the most striking mark of reversion in modern communities, the case of the American colonies might be cited as an example of such a reversion on an unusually large scale, though it was not a reversion of very large scope.

The leisure class is in great measure sheltered from the stress of those economic exigencies which prevail in any modern, highly organized industrial community. The exigencies of the struggle for the means of life are less exacting for this class than for any other; and as a consequence of this privileged position we should expect to find it one of the least responsive of the classes of society to the demands which the situation makes for a further growth of institutions and a readjustment to an altered industrial situation. The leisure class is the conservative class. The exigencies of the general economic situation of the community do not freely or directly impinge upon the members of this class. They are not required under penalty of forfeiture to change their habits of life and their theoretical views of the external world to suit the demands of an altered industrial technique, since they are not in the full sense an organic part of the industrial community. Therefore these exigencies do not readily produce, in the members of this class, that degree of uneasiness with the existing order which alone can lead any body of men to give up views and methods of life that have become habitual to them. The office of the leisure class in social evolution is to retard the movement and to conserve what is obsolescent. This proposition is by no means novel; it has long been one of the commonplaces of popular opinion.

The prevalent conviction that the wealthy class is by nature conservative has been popularly accepted without much aid from any theoretical view as to the place and relation of that class in the cultural development. When an explanation of this class conservatism is offered, it is commonly the invidious one that the wealthy class opposes innovation because it has a vested interest, of an unworthy sort, in maintaining the present conditions. The explanation here put forward imputes no unworthy motive. The opposition of the class to changes in the cultural scheme is instinctive, and does not rest primarily on an interested calculation of material advantages; it is an instinctive revulsion at any departure from the accepted way of doing and of looking at things—a revulsion common to all men and only to be overcome by stress of circumstances. All change in habits of life and of thought is irksome. The difference in this respect between the wealthy and the common run of mankind lies not so much in the motive which prompts to conservatism as in the degree of exposure to the economic forces that urge a change. The members of the wealthy class do not yield to the demand for innovation as readily as other men because they are not constrained to do so.

This conservatism of the wealthy class is so obvious a feature that it has even come to be recognized as a mark of respectability. Since conservatism is a characteristic of the wealthier and therefore more reputable portion of the community, it has acquired a certain honorific or decorative value. It has become prescriptive to such an extent that an adherence to conservative views is comprised as a matter of course in our notions of respectability; and it is imperatively incumbent on all who would lead a blameless life in point of social repute. Conservatism, being an upper-class characteristic, is decorous; and conversely, innovation, being a lower-class phenomenon, is vulgar. The first and most unreflected element in that instinctive revulsion and reprobation with which we turn from all social innovators is this sense of the essential vulgarity of the thing. So that even in cases where one recognizes the substantial merits of the case for which the innovator is spokesman—as may easily happen if the evils which he seeks to remedy are sufficiently remote in point of time or space or personal contact—still one cannot but be sensible of the fact that the innovator is a person with whom it is at least distasteful to be associated, and from whose social contact one must shrink. Innovation is bad form.

The fact that the usages, actions, and views of the well-to-do leisure class acquire the character of a prescriptive canon of conduct for the rest of society, gives added weight and reach to the conservative influence of that class. It makes it incumbent upon all reputable people to follow their lead. So that, by virtue of its high position as the avatar of good form, the wealthier class comes to exert a retarding influence upon social development far in excess of that which the simple numerical strength of the class would assign it. Its prescriptive example acts to greatly stiffen the resistance of all other classes against any innovation, and to fix men's affections upon the good institutions handed down from an earlier generation.

There is a second way in which the influence of the leisure class acts in the same direction, so far as concerns hindrance to the adoption of a conventional scheme of life more in accord with the exigencies of the time. This second method of upper-class guidance is not in strict consistency to be brought under the same category as the instinctive conservatism and aversion to new modes of thought just spoken of; but it may as well be dealt with here, since it has at least this much in common with the conservative habit of mind that it acts to retard innovation and the growth of social structure. The code of proprieties, conventionalities, and usages in vogue at any given time and among any given people has more or less of the character of an organic whole; so that any appreciable change in one point of the scheme involves something of a change or readjustment at other points also, if not a reorganization all along the line. When a change is made which immediately touches only a minor point in the scheme, the consequent derangement of the structure of conventionalities may be inconspicuous; but even in such a case it is safe to say that some derangement of the general scheme, more or less far-reaching, will follow. On the other hand, when an attempted reform involves the suppression or thorough-going remodeling of an institution of first-rate importance in the conventional scheme, it is immediately felt that a serious derangement of the entire scheme would result; it is felt that a readjustment of the structure to the new form taken on by one of its chief elements would be a painful and tedious, if not a doubtful process.

In order to realize the difficulty which such a radical change in any one feature of the conventional scheme of life would involve, it is only necessary to suggest the suppression of the monogamic family, or of the agnatic system of consanguinity, or of private property, or of the theistic faith, in any country of the Western civilization; or suppose the suppression of ancestor worship in China, or of the caste system in India, or of slavery in Africa, or the establishment of equality of the sexes in Mohammedan countries. It needs no argument to show that the derangement of the general structure of conventionalities in any of these cases would be very considerable. In order to effect such an innovation a very far-reaching alteration of men's habits of thought would be involved also at other points of the scheme than the one immediately in question. The aversion to any such innovation amounts to a shrinking from an essentially alien scheme of life.

The revulsion felt by good people at any proposed departure from the accepted methods of life is a familiar fact of everyday experience. It is not unusual to hear those persons who dispense salutary advice and admonition to the community express themselves forcibly upon the far-reaching pernicious effects which the community would suffer from such relatively slight changes as the disestablishment of the Anglican Church, an increased facility of divorce, adoption of female suffrage, prohibition of the manufacture and sale of intoxicating beverages, abolition or restriction of inheritance, etc. Any one of these innovations would, we are told, "shake the social structure to its base," "reduce society to chaos," "subvert the foundations of morality," "make life intolerable," "confound the order of nature," etc. These various locutions are, no doubt, of the nature of hyperbole; but, at the same time, like all overstatement, they are evidence of a lively sense of the gravity of the consequences which they are intended to describe. The effect of these and like innovations in deranging the accepted scheme of life is felt to be of much graver consequence than the simple alteration of an isolated item in a series of contrivances for the convenience of men in society. What is true in so obvious a degree of innovations of first-rate importance is true in a less degree of changes of a smaller immediate importance. The aversion to change is in large part an aversion to the bother of making the readjustment which any given change will necessitate; and this solidarity of the system of institutions of any given culture or of any given people strengthens the instinctive resistance offered to any change in men's habits of thought, even in matters which, taken by themselves, are of minor importance.

A consequence of this increased reluctance, due to the solidarity of human institutions, is that any innovation calls for a greater expenditure of nervous energy in making the necessary readjustment than would otherwise be the case. It is not only that a change in established habits of thought is distasteful. The process of readjustment of the accepted theory of life involves a degree of mental effort—a more or less protracted and laborious effort to find and to keep one's bearings under the altered circumstances. This process requires a certain expenditure of energy, and so presumes, for its successful accomplishment, some surplus of energy beyond that absorbed in the daily struggle for subsistence. Consequently it follows that progress is hindered by underfeeding and excessive physical hardship, no less effectually than by such a luxurious life as will shut out discontent by cutting off the occasion for it. The abjectly poor, and all those persons whose energies are entirely absorbed by the struggle for daily sustenance, are conservative because they cannot afford the effort of taking thought for the day after tomorrow; just as the highly prosperous are conservative because they have small occasion to be discontented with the situation as it stands today.

From this proposition it follows that the institution of a leisure class acts to make the lower classes conservative by withdrawing from them as much as it may of the means of sustenance, and so reducing their consumption, and consequently their available energy, to such a point as to make them incapable of the effort required for the learning and adoption of new habits of thought. The accumulation of wealth at the upper end of the pecuniary scale implies privation at the lower end of the scale. It is a commonplace that, wherever it occurs, a considerable degree of privation among the body of the people is a serious obstacle to any innovation.

This direct inhibitory effect of the unequal distribution of wealth is seconded by an indirect effect tending to the same result. As has already been seen, the imperative example set by the upper class in fixing the canons of reputability fosters the practice of conspicuous consumption. The prevalence of conspicuous consumption as one of the main elements in the standard of decency among all classes is of course not traceable wholly to the example of the wealthy leisure class, but the practice and the insistence on it are no doubt strengthened by the example of the leisure class. The requirements of decency in this matter are very considerable and very imperative; so that even among classes whose pecuniary position is sufficiently strong to admit a consumption of goods considerably in excess of the subsistence minimum, the disposable surplus left over after the more imperative physical needs are satisfied is not infrequently diverted to the purpose of a conspicuous decency, rather than to added physical comfort and fullness of life. Moreover, such surplus energy as is available is also likely to be expended in the acquisition of goods for conspicuous consumption or conspicuous hoarding. The result is that the requirements of pecuniary reputability tend (1) to leave but a scanty subsistence minimum available for other than conspicuous consumption, and (2) to absorb any surplus energy which may be available after the bare physical necessities of life have been provided for. The outcome of the whole is a strengthening of the general conservative attitude of the community. The institution of a leisure class hinders cultural development immediately (1) by the inertia proper to the class itself, (2) through its prescriptive example of conspicuous waste and of conservatism, and (3) indirectly through that system of unequal distribution of wealth and sustenance on which the institution itself rests.

To this is to be added that the leisure class has also a material interest in leaving things as they are. Under the circumstances prevailing at any given time this class is in a privileged position, and any departure from the existing order may be expected to work to the detriment of the class rather than the reverse. The attitude of the class, simply as influenced by its class interest, should therefore be to let well enough alone. This interested motive comes in to supplement the strong instinctive bias of the class, and so to render it even more consistently conservative than it otherwise would be.

All this, of course, has nothing to say in the way of eulogy or deprecation of the office of the leisure class as an exponent and vehicle of conservatism or reversion in social structure. The inhibition which it exercises may be salutary or the reverse. Whether it is the one or the other in any given case is a question of casuistry rather than of general theory. There may be truth in the view (as a question of policy) so often expressed by the spokesmen of the conservative element, that without some such substantial and consistent resistance to innovation as is offered by the conservative well-to-do classes, social innovation and experiment would hurry the community into untenable and intolerable situations; the only possible result of which would be discontent and disastrous reaction. All this, however, is beside the present argument.

But apart from all deprecation, and aside from all question as to the indispensability of some such check on headlong innovation, the leisure class, in the nature of things, consistently acts to retard that adjustment to the environment which is called social advance or development. The characteristic attitude of the class may be summed up in the maxim "Whatever is, is right"; whereas the law of natural selection, as applied to human institutions, gives the axiom "Whatever is, is wrong." Not that the institutions of today are wholly wrong for the purposes of the life of today, but they are, always and in the nature of things, wrong to some extent. They are the result of a more or less inadequate adjustment of the methods of living to a situation which prevailed at some point in the past development; and they are therefore wrong by something more than the interval which separates the present situation from that of the past. *Right* and *wrong* are of course here used without conveying any reflection as to what ought or ought not to be. They are applied simply from the (morally colorless) evolutionary standpoint, and are intended to designate compatibility or incompatibility with the effective evolutionary process. The institution of a leisure class, by force of class interest and instinct, and by precept and prescriptive example, makes for the perpetuation of the existing maladjustment of institutions, and even favors a reversion to a somewhat more archaic scheme of life; a scheme which would be still farther out of adjustment with the exigencies of life under the existing situation even than the accredited, obsolescent scheme that has come down from the immediate past.

But after all has been said on the head of conservation of the good old ways, it remains true that institutions change and develop. There is a cumulative growth of customs and habits of thought; a selective adaptation of conventions and methods of life. Something is to be said of the office of the leisure class in guiding this growth as well as in retarding it; but little can be said here of its relation to institutional growth except as it touches the institutions that are primarily and immediately of an economic character. These institutions—the economic structure—may be roughly distinguished into two classes or categories, according as they serve one or the other of two divergent purposes of economic life.

To adapt the classical terminology, they are institutions of acquisition or of production; or to revert to terms already employed in a different connection in earlier chapters, they are pecuniary or industrial institutions; or in still other terms, they are institutions serving either the invidious or the noninvidious economic interest. The former category have to do with "business," the latter with industry, taking the latter word in the mechanical sense. The latter class are not often recognized as institutions, in great part because they do not immediately concern the ruling class, and are, therefore, seldom the subject of legislation or of deliberate convention. When they do receive attention they are commonly approached from the pecuniary or business side; that being the side or phase of economic life that chiefly occupies men's deliberations in our time, especially the deliberations of the upper classes. These classes have little else than a business interest in things economic, and on them at the same time it is chiefly incumbent to deliberate upon the community's affairs.

The relation of the leisure (that is, propertied nonindustrial) class to the economic process is a pecuniary relation—a relation of acquisition, not of production; of exploitation, not of serviceability. Indirectly their economic office may, of course, be of the utmost importance to the economic life process; and it is by no means here intended to depreciate the economic function of the propertied class or of the captains of industry. The purpose is simply to point out what is the nature of the relation of these classes to the industrial process and to economic institutions. Their office is of a parasitic character, and their interest is to divert what substance they may to their own use, and to retain whatever is under their hand. The conventions of the business world have grown up under the selective surveillance of this principle of predation or parasitism. They are conventions of ownership; derivatives, more or less remote, of the ancient predatory culture. But these pecuniary institutions do not entirely fit the situation of today, for they have grown up under a past situation differing somewhat from the present. Even for effectiveness in the pecuniary way, therefore, they are not as apt as might be. The changed industrial life requires changed methods of acquisition; and the pecuniary classes have some interest in so adapting the pecuniary institutions as to give them the best effect for acquisition of private gain that is compatible with the continuance of the industrial process out of which this gain arises.

Hence there is a more or less consistent trend in the leisure-class guidance of institutional growth, answering to the pecuniary ends which shape leisure-class economic life.

The effect of the pecuniary interest and the pecuniary habit of mind upon the growth of institutions is seen in those enactments and conventions that make for security of property, enforcement of contracts, facility of pecuniary transactions, vested interests. Of such bearing are changes affecting bankruptcy and receiverships, limited liability, banking and currency, coalitions of laborers or employers, trusts and pools. The community's institutional furniture of this kind is of immediate consequence only to the propertied classes, and in proportion as they are propertied; that is to say, in proportion as they are to be ranked with the leisure class. But indirectly these conventions of business life are of the gravest consequence for the industrial process and for the life of the community. And in guiding the institutional growth in this respect, the pecuniary classes, therefore, serve a purpose of the most serious importance to the community, not only in the conservation of the accepted social scheme, but also in shaping the industrial process proper.

The immediate end of this pecuniary institutional structure and of its amelioration is the greater facility of peaceable and orderly exploitation; but its remoter effects far outrun this immediate object. Not only does the more facile conduct of business permit industry and extraindustrial life to go on with less perturbation; but the resulting elimination of disturbances and complications calling for an exercise of astute discrimination in everyday affairs acts to make the pecuniary class itself superfluous. As fast as pecuniary transactions are reduced to routine, the captain of industry can be dispensed with. This consummation, it is needless to say, lies yet in the indefinite future. The ameliorations wrought in favor of the pecuniary interest in modern institutions tend, in another field, to substitute the "soulless" joint-stock corporation for the captain, and so they make also for the dispensability of the great leisure-class function of ownership. Indirectly, therefore, the bent given to the growth of economic institutions by the leisure-class influence is of very considerable industrial consequence.

QUESTIONS

1. Why does Veblen think institutions reflect the past instead of the present?

2. What does Veblen mean when he says that "the forces which count toward a readjustment of institutions in any modern industrial community are chiefly economic forces?" (210)

3. What social attitude is Veblen commenting on when he says, "Innovation is bad form"? (212)

4. According to Veblen, how does the wealthier class "exert a retarding influence upon social development" out of proportion to its number? (213)

5. What does Veblen mean by "conspicuous decency"? (215)

FOR FURTHER REFLECTION

1. Is Veblen correct in saying, "The accumulation of wealth at the upper end of the pecuniary scale implies privation at the lower end of the scale"?

2. Does Veblen's explanation of "conspicuous consumption" explain to your satisfaction why many people spend beyond their means?

3. Is it true, as Veblen argues, that generally the poor resist social change?

JOHN R. COMMONS

J ohn R. Commons (1862–1945) was one of the founders—with Thorstein
Veblen—of the "institutionalist" school within the academic discipline of
economics. This approach introduced a new mode of theoretical analysis,
connecting economic with legal, political, and sociological perspectives. He
made important contributions to labor history and played an instrumental role
in drafting landmark social-welfare legislation for the state of Wisconsin, which
in turn strongly influenced national legislation, such as the Social Security Act,
enacted as part of the New Deal.

Commons was born in a small town in western Ohio and after graduating from
Oberlin College in 1888, he entered Johns Hopkins University to study for a
PhD in economics under Richard T. Ely. However, Commons left Johns Hopkins
without completing his degree. He held a series of short-term teaching positions
at various colleges and universities and served on several governmental
commissions before finally landing at the University of Wisconsin in 1904. While
there he continued his civic involvement at both the state and the national
level. Commons's major works include two histories of the labor movement in
America—*A Documentary History of American Industrial Society* (10 vols.;
1910–1911) and *History of Labour in the United States* (4 vols.; 1918–1935).
Other important works are *Institutional Economics* (1934) and *The Economics
of Collective Action*, which was published posthumously. In 1918, he was
elected president of the American Economic Association. He retired from
teaching in the early 1930s, but remained active with scholarship and writing
until his death.

The following selection is taken from *The Economics of Collective Action*. In it,
Commons explains his concept of a "transaction," one of his chief theoretical
contributions to the institutional approach to economics. Commons views
a transaction not just as a simple exchange between a buyer and seller,
but rather as a complex set of relations embedded within a social—and
especially juridical—institutional framework. Though his name is no longer
very well known, the modern concept of a "transaction cost" may be traced to
Commons's analysis.

Transactions

P rivate property, owned by individuals for executing the will of the owner, was assumed and taken for granted, without investigation, by the nineteenth-century economists. The kind of property with which they were familiar was "corporeal" property, the rights of ownership of lands and physical commodities, which were the products of labor. Their buying and selling was merely a "voluntary exchange" of one item of physical property for another item.

But the incoming of joint stock corporations, labor unions, and universal suffrage without property qualifications changed the legal foundations of economics. Corporations now began to own the bulk of corporeal property as valued on the markets, and individuals owned the stocks and bonds of the corporations. Laborers, backed by the new universal suffrage, obtained legal rights to organize and bargain collectively with corporations and individual owners. Political parties became the organizations through which these legal foundations of economics were maintained or changed.

In this process three types of transactions may be distinguished instead of the one type of voluntary exchange of physical commodities by individuals. These are the *rationing* transactions by the "policy makers" of the organization—boards of directors of corporations, or similar directors of labor unions and administrative political governments—in laying down working rules; the *managerial* transactions between superiors and inferiors, mainly wage earners and salary earners in the production of wealth; and the *bargaining* transactions on the markets, which transfer ownerships of corporeal property and the new kinds of incorporeal and intangible property of bonds and stocks of corporations.

All these varieties of transactions are in operation at the same time, and the problem is not the total elimination of any one kind, but the balance among the three in the processes of economic activity. The latest to

This selection is taken from part 1, chapter 3 of The Economics of Collective Action.

come historically into prominence were the bargaining transactions; the most ancient were the managerial transactions. Rationing transactions, which are also of ancient origin, have latterly become of major importance through the activities of corporations, unions, and governments.

The free bargaining transactions among individuals were the legal foundations of the early science of economics. But exactly what it was that the bargainers "exchanged" in these transactions was not made clear at the hands of the economists. There developed a double meaning of the word "commodities": a proprietary meaning, intended by the courts, of the acquisition and alienation of ownership; and a technological meaning, used by the economists, for the production, transportation, and physical delivery of the thing owned. The proprietary meaning was assets, the legal capacity to pay debts and taxes which were known as liabilities. The technological meaning was wealth, the product of labor, and the enjoyment of consumers.

That the two meanings of wealth and assets were widely separated became evident at times, but did not become the main political and economic issue until after the widest of all separations, which began in the year 1929.

The ownership meaning had become the foundation of the credit system and its method of creating credit money in place of metallic money, by the businessmen and the banks. This ownership meaning had been working itself into economics by decisions of the courts in enforcing contracts, and, therefore, had become dominant over the technological meanings of the economists. For example, I deliver to you a horse, you deliver the money. It is an exchange. But I may not own the horse. You may not own the money. Only the owner of the horse can sell it and give legal title. The owner of money is different, however. A thief can give, under certain circumstances, a legal title to the money which he has stolen and with which he pretends to buy a horse. Money becomes a privileged kind of asset. It alone pays taxes and debts. For this reason everybody tries to get the ownership of money. It cannot be taken even by its rightful owner if the payee accepted it in good faith, even from a thief who had stolen it.

It is not even the owner or a thief who transfers the ownership of property and gives a good title of ownership. It is sovereignty, the law of the land, as worked out by court decisions through the centuries in the form of the "common law." Business economics has more or less clearly distinguished between a "transaction" and an "exchange." This conforms to the distinction made in courts of law, which, after all, are closer to business practices every day than are the economists. A bargaining transaction is the negotiations and agreement which transfer *ownerships* under the "operation of law." An "exchange" is reduced to the mechanical and labor process that physically delivers the object under commands of the owner.

The accepted formula of early economists that "goods exchange for goods" fits only a primitive "barter economy." They omitted the bank credit system and the decisions of courts. Shoes are not exchanged for wheat, but both shoes and wheat are today sold for a checking account at a bank, known as a "bank deposit." Even bank "deposit" is a misnomer. It is a bank debt owed by the bank, payable on demand to the "depositor" who, in turn, is not a depositor, but a creditor. By drawing a check on that account he who has sold the shoes in "exchange" for somebody else's check on a bank goes out into other markets and buys with his own check whatever he wishes and can command in exchange. The banking and credit system of the world has destroyed the simplified barter economy of traditional economics. "Goods" do not exchange for "goods"; they are generally sold for a checking account, which is a creditor-debtor relation of contracts enforced by the courts.

The obsolete formula of a barter economy stumbled on this double meaning of the word "commodity"—the double meaning of ownership and the thing owned—assets and wealth. When the manufacturer sells his shoes, or the farmer sells his wheat, it becomes a "commodity," meaning anything that is bought and sold. But he does not sell the shoes, he alienates his ownership of the shoes, and he does not sell the wheat, he transfers its ownership.

The term "price" thus also has a double meaning. It meant, in ordinary language, the amount of physical money paid for a physical thing, as the price of a pair of shoes or a bushel of wheat. But it means, in the legal economics of the courts, the "consideration," that is, the service which the owner of the money rendered to the owner of the shoes by alienating his ownership of money in consideration of the service rendered by alienation of the ownership of the shoes. Each owner alienates his ownership, and each owner acquires another ownership. Prices are paid, not for physical objects, but for *ownership* of those objects.

This is a hard saying, and not ordinary language. For example, I buy a pair of shoes for five dollars. I physically transfer five dollars, and the merchant physically hands me the shoes. The price of the shoes is five dollars in actual money. This is so-called "common sense." But it is much more important that I go away with the ownership of the shoes, and the merchant goes to the bank with the ownership of the money and transfers its ownership to the bank. There has been the alienation and acquisition of two ownerships. Critical economists have declared that ours is an "acquisitive" economy and not a "producing economy." It is both. It is also an "alienation economy." We acquire ownership of money by alienating ownership of things that are produced.

When the merchant sells his shoes to me in exchange for a bank check, which is approximately nine-tenths of modern money, he does not get merely a piece of paper, he gets lawful ownership of a debt owed by my banker to me as a depositor, and I transfer to the merchant my ownership of that much of my deposits at the bank. That banker's debt, owed to me and now owed to the merchant, was, strangely enough, also considered to be a "commodity" like the wheat or shoes, simply because it also could be bought and sold.

This remarkable fact by which a debt becomes a "commodity," like wheat or shoes, is an invention of the lawyers and courts, beginning only as late as the seventeenth century in England, but continuing to the present day by new additions under the general name "negotiability," and the debt owned by the creditor of the bank is a "negotiable instrument," not wheat or shoes. It serves as money, or general purchasing power, and modern "money" is mainly negotiable debts owed by bankers. The barter economy knew nothing of such a "commodity" as bankers' debts, but the early economists treated these negotiable instruments as if they were wheat and shoes, although they were not the products of labor, but were the products of sovereignty.

There was another kind of commodity, the "precious metals," which were a product of labor, like shoes and wheat. The early economists carried their formula of a barter economy over to the exchange value of the precious metals, gold or silver, which were also commodities. But there is a difference between "bullion" and "coin." Bullion is a commodity, but coin is lawful money, made so by sovereigns as the means of paying debts, both the compulsory debts of taxes owed to the sovereign and the voluntary debts owed to individuals whose payment was also compulsorily enforced by the courts. Coin and bullion were eventually made equivalent in value by "free and unlimited" coinage, whereby the owner of bullion could convert it into lawful money without expense to himself but at the expense of the government. Silver was "demonetized" in some countries and not in others, which meant that silver was reduced to a commodity and could not be converted, without expense or in unlimited quantities, into lawful money that would pay debts enforced by sovereignty. Finally, gold itself is substantially demonetized in all countries by withdrawing from individuals the privilege of "free and unlimited coinage." Governments become even the sole and monopolistic owners of gold bullion, and do not bother to coin it. The American government owns more than half of the world's supply, which it locks up underground and issues "certificates" of ownership, which are themselves legal tender. Governments buy and sell gold bullion at prices stated in terms of something else. That "something else," strangely enough, is not metallic money, and is not paper money nor even bank checks. It is a "money of account," meaning, thereby, a "unit of account" on the books, the dollar, or the franc, established by law as legal tender in payment of debts. It measures the amount of metallic bullion as well as the amount of paper money, of bank debts, and of all debts and the monetary value of all commodities. This unit of account is maintained by custom and law, in the language of weight of gold or silver coin, although the metal itself has long since been taken out of circulation.

These highly complicated interferences with the simplified barter economy may be summarized in the distinction between a *transaction* and an *exchange*. A bargaining transaction is a double transfer of ownerships. The word "exchange" had, and continues to have, the double meaning of the legal transfers of ownership and the labor transfer of things owned. A bargaining transaction, as readily understood in business affairs, is the legal transfer of two ownerships, to be followed by two physical transfers of the things owned, whether the "thing" be a physical object like shoes and wheat, or a negotiable debt, like a bank check or a government debt.

The physical and labor transfers have come to be comprehended in modern economics under the name of managerial transactions, while the legal transfers are the bargaining transactions and the rationing transactions. Bargaining transactions transfer ownerships in the familiar open or free markets; the terms of the transfers, including both price and the amounts to be sold, are arrived at by negotiation. Rationing transactions transfer ownerships where either the quantity or the price, or both, are determined by some authorized superior power. Ownerships are transferred by rationing in two principal fields: in the controlled markets of dictatorships and now in wartime economies; and within the integrated industrial concerns or combinations where ownerships of goods or services pass from one company to another without market bids.

Historically, bargaining transactions come latest, but for convenience, we consider them first. According to economists, a "market" consists of a number of "exchangers" making offers and bids to each other for the physical delivery of commodities. But, according to lawful economics these "exchangers" are sellers for money and buyers with money, and the accurate name of their dealings is alienation and acquisition of the two ownerships. This ownership is "property," meaning the "rights" of property. They are alienating and acquiring property rights in a commodity. What they offer to sell and buy are the *ownerships* of the commodities, and not directly the objects owned. *After* they have acquired ownership, then they are in position to do as they lawfully please with the objects which they now legally own. But, according to legal economics, the owners of the wheat or pigs, for example, or even of one's own labor, offer to sell their ownerships, and the buyers are owners of gold or owners of bank debts (deposits) payable on demand, who offer to sell their ownerships of gold or of bankers' negotiable debts to the sellers in consideration of the release of their ownerships of wheat, pigs, or labor. Owners offer to alienate their ownerships through exchange.

If we further examine the word "commodity," as used by economists and common sense, we can see these two meanings before us every day. A commodity is not merely a physical thing like a horse, or an automobile, or a loaf of bread. It is also the lawful ownership of the horse, automobile, or bread. Of what use is an automobile to me if I steal it? I can, indeed, use it at seventy miles per hour, but I have my eye on sovereignty in the shape of every policeman ahead, or on the sheriffs and deputies who are following and lawfully shooting at me or at my rubber tires. All this is done to me because I have not acquired ownership by previously inducing the lawful owner willingly to alienate his ownership to me. I might have bought the *use* of the car without acquiring its ownership, as when I rent a car. This use also is a "commodity," but with a legal time limit, whereas if I bought the car, there is no time limit except my own will and the wearing out of the car. It is sovereignty that makes things lawfully useful.

It was not until recent years that the Federal Reserve Board recognized, in its statistics, that the demand and supply of money in the United States is the demand and supply of *ownerships* in this country. The Board introduced the item of "earmarked" gold, to indicate metallic money owned abroad and not entering into the supply of gold on the American markets. It is *physically* here, but not *legally* nor *economically* here.

One of the legal technicalities of economic significance is what may be named the negotiational psychology of the law, by means of which the intentions of the participants are discovered. These intentions may require actual investigation in cases of criminal law, usually by circumstantial evidence, but in cases of proprietary law it is sufficient to read into the minds of bargaining participants the intention to do what was right and lawful under the circumstances of time and place, as similar participants who were lawful men would have intended to do. This comparative behavioristic psychology is investigated or assumed under the name of custom, or usage.

When we reduce all of the prospective buyers and sellers upon a given market to those who participate in one bargaining transaction as our smallest unit of investigation, then they are the "best" two buyers and the "best" two sellers, meaning the two buyers who offer the highest prices and the two sellers who offer to accept the lowest prices, in consideration of transfers of ownership. All others are, for the moment, excluded as "potential" competitors. The best two sellers are those able to sell at the lowest price. They compete for choice of alternatives offered by the best two buyers, those able to buy at the highest prices, while, in turn, the best two buyers are competing for choice of alternatives offered by the best two sellers. The actual transfer of ownership by sovereignty, in that one transaction, is made by reading "purpose" or "intention" into the minds of one actual buyer and one actual seller. When they are "off the market," by "closing the negotiations," then, for the next transaction, the best pair of those who were potential now become actual, until all are off the market.

Thus, instead of the "exchange" of physical things between two parties as contemplated in the former physical economics, there are five parties, all of whom are "potential" and then they are successively "actual" participants in the lawful alienation and acquisition of ownerships. I use the term "futurity" instead of the physical term "potential." Consequently there are four expectant economic relations on the market. There are two expectant buyers who are competitors, and two expectant sellers who are competitors. But the two buyers are offering opportunities to sell for the two sellers; and the two sellers are offering opportunities to buy for the two buyers. Then the actual seller and actual buyer, whose intentions lead sovereignty actually to transfer ownerships at a price or "consideration," are the two who actually close the negotiations by agreeing upon the terms of the transaction. But throughout the negotiations, there is a future judge ready to issue commands to any of the buyers or sellers in the name of sovereignty, if any dispute arises. Eventually there is a future Supreme Court to which appeal may be made on any alleged act of injustice by the trial court, or by the legislature or executive which has given directions to the trial court.

In order to make visible this complex relationship in one hypothetical transaction of five parties we may construct a formula somewhat as follows:

Trial Judge—Supreme Court

B	B^1	buyers
$100	$90	

S	S^1	sellers
$110	$120	

In this one supposed transaction there are four possible grounds of dispute regarding the transfers of ownership by those who may turn out to be the actual seller and buyer, and each of these disputes may finally be decided by the Supreme Court, and thereafter taken for granted, that is, "customary."

First is the issue of *competition*, as to whether the competitors have acted fairly toward each other.

Second is the issue of *equal opportunity*, as to whether the actual buyer discriminates unfairly between the sellers, or the actual seller discriminates unfairly between the buyers, by charging or paying different prices under similar circumstances.

Third is the issue of *bargaining power*, as to whether the price, or consideration, agreed upon by the actual buyer and seller was determined with or without duress, coercion, unfair competition, or unequal opportunity, known as a fair or reasonable price or value. These, as we have said, are treated technically as the "law of fair and unfair competition."

Fourth is the constitutional issue of *"due process* of law," which might be named the due "operation of law," as to whether the trial court, the executive, or legislature, unjustifiably deprived any one of the participants of his liberty or property.

The issues over these four relations involved in the transfers of ownership are all inextricably dependent on each other, such that a change in one will probably change the other three.

Thus the unit of investigation in economics is not an individual, it is a transaction involving, in this bargaining transaction, five individuals. This complicated transaction is short-circuited by economists and laymen who call it an "exchange." The difference is between individualistic economics and institutional economics, and between static economics and dynamic economics. The individual is important enough, but *economic science investigates what he is confronted with and what he does* in getting a living and getting rich by transfers of ownership. He is confronted by sovereignty which does the creating and transferring of ownerships. Sovereignty imposes the duties of avoidance and forbearance which create ownership, and the duties of performance and payment which transfer ownerships. The individual is confronted by competitors who are trying to take from him his living or riches by fair or unfair methods. He is confronted by discriminations which may unfairly deprive him of equal opportunity with others in getting a living or getting rich. He is confronted by the bargaining power of others compared with his own bargaining power. He is tied into an expected repetition of transactions within which he must find as much liberty and property as he can.

Finally, the closing of the negotiations between the actual buyer and actual seller creates two lawful debts, a debt of performance owed by the seller and a debt of payment owed by the buyer. The seller is under obligation to deliver the commodity to the buyer at a certain place within a specified time. The buyer is under similar obligation to make the payment immediately or at a future designated place and time.

These debts of payment also can be bought and sold, on what is known as the "money market" or the "capital market." Indeed it may rightly be said, as it has been said in effect, that the greatest of all inventions in the field of economics was the discovery that a debt could be bought and sold like a physical commodity. Debts were originally only debts of honor or a personal obligation, not imposed by sovereignty, and it seemed at that time to be preposterous that such a moral or personal duty could be sold by the creditor to a stranger, just as it now would seem preposterous to sell to a stranger a woman's promise to marry. That was the very prejudice which lawyers had to overcome when they invented the "negotiability" of debts in the seventeenth century. The nobility, indeed, did claim that their debts were not merchants' debts but were debts of honor which could not be sold to strangers. The matter was settled nearly two hundred years ago in England, when the court refused to listen to a grandee who argued that he was not a merchant.

Thus, besides the four grounds of dispute in bargaining transactions, there are four economic facts which are inseparable, namely, transfers of ownership by sovereignty, the monetary prices to be paid in acquiring ownerships, and the two debts of performance and payment created by the transaction. These debts may be named "rules of action" or "working rules" agreed upon by the participants and enforceable by the courts in case of dispute. Each participant must arrange his business so as to fulfill his debts of performance and payment when due. These four facts constitute the modern credit system, the foundation of capitalism. Briefly, they are alienations, prices, debts, performances, and payments, inseparately tied together in a bargaining transaction.

In point of time sequence, the bargaining transaction has three stages: first, the negotiations, which are closed when the agreement on intentions is reached; then the contract or "commitment," which imposes the obligations of performance and payment upon the parties in future time; finally the administration or performance of the obligations agreed upon, which, when completed by both parties, closes the transaction.

In point of time duration, bargaining transactions are cash, short-time, and long-time transactions. In cash transactions the negotiations, the transaction, and the performance and payment are all begun and closed together, without a measurable interval of time. In the short-time and long-time debts of hours, days, and years there are measurable lapses of time between the closing of the negotiations which originate the transaction and the final closing of the transaction itself by execution of the duties of performance and payment, during which lapse of time interest is paid.

The kinds of debts, above mentioned, are simply economic duties arising at law from the acquisition of ownerships. The fulfillment of these duties is effected by an entirely different transaction, which, in recent time, has come to be known as a managerial transaction, such as the dealings between a foreman and a laborer, a master and servant. This also has a legal foundation. Before a managerial transaction can lawfully be carried through, legal ownership must be obtained. This is obtained by lawful bargaining transactions. With legal ownership thus obtained, the owner has the legal power to issue commands and require obedience of laborers. While the law of bargaining transactions sets up an ethical ideal of persuasion between individuals who are equally free, the law of managerial transactions rests on the legal right of the owner to issue commands to laborers and on the correlative duty of obedience by the laborers to the commands of owners.

This is because the law of managerial transactions runs back into antiquity beyond the law of bargaining transactions, which, in our jurisprudence, has a history of only about three hundred years. The law of managerial transactions is plainly a law of inequality compared with the assumptions of equality in bargaining transactions. The present-day assumption is that when the free laborer enters upon the premises of the owner, not as a visitor or a thief, but with the joint intention of owner and laborer to become a producer of wealth, he thereby accepts the obligation to obey the commands of the owner, delegated perhaps to foremen. He is, in law, a "servant," as was literally the *servus* or slave. But he differs from the slave in that the court will not compel him to work, that is, will not compel him to fulfill his obligation of contract, because he has now acquired both the right to run away from his job without penalty, and the right to refuse to enter upon the premises without a previous understanding of what the job will be.

It is these rights to withhold his services that give to him bargaining power. They were denied, in the American history of slavery, by the Dred Scott decision of the Supreme Court (1857), but reversed by the Civil War and the Thirteenth and Fourteenth Amendments to the Constitution. But there still remain, during the period of time while the laborer is on the premises of the owner, the ancient obligations arising from the law of command and obedience. This is violated by the "sit-down" strike. The owner is free to "hire and fire" at will, an economic inducement, and the laborer is free to serve or quit at will, the reciprocal economic inducement. These are the preceding bargaining transactions. But these do not give him freedom while he is on the owner's premises.

By this law of managerial transactions the seller of property rights is placed in a position to fulfill his duty of *performance*, and the buyer his duty of *payment*, by "hiring and firing" laborers and by commanding their obedience.

Rationing transactions, the third type of transactions, are even more primitive than bargaining and managerial transactions. They were the decrees of sovereignty apportioning among subordinates, without their consent, and without bargaining, which in recent times would be bribery, the benefits and burdens of the joint production of wealth by the joint action of all producers of wealth. The historical example is taxation, and a modern example is taxation for the support of education. The burden of taxes is apportioned by sovereignty without consent or bargaining on the part of individual taxpayers. So with the children who are sent to school by commands of sovereignty. The parents, without their individual consent or bargaining, are deprived of their physical control over their children during specified hours, days, and ages. A fascist or communist dictatorship extends this economics of domestic law to all the transactions of economics. Modern totalitarianism is rationing transactions imposed by those in power, the "superiors," upon those deprived of power, the "inferiors."

A fiction has long prevailed that in countries of legislative sovereignty these same taxpayers and parents have given their consent through their representatives in the legislature. But taxpayers and parents have not individually or voluntarily given their consent, as they are supposed to do in bargaining transactions. The false analogy is a confusion of collective action with individual action. Sovereignty is the collective action which has monopolized powers extending to violence, and there cannot be found any individual taxpayer or parent who by bargaining has consented to be compelled by threat of violence to pay the specified taxes or give up the specified control of his children. If he tried to bargain with the policeman, one or both would go to jail on a charge of bribery. The appropriate statement, avoiding fictions, is collective action in control of individual action. This kind of collective action has, by economists and usage, been given the name of "rationing." But we need to know the method by which sovereignty acts in its process of rationing. Such activity may be distinguished as rationing transactions.

Such transactions may be seen in any legislative assembly, depending upon the constitutional organization of the legislature. The members are arguing, debating, exchanging views, and finally closing the negotiations by majority vote. They may, by fictitious analogy, be said to be "trading votes," but they are not lawfully alienating or acquiring ownerships as they do in bargaining transactions. Trading votes is lawful negotiation, and not bribery, within a legislative assembly.

Dictatorship is only another and more primitive form of rationing transactions. No dictator can arbitrarily impose his sole will upon a nation. He consults his associates, or his monopolistic party, or his military chiefs, as to what shall be the particular rationing of benefits and burdens among those individuals who are subject to this dictatorial form of sovereignty. The rationing negotiation is perhaps closed by his one vote instead of by a majority vote. And it is probable that a majority vote in a democracy is, at times, as dictatorial over minorities as is the vote of a dictator over majorities. Indeed, historical analysis reveals that the judicial sovereignty in America was created and is now sustained by the combined religious, political, and economic *minorities* as their protection against the democracy of majority rule.

Interestingly enough these rationing transactions are discoverable in all collective action, as may be seen in the board of directors of a corporation, or in a cooperative association, in making up its budget for the coming year. The board apportions, without individual consent or bargaining with subordinates, the expected benefits and burdens of the concern. The execution of this rationing, within the budget limits, is carried out by means of managerial transactions. Collective action in control of individuals becomes a hierarchy of collective action in control of the bargaining, managerial, and rationing transactions of individuals.

One of the main advantages of the modern large corporations is in the elimination of bargaining transactions by enlarging the scope of managerial and rationing transactions. It is carried furthest by a so-called "integrated" industry. The substance of this elimination of bargaining transactions is in the consolidation of ownerships with a coordinated legal control by a board of directors at the top. In the United States Steel Corporation, a hundred, or perhaps several hundred, formerly separate ownerships are consolidated under a so-called "holding company," meaning an owning company. Its activity, within its own jurisdiction of ownership, is exercised by rationing and managerial transactions.

Since I make transactions the units of economic science, it is well at this point to offer a diagrammatic presentation of the scope of transactions. Its detailed application will appear at many points. Of course, facts do not thus neatly assort themselves in boxes, but the boxes help to arrange our ideas.

Scope of Transactions

TIME SEQUENCE	KINDS OF TRANSACTIONS (Status of Participants)			KINDS OF ECONOMICS
	Bargaining (Legal equals)	Managerial (Legal superior & inferior)	Rationing (Legal superior & inferior)	
1. *Negotiational psychology* (inducements, intentions, purpose)	Persuasion or Coercion	Command and Obedience	Command and Obedience	Qualitative (not measured)
2. *Commitments for future action* (agreement, contracts, obligations, rules of action)	Debts of Performance and Payment	Production of Wealth	Distribution of Wealth	Qualitative (not measured)
3. *Execution of the commitments* (administration, management, sovereignty)	Prices and Quantities	Input and Output	Budgets Taxes Price-fixing Wage-fixing	Qualitative (measured)

QUESTIONS

1. Why does Commons argue that economics needs to make a "distinction between a *transaction* and an *exchange*"? (226)

2. According to Commons, how does law have "economic significance"? (227)

3. Why does Commons make the claim that "the greatest of all inventions in the field of economics was the discovery that a debt could be bought and sold like a physical commodity"? (229)

4. Why does Commons refer to the modern credit system as "the foundation of capitalism"? (230)

5. Why does Commons make transactions "the units of economic science"? (233)

FOR FURTHER REFLECTION

1. Of the three types of transaction delineated by Commons, which do you think suffers from too much or too little legal oversight?

2. Does Commons's description of the law of managerial transactions conform to your experiences of the relationship between an employer and employee?

3. Does the legal system shape the economic system, or does the economic system shape the legal system?

JOSEPH A. SCHUMPETER

Joseph A. Schumpeter (1883–1950), one of the most learned and respected economists of the twentieth century, was largely responsible for bringing the Marxian emphasis on the historical evolution of economic systems into the mainstream of economic thought. He is perhaps best known for his analysis of the crucial role of the entrepreneur, as opposed to the provider of capital, in fostering the innovation and "creative destruction" that he claimed are the main engines of growth in a modern capitalist economy.

Schumpeter was born in a small town in Moravia, now part of the Czech Republic. His father, who owned a factory, died when Joseph was four years old. Afterward, he and his mother moved to Vienna, where she eventually remarried into the aristocracy, enabling her son to attend first the exclusive Theresianum secondary school and then the University of Vienna, where he studied law and economics. After earning his PhD in 1906, Schumpeter traveled and embarked on a variety of activities before obtaining professorships first in Austria and later in Germany, punctuated by brief stints in politics— as finance minister of the post–World War I Austrian government—and in business—as president of a private Viennese bank. In 1932 he left the University of Bonn and emigrated to the United States, accepting a permanent position at Harvard, where he taught until just before his death. Schumpeter's highly influential books include *The Theory of Economic Development* (1912) and *Capitalism, Socialism, and Democracy* (1942). His magisterial, if incomplete, *History of Economic Analysis* was published posthumously in 1954.

Capitalism, Socialism, and Democracy contains brilliant analyses of the teachings of Karl Marx as well as of the principles underlying social and economic development, in general, and planned versus free-market economies, in particular. In the following excerpts, Schumpeter advances the thesis that the economic success of capitalism carries with it the seeds of its own undoing and will lead to its downfall in the long run.

The Civilization of Capitalism

L eaving the precincts of purely economic considerations, we now turn to the cultural complement of the capitalist economy—to its sociopsychological *superstructure*, if we wish to speak the Marxian language—and to the mentality that is characteristic of capitalist society and in particular of the bourgeois class. In desperate brevity, the salient facts may be conveyed as follows.

Fifty thousand years ago man confronted the dangers and opportunities of his environment in a way which some "prehistorians," sociologists, and ethnologists agree was roughly equivalent to the attitude of modern primitives. Two elements of this attitude are particularly important for us: the "collective" and "affective" nature of the primitive mental process and, partly overlapping, the role of what, not quite correctly, I shall here call magic. By the first I designate the fact that in small and undifferentiated or not much differentiated social groups, collective ideas impose themselves much more stringently on the individual mind than they do in big and complex groups; and that conclusions and decisions are arrived at by methods which for our purpose may be characterized by a negative criterion: the disregard of what we call logic and, in particular, of the rule that excludes contradiction. By the second I designate the use of a set of beliefs which are not indeed completely divorced from experience—no magic device can survive an unbroken sequence of failures—but which insert, into the sequence of observed phenomena, entities or influences derived from nonempirical sources. The similarity of this type of mental process with the mental processes of neurotics has been pointed out by [Gabriel] Dromard (1911; his term, *délire d'interpretation*, is particularly suggestive) and [Sigmund] Freud (*Totem und Tabu*, 1913). But it does not follow that it is foreign to the mind of normal man of our own time. On the contrary, any discussion of political issues may convince the reader

This selection is taken from chapter 11 of Capitalism, Socialism, and Democracy.

that a large and—for action—most important body of our own processes is of exactly the same nature.

Rational thought or behavior and a rationalistic civilization therefore do not imply absence of the criteria mentioned but only a slow though incessant widening of the sector of social life within which individuals or groups go about dealing with a given situation, first, by trying to make the best of it more or less—never wholly—according to their own lights; second, by doing so according to those rules of consistency which we call logic; and third, by doing so on assumptions which satisfy two conditions: that their number be a minimum and that every one of them be amenable to expression in terms of potential experience.

All this is very inadequate of course but it suffices for our purpose. There is however one more point about the concept of rationalist civilizations that I will mention here for future reference. When the habit of rational analysis of, and rational behavior in, the daily tasks of life has gone far enough, it turns back upon the mass of collective ideas and criticizes and to some extent "rationalizes" them by way of such questions as why there should be kings and popes or subordination or tithes or property. Incidentally, it is important to notice that, while most of us would accept such an attitude as the symptom of a "higher stage" of mental development, this value judgment is not necessarily and in every sense borne out by the results. The rationalist attitude may go to work with information and technique so inadequate that actions—and especially a general surgical propensity—induced by it may, to an observer of a later period, appear to be, even from a purely intellectual standpoint, inferior to the actions and antisurgical propensities associated with attitudes that at the time most people felt inclined to attribute to a low IQ. A large part of the political thought of the seventeenth and eighteenth centuries illustrates this ever-forgotten truth. Not only in depth of social vision but also in logical analysis later "conservative" countercriticism was clearly superior although it would have been a mere matter of laughter for the writers of the enlightenment.

Now the rational attitude presumably forced itself on the human mind primarily from economic necessity; it is the everyday economic task to which we as a race owe our elementary training in rational thought and behavior—I have no hesitation in saying that all logic is derived from the pattern of the economic decision or, to use a pet phrase of mine, that the economic pattern is the matrix of logic. This seems plausible for the following reason. Suppose that some "primitive" man uses that most elementary of all machines, already appreciated by our gorilla cousins, a stick, and that this stick breaks in his hand. If he tries to remedy the damage by reciting a magic formula—he might for instance murmur, "Supply and demand" or "Planning and control" in the expectation that if he repeats this exactly nine times the two fragments will unite again—then he is within the precincts of prerational thought. If he gropes for the best way to join the fragments or to procure another stick, he is being rational in our sense. Both attitudes are possible of course. But it stands to reason that in this and most other economic actions the failure of a magic formula to work will be much more obvious than could be any failure of a formula that was to make our man victorious in combat or lucky in love or to lift a load of guilt from his conscience. This is due to the inexorable definiteness and, in most cases, the quantitative character that distinguish the economic from other spheres of human action, perhaps also to the unemotional drabness of the unending rhythm of economic wants and satisfactions. Once hammered in, the rational habit spreads under the pedagogic influence of favorable experiences to the other spheres and there also opens eyes for that amazing thing, the Fact.

This process is independent of any particular garb, hence also of the capitalistic garb, of economic activity. So is the profit motive and self-interest. Precapitalist man is in fact no less "grabbing" than capitalist man. Peasant serfs for instance or warrior lords assert their self-interest with a brutal energy all their own. But capitalism develops rationality and adds a new edge to it in two interconnected ways.

First it exalts the monetary unit—not itself a creation of capitalism—into a unit of account. That is to say, capitalist practice turns the unit of money into a tool of rational cost-profit calculations, of which the towering monument is double-entry bookkeeping. Without going into this, we will notice that, primarily a product of the evolution of economic rationality, the cost-profit calculus in turn reacts upon that rationality; by crystallizing and defining numerically, it powerfully propels the logic of enterprise. And thus defined and quantified for the economic sector, this type of logic or attitude or method then starts upon its conqueror's career subjugating—rationalizing—man's tools and philosophies, his medical practice, his picture of the cosmos, his outlook on life, everything in fact including his concepts of beauty and justice and his spiritual ambitions.

In this respect it is highly significant that modern mathematico-experimental science developed, in the fifteenth, sixteenth, and seventeenth centuries, not only along with the social process usually referred to as the Rise of Capitalism, but also outside of the fortress of scholastic thought and in the face of its contemptuous hostility. In the fifteenth century mathematics was mainly concerned with questions of commercial arithmetic and the problems of the architect. The utilitarian mechanical device, invented by men of the craftsman type, stood at the source of modern physics. The rugged individualism of Galileo was the individualism of the rising capitalist class. The surgeon began to rise above the midwife and the barber. The artist who at the same time was an engineer and an entrepreneur—the type immortalized by such men as Vinci, Alberti, Cellini; even Dürer busied himself with plans for fortifications—illustrates best of all what I mean. By cursing it all, scholastic professors in the Italian universities showed more sense than we give them credit for. The trouble was not with individual unorthodox propositions. Any decent schoolman could be trusted to twist his texts so as to fit the Copernican system. But those professors quite rightly sensed the spirit behind such exploits—the spirit of rationalist individualism, the spirit generated by rising capitalism.

Second, rising capitalism produced not only the mental attitude of modern science, the attitude that consists in asking certain questions and in going about answering them in a certain way, but also the men and the means. By breaking up the feudal environment and disturbing the intellectual peace of manor and village (though there always was, of course, plenty to discuss and to fall out about in a convent), but especially by creating the social space for a new class that stood upon individual achievement in the economic field, it in turn attracted to that field the strong wills and the strong intellects. Precapitalist economic life left no scope for achievement that would carry over class boundaries or, to put it differently, be adequate to create social positions comparable to those of the members of the then ruling classes. Not that it precluded ascent in general. But business activity was, broadly speaking, essentially subordinate, even at the peak of success within the craft guild, and it hardly ever led out of it. The main avenues to advancement and large gain were the church—nearly as accessible throughout the Middle Ages as it is now—to which we may add the chanceries of the great territorial magnates, and the hierarchy of warrior lords—quite accessible to every man who was physically and psychically fit until about the middle of the twelfth century, and not quite inaccessible thereafter. It was only when capitalist enterprise—first commercial and financial, then mining, finally industrial—unfolded its possibilities that supernormal ability and ambition began to turn to business as a third avenue. Success was quick and conspicuous, but it has been much exaggerated as regards the social weight it carried at first. If we look closely at the career of Jacob Fugger, for instance, or of Agostino Chigi, we easily satisfy ourselves that they had very little to do with steering the policies of Charles V or of Pope Leo X and that they paid heavily for such privileges as they enjoyed. Yet entrepreneurial success was fascinating enough for everyone excepting the highest strata of feudal society to draw most of the best brains and thus to generate further success—to generate additional steam for the rationalist engine. So, in this sense, capitalism—and not merely economic activity in general—has after all been the propelling force of the rationalization of human behavior.

And now we are at long last face to face with the immediate goal to which that complex yet inadequate argument was to lead. Not only the modern mechanized plant and the volume of the output that pours forth from it, not only modern technology and economic organization, but all the features and achievements of modern civilization are, directly or indirectly, the products of the capitalist process. They must be included in any balance sheet of it and in any verdict about its deeds or misdeeds.

There is the growth of rational science and the long list of its applications. Airplanes, refrigerators, television, and that sort of thing are immediately recognizable as results of the profit economy. But although the modern hospital is not as a rule operated for profit, it is nonetheless the product of capitalism not only, to repeat, because the capitalist process supplies the means and the will, but much more fundamentally because capitalist rationality supplied the habits of mind that evolved the methods used in these hospitals. And the victories, not yet completely won but in the offing, over cancer, syphilis, and tuberculosis will be as much capitalist achievements as motorcars or pipelines or Bessemer steel have been. In the case of medicine, there is a capitalist profession behind the methods, capitalist both because to a large extent it works in a business spirit and because it is an emulsion of the industrial and commercial bourgeoisie. But even if that were not so, modern medicine and hygiene would still be byproducts of the capitalist process just as is modern education.

There is the capitalist art and the capitalist style of life. If we limit ourselves to painting as an example, both for brevity's sake and because in that field my ignorance is slightly less complete than it is in others, and if (wrongly, as I think) we agree to start an epoch with Giotto's Arena frescoes and then follow the line (nothing short of damnable though such "linear" arguments are) Giotto—Masaccio—Vinci—Michelangelo—Greco, no amount of emphasis on mystical ardors in the case of Greco can obliterate my point for anyone who has eyes that see. And Vinci's experiments are offered to doubters who wish, as it were, to touch the capitalist rationality with their fingertips. This line if projected (yes, I know) could be made to land us (though perhaps gasping) in the contrast between Delacroix and Ingres. Well, and there we are; Cézanne, Van Gogh, Picasso, or Matisse will do the rest. Expressionist liquidation of the object forms an admirably logical conclusion. The story of the capitalist novel (culminating in the Goncourt novel: "documents written up") would illustrate still better. But that is obvious. The evolution of the capitalist style of life could be easily—and perhaps most tellingly—described in terms of the genesis of the modern lounge suit.

There is finally all that may be grouped around the symbolic centerpiece of Gladstonian liberalism. The term Individualist Democracy would do just as well—better in fact because we want to cover some things that Gladstone would not have approved and a moral and spiritual attitude which, dwelling in the citadel of faith, he actually hated. At that I could leave this point if radical liturgy did not consist largely in picturesque denials of what I mean to convey. Radicals may insist that the masses are crying for salvation from intolerable sufferings and rattling their chains in darkness and despair, but of course there never was so much personal freedom of mind and body *for all*, never so much readiness to bear with and even to finance the mortal enemies of the leading class, never so much active sympathy with real and faked sufferings, never so much readiness to accept burdens, as there is in modern capitalist society; and whatever democracy there was, outside of peasant communities, developed historically in the wake of both modern and ancient capitalism. Again plenty of facts can be adduced from the past to make up a counterargument that will be effective but is irrelevant in a discussion of present conditions and future alternatives. If we do decide to embark upon historical disquisition at all, then even many of those facts which to radical critics may seem to be the most eligible ones for their purpose will often look differently if viewed in the light of a comparison with the corresponding facts of pre-capitalist experience. And it cannot be replied that "those were different times." For it is precisely the capitalist process that made the difference.

Two points in particular must be mentioned. I have pointed out before that social legislation or, more generally, institutional change for the benefit of the masses is not simply something which has been forced upon capitalist society by an ineluctable necessity to alleviate the ever-deepening misery of the poor but that, besides raising the standard of living of the masses by virtue of its automatic effects, the capitalist process also provided for that legislation the means "and the will." The words in quotes require further explanation that is to be found in the principle of spreading rationality. The capitalist process rationalizes behavior and ideas and by so doing chases from our minds, along with metaphysical belief, mystic and romantic ideas of all sorts. Thus it reshapes not only our methods of attaining our ends but also these ultimate ends themselves. "Free thinking" in the sense of materialistic monism, laicism, and pragmatic acceptance of the world this side of the grave follow from this not indeed by logical necessity but nevertheless very naturally. On the one hand, our inherited sense of duty, deprived of its traditional basis, becomes focused in utilitarian ideas about the betterment of mankind which, quite illogically to be sure, seem to withstand rationalist criticism better than, say, the fear of God does. On the other hand, the same rationalization of the soul rubs off all the glamour of superempirical sanction from every species of classwise rights. This then, together with the typically capitalist enthusiasm for Efficiency and Service—so completely different from the body of ideas which would have been associated with those terms by the typical knight of old—breeds that "will" within the bourgeoisie itself. Feminism, an essentially capitalist phenomenon, illustrates the point still more clearly. The reader will realize that these tendencies must be understood "objectively" and that therefore no amount of antifeminist or antireformist *talk* or even of temporary opposition to any particular measure proves anything against this analysis. These things are the very symptoms of the tendencies they pretend to fight. Of this, more in the subsequent chapters.

Also, capitalist civilization is rationalistic "and antiheroic." The two go together of course. Success in industry and commerce requires a lot of stamina, yet industrial and commerical activity is essentially unheroic in the knight's sense—no flourishing of swords about it, not much physical prowess, no chance to gallop the armored horse into the enemy, preferably a heretic or heathen—and the ideology that glorifies the idea of fighting for fighting's sake and of victory for victory's sake understandably withers in the office among all the columns of figures. Therefore, owning assets that are apt to attract the robber or the tax gatherer and not sharing or even disliking warrior ideology that conflicts with its "rational" utilitarianism, the industrial and commercial bourgeoisie is fundamentally pacifist and inclined to insist on the application of the moral precepts of private life to international relations. It is true that, unlike most but like some other features of capitalist civilization, pacifism and international morality have also been espoused in noncapitalist environments and by precapitalist agencies, in the Middle Ages by the Roman Church for instance. Modern pacifism and modern international morality are nonetheless products of capitalism.

In view of the fact that Marxian doctrine—especially neo-Marxian doctrine and even a considerable body of nonsocialist opinion—is, as we have seen in the first part of this book, strongly opposed to this proposition, it is necessary to point out that the latter is not meant to deny that many a bourgeoisie has put up a splendid fight for hearth and home, or that almost purely bourgeois commonwealths were often aggressive when it seemed to pay—like the Athenian or the Venetian commonwealths—or that no bourgeoisie ever disliked war profits and advantages to trade accruing from conquest or refused to be trained in warlike nationalism by its feudal masters or leaders or by the propaganda of some specially interested group. All I hold is, first, that such instances of capitalist combativeness are not, as Marxism has it, to be explained—exclusively or primarily—in terms of class interests or class situations that systematically engender capitalist wars of conquest; second, that there is a difference between doing that which you consider your normal business in life, for which you prepare yourself in season and out of season and in terms of which you define your success or failure, and doing what is not in your line, for which your normal work and your mentality do not fit you and success in which will increase the prestige of the most unbourgeois of professions; and third, that this difference steadily tells—in international as well as in domestic affairs—against the use of military force and for peaceful arrangements, even where the balance of pecuniary advantage is clearly on the side of war which, under modern circumstances, is not in general very likely. As a matter of fact, the more completely capitalist the structure and attitude of a nation, the more pacifist—and the more prone to count the costs of war—we observe it to be. Owing to the complex nature of every individual pattern, this could be fully brought out only by detailed historical analysis. But the bourgeois attitude to the military (standing armies), the spirit in which and the methods by which bourgeois societies wage war, and the readiness with which, in any serious case of prolonged warfare, they submit to nonbourgeois rule are conclusive in themselves. The Marxist theory that imperialism is the last stage of capitalist evolution therefore fails quite irrespective of purely economic objections.

But I am not going to sum up as the reader presumably expects me to. That is to say, I am not going to invite him, before he decides to put his trust in an untried alternative advocated by untried men, to look once more at the impressive economic and the still more impressive cultural achievement of the capitalist order and at the immense promise held out by both. I am not going to argue that that achievement and that promise are in themselves sufficient to support an argument for allowing the capitalist process to work on and, as it might easily be put, to lift poverty from the shoulders of mankind.

There would be no sense in this. Even if mankind were as free to choose as a businessman is free to choose between two competing pieces of machinery, no determined value judgment necessarily follows from the facts and relations between facts that I have tried to convey. As regards the economic performance, it does not follow that men are "happier" or even "better off" in the industrial society of today than they were in a medieval manor or village. As regards the cultural performance, one may accept every word I have written and yet hate it—its utilitarianism and the wholesale destruction of Meanings incident to it—from the bottom of one's heart. Moreover, as I shall have to emphasize again in our discussion of the socialist alternative, one may care less for the efficiency of the capitalist process in producing economic and cultural values than for the kind of human beings that it turns out and then leaves to their own devices, free to make a mess of their lives. There is a type of radical whose adverse verdict about capitalist civilization rests on nothing except stupidity, ignorance, or irresponsibility, who is unable or unwilling to grasp the most obvious facts, let alone their wider implications. But a completely adverse verdict may also be arrived at on a higher plane.

However, whether favorable or unfavorable, value judgments about capitalist performance are of little interest. For mankind is not free to choose. This is not only because the mass of people are not in a position to compare alternatives rationally and always accept what they are being told. There is a much deeper reason for it. Things economic and social move by their own momentum and the ensuing situations compel individuals and groups to behave in certain ways whatever they may wish to do—not indeed by destroying their freedom of choice but by shaping the choosing mentalities and by narrowing the list of possibilities from which to choose. If this is the quintessence of Marxism then we all of us have got to be Marxists. In consequence, capitalist performance is not even relevant for prognosis. Most civilizations have disappeared before they had time to fill to the full the measure of their promise.

QUESTIONS

1. What is meant by the title "The Civilization of Capitalism"?

2. What does Schumpeter mean when he says that "the economic pattern is the matrix of logic"? (237)

3. Why does Schumpeter argue that capitalism has been "the propelling force of the rationalization of human behavior"? (239)

4. On what grounds does Schumpeter refute the Marxist theory that "imperialism is the last stage of capitalist evolution"? (243)

5. If rising capitalism generates "the spirit of rationalist individualism," why does Schumpeter conclude by saying that "mankind is not free to choose"? (239, 243)

FOR FURTHER REFLECTION

1. Do you agree with Schumpeter's assertion that "all the features and achievements of modern civilization are, directly or indirectly, the products of the capitalist process"?

2. Is Schumpeter correct in regarding feminism as "an essentially capitalist phenomenon"?

3. Does modern history support Schumpeter's assertion that "the more completely capitalist the structure and attitude of a nation, the more pacifist—and the more prone to count the costs of war—we observe it to be"?

John Maynard Keynes (1883–1946), born into a Cambridge academic family, was one of the most important economists of the twentieth century. He achieved positions of power and influence in English society wherever he turned his hand, whether in academia, in government, in business, or in the arts. Keynes's writings form the foundation for the modern discipline of macroeconomics and have shaped public debate on government spending policies from the 1930s until today.

Keynes began his career at Cambridge under the sway of Alfred Marshall, who convinced him to study economics. After graduating from Cambridge, Keynes went to work for the British government in the India Office, before returning to Cambridge to teach economics. During these years, and indeed throughout his life, Keynes was associated with the artists and writers known as the Bloomsbury Group, which included Virginia Woolf and E. M. Forster. When the First World War broke out, he was hired as a consultant for the Treasury, where he played a key role in financing the British war effort. After the war, he participated in the Versailles Peace Conference, but was deeply disillusioned by the results. His 1919 book, *The Economic Consequences of the Peace*, in which he predicted the disastrous political effects of the vindictive Versailles Treaty, made him a household name in Europe and America. During World War II, he again worked on financing Britain's war effort, and was an influential participant in the 1944 Bretton Woods Conference.

Keynes's most original theoretical contributions are contained in *The General Theory of Employment, Interest and Money* (1936), in which he diagnosed the Great Depression as a "low-employment equilibrium" of excess production capacity and insufficient demand—a combination classical economic theory claimed was impossible. As a remedy, he proposed that governments should fight recessions through deficit spending, thus giving a "stimulus" to aggregate demand. These ideas achieved the status of conventional wisdom within the international economics community for decades. Keynes's influence declined during the late 1970s, when Keynesian policies were blamed for causing high unemployment and inflation ("stagflation"). But they are again being vigorously debated as a result of the 2008 financial crisis. The following selection comes from a 1937 article in which Keynes replies to his critics.

The General Theory
of Employment (selection)

We have, as a rule, only the vaguest idea of any but the most direct consequences of our acts. Sometimes we are not much concerned with their remoter consequences, even though time and chance may make much of them. But sometimes we are intensely concerned with them, more so, occasionally, than with the immediate consequences. Now of all human activities which are affected by this remoter preoccupation, it happens that one of the most important is economic in character, namely, Wealth. The whole object of the accumulation of Wealth is to produce results, or potential results, at a comparatively distant, and sometimes at an *indefinitely* distant, date. Thus the fact that our knowledge of the future is fluctuating, vague, and uncertain, renders Wealth a peculiarly unsuitable subject for the methods of the classical economic theory. This theory might work very well in a world in which economic goods were necessarily consumed within a short interval of their being produced. But it requires, I suggest, considerable amendment if it is to be applied to a world in which the accumulation of wealth for an indefinitely postponed future is an important factor; and the greater the proportionate part played by such wealth accumulation the more essential does such amendment become.

By "uncertain" knowledge, let me explain, I do not mean merely to distinguish what is known for certain from what is only probable. The game of roulette is not subject, in this sense, to uncertainty; nor is the prospect of a victory bond being drawn. Or, again, the expectation of life is only slightly uncertain. Even the weather is only moderately uncertain. The sense in which I am using the term is that in which the prospect of a European war is uncertain, or the price of copper and the rate of interest twenty years hence, or the obsolescence of a new invention, or the position of private wealth owners in the social system in 1970. About these matters there is no scientific basis on which to form any calculable probability whatever. We simply do not know. Nevertheless, the necessity for action and for decision compels us as practical men to do our best to overlook this awkward fact and to behave exactly as we should if we had behind us a good Benthamite calculation of a series of prospective advantages and disadvantages, each multiplied by its appropriate probability, waiting to be summed.

How do we manage in such circumstances to behave in a manner which saves our faces as rational, economic men? We have devised for the purpose a variety of techniques, of which much the most important are the three following:

1. We assume that the present is a much more serviceable guide to the future than a candid examination of past experience would show it to have been hitherto. In other words we largely ignore the prospect of future changes about the actual character of which we know nothing.

2. We assume that the *existing* state of opinion as expressed in prices and the character of existing output is based on a *correct* summing up of future prospects, so that we can accept it as such unless and until something new and relevant comes into the picture.

3. Knowing that our own individual judgment is worthless, we endeavor to fall back on the judgment of the rest of the world which is perhaps better informed. That is, we endeavor to conform with the behavior of the majority or the average. The psychology of a society of individuals each of whom is endeavoring to copy the others leads to what we may strictly term a *conventional* judgment.

Now a practical theory of the future based on these three principles has certain marked characteristics. In particular, being based on so flimsy a foundation, it is subject to sudden and violent changes. The practice of calmness and immobility, of certainty and security, suddenly breaks down. New fears and hopes will, without warning, take charge of human conduct. The forces of disillusion may suddenly impose a new conventional basis of valuation. All these pretty, polite techniques, made for a well-paneled boardroom and a nicely regulated market, are liable to collapse. At all times the vague panic fears and equally vague and unreasoned hopes are not really lulled, and lie but a little way below the surface.

Perhaps the reader feels that this general, philosophical disquisition on the behavior of mankind is somewhat remote from the economic theory under discussion. But I think not. Though this is how we behave in the marketplace, the theory we devise in the study of how we behave in the marketplace should not itself submit to marketplace idols. I accuse the classical economic theory of being itself one of these pretty, polite techniques which tries to deal with the present by abstracting from the fact that we know very little about the future.

I daresay that a classical economist would readily admit this. But, even so, I think he has overlooked the precise nature of the difference which his abstraction makes between theory and practice, and the character of the fallacies into which he is likely to be led.

This is particularly the case in his treatment of Money and Interest. And our first step must be to elucidate more clearly the functions of Money.

Money, it is well known, serves two principal purposes. By acting as a money of account it facilitates exchanges without its being necessary that it should ever itself come into the picture as a substantive object. In this respect it is a convenience which is devoid of significance or real influence. In the second place, it is a store of wealth. So we are told, without a smile on the face. But in the world of the classical economy, what an insane use to which to put it! For it is a recognized characteristic of money as a store of wealth that it is barren; whereas practically every other form of storing wealth yields some interest or profit. Why should anyone outside a lunatic asylum wish to use money as a store of wealth?

Because, partly on reasonable and partly on instinctive grounds, our desire to hold Money as a store of wealth is a barometer of the degree of our distrust of our own calculations and conventions concerning the future. Even though this feeling about Money is itself conventional or instinctive, it operates, so to speak, at a deeper level of our motivation. It takes charge at the moments when the higher, more precarious conventions have weakened. The possession of actual money lulls our disquietude; and the premium which we require to make us part with money is the measure of the degree of our disquietude.

The significance of this characteristic of money has usually been overlooked; and insofar as it has been noticed, the essential nature of the phenomenon has been misdescribed. For what has attracted attention has been the *quantity* of money which has been hoarded; and importance has been attached to this because it has been supposed to have a direct proportionate effect on the price-level through affecting the velocity of circulation. But the *quantity* of hoards can only be altered either if the total quantity of money is changed or if the quantity of current money income (I speak broadly) is changed; whereas fluctuations in the degree of confidence are capable of having quite a different effect, namely, in modifying not the amount that is actually hoarded, but the amount of the premium which has to be offered to induce people not to hoard. And changes in the propensity to hoard, or in the state of liquidity preference as I have called it, primarily affect, not prices, but the rate of interest; any effect on prices being produced by repercussion as an ultimate consequence of a change in the rate of interest.

This, expressed in a very general way, is my theory of the rate of interest. The rate of interest obviously measures—just as the books on arithmetic say it does—the premium which has to be offered to induce people to hold their wealth in some form other than hoarded money. The quantity of money and the amount of it required in the active circulation for the transaction of current business (mainly depending on the level of money income) determine how much is available for inactive balances, i.e., for hoards. The rate of interest is the factor which adjusts at the margin the demand for hoards to the supply of hoards.

Now let us proceed to the next stage of the argument. The owner of wealth, who has been induced not to hold his wealth in the shape of hoarded money, still has two alternatives between which to choose. He can lend his money at the current rate of money-interest or he can purchase some kind of capital asset. Clearly in equilibrium these two alternatives must offer an equal advantage to the marginal investor in each of them. This is brought about by shifts in the money prices of capital assets relative to the prices of money loans. The prices of capital assets move until, having regard to their prospective yields and account being taken of all those elements of doubt and uncertainty, interested and disinterested advice, fashion, convention, and what else you will which affect the mind of the investor, they offer an equal apparent advantage to the marginal investor who is wavering between one kind of investment and another.

This, then, is the first repercussion of the rate of interest, as fixed by the quantity of money and the propensity to hoard, namely, on the prices of capital assets. This does not mean, of course, that the rate of interest is the only fluctuating influence on these prices. Opinions as to their prospective yield are themselves subject to sharp fluctuations, precisely for the reason already given, namely, the flimsiness of the basis of knowledge on which they depend. It is these opinions taken in conjunction with the rate of interest which fix their price.

Now for stage three. Capital assets are capable, in general, of being newly produced. The scale on which they are produced depends, of course, on the relation between their costs of production and the prices which they are expected to realize in the market. Thus if the level of the rate of interest taken in conjunction with opinions about their prospective yield raise the prices of capital assets, the volume of current investment (meaning by this the value of the output of newly produced capital assets) will be increased; while if, on the other hand, these influences reduce the prices of capital assets, the volume of current investment will be diminished.

It is not surprising that the volume of investment, thus determined, should fluctuate widely from time to time. For it depends on two sets of judgments about the future, neither of which rests on an adequate or secure foundation—on the propensity to hoard and on opinions of the future yield of capital assets. Nor is there any reason to suppose that the fluctuations in one of these factors will tend to offset the fluctuations in the other. When a more pessimistic view is taken about future yields, that is no reason why there should be a diminished propensity to hoard. Indeed, the conditions which aggravate the one factor tend, as a rule, to aggravate the other. For the same circumstances which lead to pessimistic views about future yields are apt to increase the propensity to hoard. The only element of self-righting in the system arises at a much later stage and in an uncertain degree. If a decline in investment leads to a decline in output as a whole, this may result (for more reasons than one) in a reduction of the amount of money required for the active circulation, which will release a larger quantity of money for the inactive circulation, which will satisfy the propensity to hoard at a lower level of the rate of interest, which will raise the prices of capital assets, which will increase the scale of investment, which will restore in some measure the level of output as a whole.

This completes the first chapter of the argument, namely, the liability of the scale of investment to fluctuate for reasons quite distinct (a) from those which determine the propensity of the individual to *save* out of a given income and (b) from those physical conditions of technical capacity to aid production which have usually been supposed hitherto to be the chief influence governing the marginal efficiency of capital.

If, on the other hand, our knowledge of the future was calculable and not subject to sudden changes, it might be justifiable to assume that the liquidity-preference curve was both stable and very inelastic. In this case a small decline in money income would lead to a large fall in the rate of interest, probably sufficient to raise output and employment to the full. In these conditions we might reasonably suppose that the whole of the available resources would normally be employed; and the conditions required by the orthodox theory would be satisfied.

My next difference from the traditional theory concerns its apparent conviction that there is no necessity to work out a theory of the demand and supply of output *as a whole*. Will a fluctuation in investment, arising for the reasons just described, have any effect on the demand for output as a whole, and consequently on the scale of output and employment? What answer can the traditional theory make to this question? I believe that it makes no answer at all, never having given the matter a single thought; the theory of effective demand, that is the demand for output as a whole, having been entirely neglected for more than a hundred years.

My own answer to this question involves fresh considerations. I say that effective demand is made up of two items—investment-expenditure determined in the manner just explained and consumption-expenditure. Now what governs the amount of consumption-expenditure? It depends mainly on the level of income. People's propensity to spend (as I call it) is influenced by many factors such as the distribution of income, their normal attitude to the future and—though probably in a minor degree—by the rate of interest. But in the main the prevailing psychological law seems to be that when aggregate income increases, consumption-expenditure will also increase but to a somewhat lesser extent. This is a very obvious conclusion. It simply amounts to saying that an increase in income will be divided in some proportion or another between spending and saving, and that when our income is increased it is extremely unlikely that this will have the effect of making us either spend less or save less than before. This psychological law was of the utmost importance in the development of my own thought, and it is, I think, absolutely fundamental to the theory of effective demand as set forth in my book. But few critics or commentators so far have paid particular attention to it.

There follows from this extremely obvious principle an important, yet unfamiliar, conclusion. Incomes are created partly by entrepreneurs producing for investment and partly by their producing for consumption. The amount that is consumed depends on the amount of income thus made up. Hence the amount of consumption goods which it will pay entrepreneurs to produce depends on the amount of investment goods which they are producing. If, for example, the public are in the habit of spending nine-tenths of their income on consumption goods, it follows that if entrepreneurs were to produce consumption goods at a cost more than nine times the cost of the investment goods they are producing, some part of their output could not be sold at a price which would cover its cost of production. For the consumption goods on the market would have cost more than nine-tenths of the aggregate income of the public and would therefore be in excess of the demand for consumption goods, which by hypothesis is only the nine-tenths. Thus entrepreneurs will make a loss until they contract their output of consumption goods down to an amount at which it no longer exceeds nine times their current output of investment goods.

The formula is not, of course, quite so simple as in this illustration. The proportion of their incomes which the public will choose to consume will not be a constant one, and in the most general case other factors are also relevant. But there is always a formula, more or less of this kind, relating the output of consumption goods which it pays to produce to the output of investment goods; and I have given attention to it in my book under the name of the *Multiplier*. The fact that an increase in consumption is apt in itself to stimulate this further investment merely fortifies the argument.

That the level of output of consumption goods, which is profitable to the entrepreneur, should be related by a formula of this kind to the output of investment goods depends on assumptions of a simple and obvious character. The conclusion appears to me to be quite beyond dispute. Yet the consequences which follow from it are at the same time unfamiliar and of the greatest possible importance.

The theory can be summed up by saying that, given the psychology of the public, the level of output and employment as a whole depends on the amount of investment. I put it in this way, not because this is the only factor on which aggregate output depends, but because it is usual in a complex system to regard as the *causa causans* that factor which is most prone to sudden and wide fluctuation. More comprehensively, aggregate output depends on the propensity to hoard, on the policy of the monetary authority as it affects the quantity of money, on the state of confidence concerning the prospective yield of capital assets, on the propensity to spend, and on the social factors which influence the level of the money wage. But of these several factors it is those which determine the rate of investment which are most unreliable, since it is they which are influenced by our views of the future about which we know so little.

This that I offer is, therefore, a theory of why output and employment are so liable to fluctuation. It does not offer a ready-made remedy as to how to avoid these fluctuations and to maintain output at a steady optimum level. But it is, properly speaking, a Theory of Employment because it explains *why*, in any given circumstances, employment is what it is. Naturally I am interested not only in the diagnosis, but also in the cure; and many pages of my book are devoted to the latter. But I consider that my suggestions for a cure, which, avowedly, are not worked out completely, are on a different plane from the diagnosis. They are not meant to be definitive; they are subject to all sorts of special assumptions and are necessarily related to the particular conditions of the time. But my main reasons for departing from the traditional theory go much deeper than this. They are of a highly general character and are meant to be definitive.

I sum up, therefore, the main grounds of my departure as follows:

(1) The orthodox theory assumes that we have a knowledge of the future of a kind quite different from that which we actually possess. This false rationalization follows the lines of the Benthamite calculus. The hypothesis of a calculable future leads to a wrong interpretation of the principles of behavior which the need for action compels us to adopt, and to an underestimation of the concealed factors of utter doubt, precariousness, hope, and fear. The result has been a mistaken theory of the rate of interest. It is true that the necessity of equalizing the advantages of the choice between owning loans and assets requires that the rate of interest should be *equal* to the marginal efficiency of capital. But this does not tell us at what *level* the equality will be effective. The orthodox theory regards the marginal efficiency of capital as setting the pace. But the marginal efficiency of capital depends on the price of capital assets; and since this

price determines the rate of new investment, it is consistent in equilibrium with only one given level of money income. Thus the marginal efficiency of capital is not determined, unless the level of money income is given. In a system in which the level of money income is capable of fluctuating, the orthodox theory is one equation short of what is required to give a solution. Undoubtedly the reason why the orthodox system has failed to discover this discrepancy is because it has always tacitly assumed that income *is* given, namely, at the level corresponding to the employment of all the available resources. In other words it is tacitly assuming that the monetary policy is such as to maintain the rate of interest at that level which is compatible with full employment. It is, therefore, incapable of dealing with the general case where employment is liable to fluctuate. Thus, instead of the marginal efficiency of capital determining the rate of interest, it is truer (though not a full statement of the case) to say that it is the rate of interest which determines the marginal efficiency of capital.

(2) The orthodox theory would by now have discovered the above defect, if it had not ignored the need for a theory of the supply and demand of output as a whole. I doubt if many modern economists really accept Say's Law that supply creates its own demand. But they have not been aware that they were tacitly assuming it. Thus the psychological law underlying the Multiplier has escaped notice. It has not been observed that the amount of consumption goods which it pays entrepreneurs to produce is a function of the amount of investment goods which it pays them to produce. The explanation is to be found, I suppose, in the tacit assumption that every individual spends the whole of his income either on consumption or on buying, directly or indirectly, newly produced capital goods. But, here again, while the older economists expressly believed this, I doubt if many contemporary economists really do believe it. They have discarded these older ideas without becoming aware of the consequences.

QUESTIONS

1. What does Keynes mean by "liquidity preference"? Why does he consider it to be of major importance in determining "not prices, but the rate of interest"? (250)

2. Why do fluctuations in the rate of interest affect the price of capital assets and the marginal efficiency of capital?

3. According to Keynes, why are output and employment "so liable to fluctuation"? (254) Why is this fluctuation of importance to Keynes's theory?

4. Why does Keynes argue that "the marginal efficiency of capital is not determined, unless the level of money income is given"? (255) What are the causes of money income fluctuation?

5. According to Keynes, what causes employment to fluctuate?

FOR FURTHER REFLECTION

1. What elements of Keynes's theory might be useful to explain aspects of the U.S. economy today?

2. How do you explain the decline of interest rates in the wake of the U.S. recession? What have been the intended and unintended economic consequences of historically low rates of interest?

3. If, as Keynes says, "The whole object of the accumulation of Wealth is to produce results, or potential results, at a comparatively distant, and sometimes at an *indefinitely* distant, date," what economic behavior would you expect during an economic contraction? What would you expect during a boom?

FRIEDRICH HAYEK

Friedrich Hayek (1899–1992), one of the most influential economists of the twentieth century and a strong advocate of libertarian political thought, was born in Vienna, Austria. After military service in World War I, Hayek studied economics at the University of Vienna where he was briefly interested in Marxism but eventually found the free-market philosophy of Carl Menger and the critique of socialism by Ludwig von Mises more compelling. He took degrees in law and political science, and then studied economics at New York University. Returning to Austria, he wrote his early works dealing with interest rates, government monetary policy, and business cycles.

In 1931 Hayek left Austria for the London School of Economics, where he taught for eighteen years and wrote his most well known book, *The Road to Serfdom* (1944). In it, Hayek made the case for less, rather than more, government involvement in the marketplace, arguing that central planning of economic affairs is an incursion on individual liberty bearing detrimental and sometimes disastrous consequences. In making this argument, Hayek established himself as an opponent of the interventionist policies of John Maynard Keynes. Hayek joined the University of Chicago's Committee on Social Thought in 1950, taught there for twelve years, and then finished his teaching career at the Universities of Freiburg and Salzburg.

Hayek was awarded the Nobel Prize in Economics in 1974. For many observers, the events of the 1980s—which included the adoption of free-market principles by the Reagan and Thatcher administrations, as well as the implosion of the Soviet communist bloc in 1989—vindicated the prescience of Hayek's theories, which seemed far out of the mainstream when he advanced them in the early 1930s. Hayek's views on economics are organically connected to his emphasis on the importance of individual liberty, making him as much a political theorist as an economist. For him, economic and political activity cannot be separated, and he refused to practice economics as a narrowly defined discipline. In the following selection from *The Road to Serfdom,* Hayek raises questions about how individual freedoms can be secured within the confines of the political and economic laws that govern the social order.

FRIEDRICH HAYEK

The Road to Serfdom (selection)

The finest opportunity ever given to the world
was thrown away because the passion for equality
made vain the hope for freedom.
—LORD ACTON

I t is significant that one of the commonest objections to competition is
that it is "blind." It is not irrelevant to recall that to the ancients blind-
ness was an attribute of their deity of justice. Although competition and
justice may have little else in common, it is as much a commendation of
competition as of justice that it is no respecter of persons. That it is impossible to foretell who will be the lucky ones or whom disaster will strike,
that rewards and penalties are not shared out according to somebody's
views about the merits or demerits of different people but depend on their
capacity and their luck, is as important as that, in framing legal rules,
we should not be able to predict which particular person will gain and
which will lose by their application. And this is nonetheless true, because
in competition chance and good luck are often as important as skill and
foresight in determining the fate of different people.

The choice open to us is not between a system in which everybody will
get what he deserves according to some absolute and universal standard
of right, and one where the individual shares are determined partly by
accident or good or ill chance, but between a system where it is the will
of a few persons that decides who is to get what, and one where it depends
at least partly on the ability and enterprise of the people concerned and
partly on unforeseeable circumstances. This is no less relevant because in
a system of free enterprise chances are not equal, since such a system is
necessarily based on private property and (though perhaps not with the

This selection is the chapter "Who, Whom?" in The Road to Serfdom.

same necessity) on inheritance, with the differences in opportunity which these create. There is, indeed, a strong case for reducing this inequality of opportunity as far as congenital differences permit and as it is possible to do so without destroying the impersonal character of the process by which everybody has to take his chance and no person's view about what is right and desirable overrules that of others.

The fact that the opportunities open to the poor in a competitive society are much more restricted than those open to the rich does not make it less true that in such a society the poor are much more free than a person commanding much greater material comfort in a different type of society. Although under competition the probability that a man who starts poor will reach great wealth is much smaller than is true of the man who has inherited property, it is not only possible for the former, but the competitive system is the only one where it depends solely on him and not on the favors of the mighty, and where nobody can prevent a man from attempting to achieve this result. It is only because we have forgotten what unfreedom means that we often overlook the patent fact that in every real sense a badly paid unskilled worker in this country has more freedom to shape his life than many a small entrepreneur in Germany or a much better paid engineer or manager in Russia. Whether it is a question of changing his job or the place where he lives, of professing certain views or of spending his leisure in a particular manner, although sometimes the price he may have to pay for following his inclinations may be high, and to many appear too high, there are no absolute impediments, no dangers to bodily security and freedom, that confine him by brute force to the task and the environment to which a superior has assigned him.

That the ideal of justice of most socialists would be satisfied if merely private income from property were abolished and the differences between the earned incomes of different people remained what they are now is true. What these people forget is that, in transferring all property in the means of production to the state, they put the state in a position whereby its action must in effect decide all other incomes. The power thus given to the state and the demand that the state should use it to "plan" means nothing else than that it should use it in full awareness of all these effects.

To believe that the power which is thus conferred on the state is merely transferred to it from others is erroneous. It is a power which is newly created and which in a competitive society nobody possesses. So long as property is divided among many owners, none of them acting independently has exclusive power to determine the income and position of particular people—nobody is tied to any one property owner except by the fact that he may offer better terms than anybody else.

What our generation has forgotten is that the system of private property is the most important guarantee of freedom, not only for those who own property, but scarcely less for those who do not. It is only because the control of the means of production is divided among many people acting independently that nobody has complete power over us, that we as individuals can decide what to do with ourselves. If all the means of production were vested in a single hand, whether it be nominally that of "society" as a whole or that of a dictator, whoever exercises this control has complete power over us.

Who can seriously doubt that a member of a small racial or religious minority will be freer with no property so long as fellow members of his community have property and are therefore able to employ him, than he would be if private property were abolished and he became owner of a nominal share in the communal property. Or that the power which a multiple millionaire, who may be my neighbor and perhaps my employer, has over me is very much less than that which the smallest *fonctionnaire* possesses who wields the coercive power of the state and on whose discretion it depends whether and how I am to be allowed to live or to work? And who will deny that a world in which the wealthy are powerful is still a better world than one in which only the already powerful can acquire wealth?

It is pathetic, yet at the same time encouraging, to find as prominent an old communist as Max Eastman rediscovering this truth:

"It seems obvious to me now—though I have been slow, I must say, in coming to the conclusion—that the institution of private property is one of the main things that have given man that limited amount of free and equalness that Marx hoped to render infinite by abolishing this institution. Strangely enough Marx was the first to see this. He is the one who informed us, looking backwards, that the evolution of private capitalism with its free market had been a precondition for the evolution of all our democratic freedoms. It never occurred to him, looking forward, that if this was so, these other freedoms might disappear with the abolition of the free market."

It is sometimes said, in answer to such apprehensions, that there is no reason why the planner should determine the incomes of individuals. The social and political difficulties involved in deciding the shares of different people in the national income are so obvious that even the most inveterate planner may well hesitate before he charges any authority with this task. Probably everybody who realizes what it involves would prefer to confine planning to production, to use it only to secure a "rational organization of industry," leaving the distribution of incomes as far as possible to impersonal forces. Although it is impossible to direct industry without exercising some influence on distribution, and although no planner will wish to leave distribution entirely to the forces of the market, they would probably all prefer to confine themselves to seeing that this distribution conforms to certain general rules of equity and fairness, that extreme inequalities are avoided, and that the relation between the remuneration of the major classes is just, without undertaking the responsibility for the position of particular people within their class or for the gradations and differentiations between smaller groups and individuals.

We have already seen that the close interdependence of all economic phenomena makes it difficult to stop planning just where we wish and that, once the free working of the market is impeded beyond a certain degree, the planner will be forced to extend his controls until they become all-comprehensive. These economic considerations, which explain why it is impossible to stop deliberate control just where we should wish, are strongly reinforced by certain social or political tendencies whose strength makes itself increasingly felt as planning extends.

Once it becomes increasingly true, and is generally recognized, that the position of the individual is determined not by impersonal forces, not as a result of the competitive effort of many, but by the deliberate decision of authority, the attitude of the people toward their position in the social order necessarily changes. There will always exist inequalities which will appear unjust to those who suffer from them, disappointments which will appear unmerited, and strokes of misfortune which those hit have not deserved. But when these things occur in a society which is consciously directed, the way in which people will react will be very different from what it is when they are nobody's conscious choice.

Inequality is undoubtedly more readily borne, and affects the dignity of the person much less, if it is determined by impersonal forces than when it is due to design. In a competitive society it is no slight to a person, no offense to his dignity, to be told by any particular firm that it has no need for his services or that it cannot offer him a better job. It is true that in periods of prolonged mass unemployment the effect on many may be very similar. But there are other and better methods to prevent that scourge than central direction. But the unemployment or the loss of income which will always affect some in any society is certainly less degrading if it is the result of misfortune and not deliberately imposed by authority. However bitter the experience, it would be very much worse in a planned society. There individuals will have to decide not whether a person is needed for a particular job but whether he is of use for anything, and how useful he is. His position in life must be assigned to him by somebody else.

While people will submit to suffering which may hit anyone, they will not so easily submit to suffering which is the result of the decision of authority. It may be bad to be just a cog in an impersonal machine; but it is infinitely worse if we can no longer leave it, if we are tied to our place and to the superiors who have been chosen for us. Dissatisfaction of everybody with his lot will inevitably grow with the consciousness that it is the result of deliberate human decision.

Once government has embarked upon planning for the sake of justice, it cannot refuse responsibility for anybody's fate or position. In a planned society we shall all know that we are better or worse off than others, not because of circumstances which nobody controls, and which it is impossible to foresee with certainty, but because some authority wills it. And all our efforts directed toward improving our position will have to aim, not at foreseeing and preparing as well as we can for the circumstances over which we have no control, but at influencing in our favor the authority which has all the power. The nightmare of English nineteenth-century political thinkers, the state in which "no avenue to wealth and honor would exist save through the government,"[1] would be realized in a completeness which they never imagined—though familiar enough in some countries which have since passed to totalitarianism.

As soon as the state takes upon itself the task of planning the whole economic life, the problem of the due station of the different individuals and groups must indeed inevitably become the central political problem. As the coercive power of the state will alone decide who is to have what, the only power worth having will be a share in the exercise of this directing power. There will be no economic or social questions that would not be political questions in the sense that their solution will depend exclusively on who wields the coercive power, on whose are the views that will prevail on all occasions.

I believe it was Lenin himself who introduced to Russia the famous phrase "who, whom?"—during the early years of Soviet rule the byword in which the people summed up the universal problem of a socialist society. Who plans whom, who directs and dominates whom, who assigns to other people their station in life, and who is to have his due allotted by others? These become necessarily the central issues to be decided solely by the supreme power.

More recently an American student of politics has enlarged upon Lenin's phrase and asserted that the problem of all government is "who gets what, when, and how." In a way this is not untrue. That all government affects the relative position of different people and that there is under any system scarcely an aspect of our lives which may not be affected by government action is certainly true. Insofar as government does anything at all, its action will always have some effect on "who gets what, when, and how."

---

1. The actual words are those of the young Disraeli.

There are, however, two fundamental distinctions to be made. First, particular measures may be taken without the possibility of knowing how they will affect particular individuals and therefore without aiming at such particular effects. This point we have already discussed. Second, it is the extent of the activities of the government which decides whether everything that any person gets any time depends on the government, or whether its influence is confined to whether some people will get some things in some way at some time. Here lies the whole difference between a free and a totalitarian system.

The contrast between a liberal and a totally planned system is characteristically illustrated by the common complaints of Nazis and socialists of the "artificial separations of economics and politics" and by their equally common demand for the dominance of politics over economics. These phrases presumably mean not only that economic forces are now allowed to work for ends which are not part of the policy of the government but also that economic power can be used independently of government direction and for ends of which the government may not approve. But the alternative is not merely that there should be only one power but that this single power, the ruling group, should have control over all human ends and particularly that it should have complete power over the position of each individual in society.

That a government which undertakes to direct economic activity will have to use its power to realize somebody's ideal of distributive justice is certain. But how can and how will it use that power? By what principles will it or ought it to be guided? Is there a definite answer to the innumerable questions of relative merits that will arise and that will have to be solved deliberately? Is there a scale of values, on which reasonable people can be expected to agree, which would justify a new hierarchical order of society and is likely to satisfy the demands for justice?

There is only one general principle, one simple rule which would indeed provide a definite answer to all these questions: equality, complete and absolute equality of all individuals in all those points which are subject to human control. If this were generally regarded as desirable (quite apart from the question whether it would be practicable, i.e., whether it would provide adequate incentives), it would give the vague idea of distributive justice a clear meaning and would give the planner definite guidance. But nothing is further from the truth than that people in general regard mechanical equality of this kind as desirable. No socialist movement which aimed at complete equality has ever gained substantial support. What socialism promised was not an absolutely equal, but a more just and more equal, distribution. Not equality in the absolute sense but "greater equality" is the only goal which is seriously aimed at.

Though these two ideals sound very similar, they are as different as possible as far as our problem is concerned. While absolute equality would clearly determine the planner's task, the desire for greater equality is merely negative, no more than an expression of dislike of the present state of affairs; and so long as we are not prepared to say that every move in the direction toward complete equality is desirable, it answers scarcely any of the questions the planner will have to decide.

This is not a quibble about words. We face here a crucial issue which the similarity of the terms used is likely to conceal. While agreement on complete equality would answer all the problems of merit the planner must answer, the formula of the approach to greater equality answers practically none. Its content is hardly more definite than the phrases "common good" or "social welfare." It does not free us from the necessity of deciding in every particular instance between the merits of particular individuals or groups, and it gives us no help in that decision. All it tells us in effect is to take from the rich as much as we can. But, when it comes to the distribution of the spoils, the problem is the same as if the formula of "greater equality" had never been conceived.

Most people find it difficult to admit that we do not possess moral standards which would enable us to settle these questions—if not perfectly, at least to greater general satisfaction than is done by the competitive system. Have we not all some idea of what is a "just price" or a "fair wage"? Can we not rely on the strong sense of fairness of the people? And even if we do not now agree fully on what is just or fair in a particular case, would popular ideas not soon consolidate into more definite standards if people were given an opportunity to see their ideals realized?

Unfortunately, there is little ground for such hopes. What standards we have are derived from the competitive regime we have known and would necessarily disappear soon after the disappearance of competition. What we mean by a just price or a fair wage is either the customary price or wage, the return which past experience has made people expect, or the price or wage that would exist if there were no monopolistic exploitation. The only important exception to this used to be the claim of the workers to the "full produce of their labor," to which so much of socialist doctrine traces back. But there are few socialists today who believe that in a socialist society the output of each industry would be entirely shared by the workers of that industry; for this would mean that workers in industries using a great deal of capital would have a much larger income than those in industries using little capital, which most socialists would regard as very unjust. And it is now fairly generally agreed that this particular claim was based on an erroneous interpretation of the facts. But once the claim of the individual worker to the whole of "his" product is disallowed, and the whole of the return from capital is to be divided among all workers, the problem of how to divide it raises the same basic issue.

What the "just price" of a particular commodity or the "fair" remuneration for a particular service is might conceivably be determined objectively if the quantities needed were independently fixed. If these were given irrespective of cost, the planner might try to find what price or wage is necessary to bring forth this supply. But the planner must also decide how much is to be produced of each kind of goods, and, in so doing, he determines what will be the just price or fair wage to pay. If the planner decides that fewer architects or watchmakers are wanted and that the need can be met by those who are willing to stay in the trade at a lower remuneration, the "fair" wage will be lower. In deciding the relative importance of the different ends, the planner also decides the relative importance of the different groups and persons. As he is not supposed to treat the people merely as a means, he must take account of these effects and consciously balance the importance of the different ends against the effects of his decision. This means, however, that he will necessarily exercise direct control over the conditions of the different people.

This applies to the relative position of individuals no less than to that of the different occupational groups. We are in general far too likely to think of incomes within a given trade or profession as more or less uniform. But the differences between the incomes, not only of the most and the least successful doctor or architect, writer or movie actor, boxer or jockey, but also of the more and the less successful plumber or market gardener, grocer or tailor, are as great as those between the propertied and the propertyless classes. And although, no doubt, there would be some attempt at standardization by creating categories, the necessity of discrimination between individuals would remain the same, whether it were exercised by fixing their individual incomes or by allocating them to particular categories.

We need say no more about the likelihood of men in a free society submitting to such control—or about their remaining free if they submitted. On the whole question, what John Stuart Mill wrote nearly a hundred years ago remains equally true today:

"A fixed rule, like that of equality, might be acquiesced in, and so might chance, or an external necessity; but that a handful of human beings should weigh everybody in the balance, and give more to one and less to another at their sole pleasure and judgement, would not be borne unless from persons believed to be more than men, and backed by supernatural terrors."

These difficulties need not lead to open clashes so long as socialism is merely the aspiration of a limited and fairly homogeneous group. They come to the surface only when a socialist policy is actually attempted with the support of the many different groups which together compose the majority of a people. Then it soon becomes the one burning question of which of the different sets of ideals shall be imposed upon all by making the whole resources of the country serve it. It is because successful planning requires the creation of a common view on the essential values that the restriction of our freedom with regard to material things touches so directly on our spiritual freedom.

Socialists, the cultivated parents of the barbarous offspring they have produced, traditionally hope to solve this problem by education. But what does education mean in this respect? Surely we have learned that knowledge cannot create new ethical values, that no amount of learning will lead people to hold the same views on the moral issues which a conscious ordering of all social relations raises. It is not rational conviction but the acceptance of a creed which is required to justify a particular plan. And, indeed, socialists everywhere were the first to recognize that the task they had set themselves required the general acceptance of a common Weltanschauung, of a definite set of values. It was in these efforts to produce a mass movement supported by such a single world view that the socialists first created most of the instruments of indoctrination of which Nazis and Fascists have made such effective use.

In Germany and Italy the Nazis and Fascists did, indeed, not have much to invent. The usages of the new political movements which pervaded all aspects of life had in both countries already been introduced by the socialists. The idea of a political party which embraces all activities of the individual from the cradle to the grave, which claims to guide his views on everything, and which delights in making all problems questions of party Weltanschauung, was first put into practice by the socialists. An Austrian socialist writer, speaking of the socialist movement of his country, reports with pride that it was its "characteristic feature that it created special organizations for every field of activities of workers and employees."[2]

Though the Austrian socialists may have gone further in this respect than others, the situation was not very different elsewhere. It was not the Fascists but the socialists who began to collect children from the tenderest age into political organizations to make sure that they grew up as good proletarians. It was not the Fascists but the socialists who first thought of organizing sports and games, football and hiking, in party clubs where the members would not be infected by other views. It was the socialists who first insisted that the party member should distinguish himself from others by the modes of greeting and forms of address. It was they who

---

2. G. Wieser, Ein Staat stirbt, Oesterreich 1934-1938 (Paris, 1938), p. 41.

by their organization of "cells" and devices for the permanent supervision of private life created the prototype of the totalitarian party. *Balilla* and *Hitlerjugend*, *Dopolavoro* and *Kraft durch Freude*, political uniforms and military party formations, are all little more than imitations of older socialist institutions.

So long as the socialist movement in a country is closely bound up with the interests of a particular group, usually the more highly skilled industrial workers, the problem of creating a common view on the desirable status of the different members of society is comparatively simple. The movement is immediately concerned with the status of one particular group, and its aim is to raise that status relatively to other groups. The character of the problem changes, however, as in the course of the progressive advance toward socialism it becomes more and more evident to everyone that his income and general position are determined by the coercive apparatus of the state, that he can maintain or improve his position only as a member of an organized group capable of influencing or controlling the state machine in his interest.

In the tug of war between the various pressure groups which arises at this stage, it is by no means necessary that the interests of the poorest and most numerous groups should prevail. Nor is it necessarily an advantage for the older socialist parties, who avowedly represented the interests of a particular group, to have been the first in the field and to have designed their whole ideology to appeal to the manual workers in industry. Their very success, and their insistence on the acceptance of the whole creed, is bound to create a powerful countermovement—not by the capitalists but by the very large and equally propertyless classes who find their relative status threatened by the advance of the elite of the industrial workers.

Socialist theory and socialist tactics, even where they have not been dominated by Marxist dogma, have been based everywhere on the idea of a division of society into two classes with common but mutually conflicting interests: capitalists and industrial workers. Socialism counted on a rapid disappearance of the old middle class and completely disregarded the rise of a new middle class, the countless army of clerks and typists, administrative workers and schoolteachers, tradesmen and small officials, and the lower ranks of the professions. For a time these classes often provided many of the leaders of the labor movement. But as it became increasingly clear that the position of those classes was deteriorating relatively to that of the industrial workers, the ideals which guided the latter lost much of their appeal to the others. While they were all socialists in the sense that they disliked the capitalist system and wanted a deliberate sharing-out of wealth according to their ideas of justice, these ideas proved to be very different from those embodied in the practice of the older socialist parties.

The means which the old socialist parties had successfully employed to secure the support of one occupational group—the raising of their relative economic position—cannot be used to secure the support of all. There are bound to arise rival socialist movements that appeal to the support of those whose relative position is worsened. There is a great deal of truth in the often heard statement that fascism and National Socialism are a sort of middle-class socialism—only that in Italy and Germany the supporters of these new movements were economically hardly a middle class any longer. It was to a large extent a revolt of a new underprivileged class against the labor aristocracy which the industrial labor movement had created.

There can be little doubt that no single economic factor has contributed more to help these movements than the envy of the unsuccessful professional man, the university-trained engineer or lawyer, and of the "white-collared proletariat" in general, of the engine driver or compositor and other members of the strongest trade unions whose income was many times theirs. Nor can there be much doubt that in terms of money income the average member of the rank and file of the Nazi movement in its early years was poorer than the average trade-unionist or member of the older socialist party—a circumstance which only gained poignancy from the fact that the former had often seen better days and were frequently still living in surroundings which were the result of this past.

The expression "class struggle à rebours," current in Italy at the time of the rise of fascism, did point to a very important aspect of the movement. The conflict between the Fascist or National Socialist and the older socialist parties must, indeed, very largely be regarded as the kind of conflict which is bound to arise between rival socialist factions. There was no difference between them about the question of its being the will of the state which should assign to each person his proper place in society. But there were, as there always will be, most profound differences about what are the proper places of the different classes and groups.

The old socialist leaders, who had always regarded their parties as the natural spearhead of the future general movement toward socialism, found it difficult to understand that with every extension in the use of socialist methods the resentment of large poor classes should turn against them. But while the old socialist parties, or the organized labor in particular industries, had usually not found it unduly difficult to come to an understanding for joint action with the employers in their particular industries, very large classes were left out in the cold. To them, and not without some justification, the more prosperous sections of the labor movement seemed to belong to the exploiting rather than to the exploited class.

The resentment of the lower middle class, from which fascism and National Socialism recruited so large a proportion of their supporters, was intensified by the fact that their education and training had in many instances made them aspire to directing positions and that they regarded themselves as entitled to be members of the directing class. While the younger generation, out of that contempt for profit making fostered by socialist teaching, spurned independent positions which involved risk and flocked in ever increasing numbers into salaried positions which promised security, they demanded a place yielding them the income and power to which in their opinion their training entitled them. While they believed in an organized society, they expected a place in that society very different from that which society ruled by labor seemed to offer. They were quite ready to take over the methods of the older socialism but intended to employ them in the service of a different class. The movement was able to attract all those who, while they agreed on the desirability of the state controlling all economic activity, disagreed with the ends for which the aristocracy of the industrial workers used their political strength.

The new socialist movement started with several tactical advantages. Labor socialism had grown in a democratic and liberal world, adapting its tactics to it and taking over many of the ideals of liberalism. Its protagonists still believed that the creation of socialism as such would solve all problems. Fascism and National Socialism, on the other hand, grew out of the experience of an increasingly regulated society's awakening to the fact that democratic and international socialism was aiming at incompatible ideals. Their tactics were developed in a world already dominated by socialist policy and the problems it creates. They had no illusions about the possibility of a democratic solution of problems which require more agreement among people than can reasonably be expected. They had no illusions about the capacity of reason to decide all the questions of the relative importance of the wants of different men or groups which planning inevitably raises, or about the formula of equality providing an answer. They knew that the strongest group which rallied enough supporters in favor of a new hierarchical order of society, and which frankly promised privileges to the classes to which it appealed, was likely to obtain the support of all those who were disappointed because they had been promised equality but found that they had merely furthered the interest of a particular class. Above all, they were successful because they offered a theory, or Weltanschauung, which seemed to justify the privileges they promised to their supporters.

QUESTIONS

1. What does Hayek mean when he says that power conferred on a state "is a power which is newly created and which in a competitive society nobody possesses"? (259)

2. Why does Hayek believe that "the system of private property is the most important guarantee of freedom," even for those who do not own property? (259)

3. According to Hayek, why will the planner be "forced to extend his controls until they become all-comprehensive"? (261)

4. According to Hayek, what is "the central political problem" of the totalitarian state? (262)

5. For Hayek, what is the difference between "a free and a totalitarian system"? Why does he equate socialism with totalitarianism? (263)

FOR FURTHER REFLECTION

1. Do you agree with Hayek that competition is to be commended because "it is no respecter of persons"?

2. Does private property guarantee freedom, as Hayek claims, or does freedom guarantee private property?

3. If "the opportunities open to the poor in a competitive society are much more restricted than those open to the rich," how should the problem of inequality be addressed?

MICHAŁ KALECKI

Michał Kalecki (1899–1970) was a Marxist economist and an economic planner in Communist Poland whose writings helped garner support for interventionist economic policies until the decline of socialist thinking among mainstream economists in the 1970s. Recently, his writings have begun to influence schools of economic thought that attempt to extend and develop the theories of John Maynard Keynes.

Kalecki was born in Łódź in what was then Russian-ruled Poland. He studied engineering at universities in Warsaw and Gdansk, and was largely self-taught in economics, reading widely in the writings of Marxist theorist and revolutionary Rosa Luxemburg. During the mid- to late-1920s, Kalecki worked as a business journalist, with a stint as a researcher at an economics institute in Warsaw. There, he obtained an extensive familiarity with the economic statistics pertaining to various industries—knowledge that would have a profound influence on his future work. His first writings on economic theory were published beginning in 1932 in the Polish-language magazine *Socialist Review*. In these articles and in his "Essay on the Theory of the Business Cycle" published the following year, Kalecki outlined a theory of the business cycle. At the same time he was developing ideas similar to those put forth by John Maynard Keynes in his *General Theory of Employment, Interest, and Money* (1936), calling for government intervention in the capitalist economy to stimulate demand during slumps. Soon thereafter, Kalecki traveled to Cambridge University where he met Keynes and formed a lifelong friendship with several of Keynes's disciples, notably Joan Robinson. Kalecki spent the war years at the Oxford University Institute of Statistics, and after the war, he worked for a time in the economics department at the United Nations in New York. In 1955 he returned to Communist Poland, where he was appointed chairman of the committee in charge of centralized planning. However his fifteen-year plan was deemed too pessimistic and his influence waned. In 1959 he retired from politics to a life of research and teaching in Poland.

The following selection was published in 1943 in a British academic journal. In it, Kalecki makes a compelling case in favor of government intervention to stimulate the economy.

Political Aspects of Full Employment

1

A solid majority of economists is now of the opinion that, even in a capitalist system, full employment may be secured by a government spending program, provided there is in existence adequate plant to employ all existing labor power, and provided adequate supplies of necessary foreign raw materials may be obtained in exchange for exports.

If the government undertakes public investment (e.g., builds schools, hospitals, and highways) or subsidizes mass consumption (by family allowances, reduction of indirect taxation, or subsidies to keep down the prices of necessities), if, moreover, this expenditure is financed by borrowing and not by taxation (which could affect adversely private investment and consumption), the effective demand for goods and services may be increased up to a point where full employment is achieved. Such government expenditure increases employment, be it noted, not only directly but indirectly as well, since the higher incomes caused by it result in a secondary increase in demand for consumption and investment goods.

2. It may be asked where the public will get the money to lend to the government if they do not curtail their investment and consumption. To understand this process it is best, I think, to imagine for a moment that the government pays its suppliers in government securities. The suppliers will, in general, not retain these securities but put them into circulation while buying other goods and services, and so on until finally these securities will reach persons or firms which retain them as interest-yielding assets. In any period of time the total increase in government securities in the possession (transitory or final) of persons and firms will be equal to the goods and services sold to the government. Thus what the economy lends to the government are goods and services whose production is "financed" by government securities. In reality the government pays for the services

not in securities but in cash, but it simultaneously issues securities and so drains the cash off; and this is equivalent to the imaginary process described above.

What happens, however, if the public is unwilling to absorb all the increase in government securities? It will offer them finally to banks to get cash (notes or deposits) in exchange. If the banks accept these offers, the rate of interest will be maintained. If not, the prices of securities will fall, which means a rise in the rate of interest, and this will encourage the public to hold more securities in relation to deposits. It follows that the rate of interest depends on banking policy, in particular on that of the central bank. If this policy aims at maintaining the rate of interest at a certain level that may be easily achieved, however large the amount of government borrowing. Such was and is the position in the present war. In spite of astronomical budget deficits, the rate of interest has shown no rise since the beginning of 1940.

3. It may be objected that government expenditure financed by borrowing will cause inflation. To this may be replied that the effective demand created by the government acts like any other increase in demand. If labor, plant, and foreign raw materials are in ample supply, the increase in demand is met by an increase in production. But if the point of full employment of resources is reached and effective demand continues to increase, prices will rise so as to equilibrate the demand for and the supply of goods and services. (In the state of overemployment of resources such as we witness at present in the war economy, an inflationary rise in prices has been avoided only to the extent to which effective demand for consumption goods has been curtailed by rationing and direct taxation.) It follows that if the government intervention aims at achieving full employment but stops short of increasing effective demand over the full employment mark, there is no need to be afraid of inflation.

2

1. The above is a very crude and incomplete statement of the economic doctrine of full employment. But, I think, it is sufficient to acquaint the reader with the essence of the doctrine and so enable him to follow the subsequent discussion of the *political* problems involved in the achievement of full employment.

It should be first stated that although most economists are now agreed that full employment may be achieved by government spending, this was by no means the case even in the recent past. Among the opposers of this doctrine there were (and still are) prominent so-called "economic experts" closely connected with banking and industry. This suggests that there is a political background in the opposition to the full employment doctrine even though the arguments advanced are economic. That is not to say that people who advance them do not believe in their economics, poor though these are. But obstinate ignorance is usually a manifestation of underlying political motives.

There are, however, even more direct indications that a first-class political issue is at stake here. In the Great Depression in the thirties, big business opposed consistently experiments for increasing employment by government spending in all countries, except Nazi Germany. This was to be clearly seen in the United States (opposition to the New Deal), in France (Blum experiment), and also in Germany before Hitler. The attitude is not easy to explain. Clearly higher output and employment benefits not only workers, but *entrepreneurs* as well, because their profits rise. And the policy of full employment outlined above does not encroach upon profits because it does not involve any additional taxation. The *entrepreneurs* in the slump are longing for a boom; why do not they accept gladly the "synthetic" boom which the government is able to offer them? It is this difficult and fascinating question with which we intend to deal in this article.

The reasons for the opposition of the "industrial leaders" to full employment achieved by government spending may be subdivided into three categories: (i) the dislike of government interference in the problem of employment as such; (ii) the dislike of the direction of government spending (public investment and subsidizing consumption); (iii) the dislike of the social and political changes resulting from the *maintenance* of full employment. We shall examine each of these three categories of objections to the government expansion policy in detail.

2. We shall deal first with the reluctance of the "captains of industry" to accept government intervention in the matter of employment. Every widening of state activity is looked upon by "business" with suspicion, but the creation of employment by government spending has a special aspect which makes the opposition particularly intense. Under a laissez-faire system the level of employment depends to a great extent on the so-called state of confidence. If this deteriorates, private investment declines, which results in a fall of output and employment (both directly and through the secondary effect of the fall in incomes upon consumption and investment). This gives the capitalists a powerful indirect control over government policy: everything which may shake the state of confidence must be carefully avoided because it would cause an economic crisis. But once the government learns the trick of increasing employment by its own purchases, this powerful controlling device loses its effectiveness. Hence budget deficits necessary to carry out government intervention must be regarded as perilous. The social function of the doctrine of "sound finance" is to make the level of employment dependent on the "state of confidence."

3. The dislike of the business leaders of a government spending policy grows even more acute when they come to consider the objects on which the money would be spent: public investment and subsidizing mass consumption.

The economic principles of government intervention require that public investment should be confined to objects which do not compete with the equipment of private business (e.g., hospitals, schools, highways, etc.). Otherwise the profitability of private investment might be impaired and the positive effect of public investment upon employment offset by the negative effect of the decline in private investment. This conception suits the businessmen very well. But the scope of public investment of this type is rather narrow, and there is a danger that the government, in pursuing this policy, may eventually be tempted to nationalize transport or public utilities so as to gain a new sphere in which to carry out investment.

One might therefore expect business leaders and their experts to be more in favor of subsidizing mass consumption (by means of family allowances, subsidies to keep down the prices of necessities, etc.) than of public investment; for by subsidizing consumption the government would not be embarking on any sort of "enterprise." In practice, however, this is not the case. Indeed, subsidizing mass consumption is much more violently opposed by these "experts" than public investment. For here a "moral" principle of the highest importance is at stake. The fundamentals of capitalist ethics require that "you shall earn your bread in sweat"—unless you happen to have private means.

4. We have considered the political reasons for the opposition against the policy of creating employment by government spending. But even if this opposition were overcome—as it may well be under the pressure of the masses—the *maintenance* of full employment would cause social and political changes which would give a new impetus to the opposition of the business leaders. Indeed, under a regime of permanent full employment, the "sack" would cease to play its role as a disciplinary measure. The social position of the boss would be undermined and the self-assurance and class-consciousness of the working class would grow. Strikes for wage increases and improvements in conditions of work would create political tension. It is true that profits would be higher under a regime of full employment than they are on the average under laissez-faire; and even the rise in wage rates resulting from the stronger bargaining power of the workers is less likely to reduce profits than to increase prices, and thus adversely affects only the *rentier* interests. But "discipline in the factories" and "political stability" are more appreciated by the business leaders than profits. Their class instinct tells them that lasting full employment is unsound from their point of view and that unemployment is an integral part of the "normal" capitalist system.

3

1. One of the important functions of Fascism, as typified by the Nazi system, was to remove the capitalist objections to full employment.

The dislike of government spending policy as such is overcome under Fascism by the fact that the state machinery is under the direct control of a partnership of big business with Fascist upstarts. The necessity for the myth of "sound finance," which served to prevent the government from offsetting a confidence crisis by spending, is removed. In a democracy, one does not know what the next government will be like. Under Fascism there is no next government.

The dislike of government spending, whether on public investment or consumption, is overcome by concentrating government expenditure on armaments. Finally, "discipline in the factories" and "political stability" under full employment are maintained by the "new order," which ranges from the suppression of the trade unions to the concentration camp. Political pressure replaces the economic pressure of unemployment.

2. The fact that armaments are the backbone of the policy of Fascist full employment has a profound influence upon its economic character. Large-scale armaments are inseparable from the expansion of the armed forces and the preparation of plans for a war of conquest. They also induce competitive rearmament of other countries. This causes the main aim of the spending to shift gradually from full employment to securing the maximum effect of rearmament. As a result employment becomes "overfull"; not only is unemployment abolished, but an acute scarcity of labor prevails. Bottlenecks arise in every sphere, and these must be dealt with by the creation of a number of controls. Such an economy has many features of a "planned economy," and is sometimes compared, rather ignorantly, with socialism. However, this type of "planning" is bound to appear whenever an economy sets itself a certain high target of production in a particular sphere, when it becomes a "target economy" of which the "armament economy" is a special case. An "armament economy" involves in particular the curtailment of consumption as compared with what it could have been under full employment.

The Fascist system starts from the overcoming of unemployment, develops into an "armament economy" of scarcity, and ends inevitably in war.

4

1. What will be the practical outcome of the opposition to "full employment by government spending" in a capitalist democracy? We shall try

to answer this question on the basis of the analysis of the reasons for this opposition given in section 2. We argued there that we may expect the opposition of the "leaders of industry" on three planes: (i) the opposition on principle to government spending based on a budget deficit; (ii) the opposition to this spending being directed either toward public investment—which may foreshadow the intrusion of the state into the new spheres of economic activity—or toward subsidizing mass consumption; (iii) the opposition to *maintaining* full employment and not merely preventing deep and prolonged slumps.

Now it must be recognized that the stage at which "business leaders" could afford to be opposed to *any* kind of government interventions to alleviate a slump is more or less past. Three factors have contributed to this: (i) very full employment during the present war; (ii) development of the economic doctrine of full employment; (iii) partly as a result of these two factors, the slogan "Unemployment never again" is now deeply rooted in the consciousness of the masses. This position is reflected in the recent pronouncements of the "captains of industry" and their experts. The necessity that "something must be done in the slump" is agreed to; but the fight continues, firstly, as to "*what* should be done in the slump" (i.e., what should be the direction of government intervention), and secondly, that "it should be done *only* in the slump" (i.e., merely to alleviate slumps rather than to secure permanent full employment).

2. In the current discussions of these problems there emerges time and again the conception of counteracting the slump by stimulating *private* investment. This may be done by lowering the rate of interest, by the reduction of income tax, or by subsidizing private investment directly in this or another form. That such a scheme should be attractive to "business" is not surprising. The *entrepreneur* remains the medium through which the intervention is conducted. If he does not feel confidence in the political situation, he will not be bribed into investment. And the intervention does not involve the government either in "playing with" (public) investment or "wasting money" on subsidizing consumption.

It may be shown, however, that the stimulation of private investment does not provide an adequate method for preventing mass unemployment. There are two alternatives to be considered here. (i) The rate of interest or income tax (or both) is reduced sharply in the slump and increased in the boom. In this case, both the period and the amplitude of the business cycle will be reduced, but employment not only in the slump but even in the boom may be far from full, i.e., the average unemployment may be considerable, although its fluctuations will be less marked. (ii) The rate of interest or income tax is reduced in a slump but *not* increased in the subsequent boom. In this case the boom will last longer, but it must end in a new slump: one reduction in the rate of interest or income tax does not, of course, eliminate the forces which cause cyclical fluctuations in a capitalist economy. In the new slump it will be necessary to reduce the rate of interest or income tax again and so on. Thus in the not-too-remote future, the rate of interest would have to be negative and income tax would have to be replaced by an income subsidy. The same would arise if it were attempted to *maintain* full employment by stimulating private investment: the rate of interest and income tax would have to be reduced continuously.

In addition to this fundamental weakness of combating unemployment by stimulating private investment, there is a practical difficulty. The reaction of the *entrepreneurs* to the measures described is uncertain. If the downswing is sharp, they may take a very pessimistic view of the future, and the reduction of the rate of interest or income tax may then for a long time have little or no effect upon investment, and thus upon the level of output and employment.

3. Even those who advocate stimulating private investment to counteract the slump frequently do not rely on it exclusively, but envisage that it should be associated with public investment. It looks at present as if "business leaders" and their experts (at least some of them) would tend to accept as a *pis aller* public investment financed by borrowing as a means of alleviating slumps. They seem, however, still to be consistently opposed to creating employment by subsidizing consumption and to *maintaining* full employment.

This state of affairs is perhaps symptomatic of the future economic regime of capitalist democracies. In the slump, either under the pressure of the masses, or even without it, public investment financed by borrowing will be undertaken to prevent large-scale unemployment. But if attempts are made to apply this method in order to maintain the high level of employment reached in the subsequent boom, strong opposition by "business leaders" is likely to be encountered. As has already been argued, lasting full employment is not at all to their liking. The workers would "get out of hand" and the "captains of industry" would be anxious to "teach them a lesson." Moreover, the price increase in the upswing is to the disadvantage of small and big *rentiers* and makes them "boom-tired."

In this situation a powerful alliance is likely to be formed between big business and *rentier* interests, and they would probably find more than one economist to declare that the situation was manifestly unsound. The pressure of all these forces, and in particular of big business—as a rule influential in government departments—would most probably induce the government to return to the orthodox policy of cutting down the budget deficit. A slump would follow in which government spending policy would again come into its own.

This pattern of a "political business cycle" is not entirely conjectural; something very similar happened in the United States in 1937–1938. The breakdown of the boom in the second half of 1937 was actually due to the drastic reduction of the budget deficit. On the other hand, in the acute slump that followed, the government promptly reverted to a spending policy.

The regime of the "political business cycle" would be an artificial restoration of the position as it existed in nineteenth-century capitalism. Full employment would be reached only at the top of the boom, but slumps would be relatively mild and short-lived.

5

1. Should a progressive be satisfied with a regime of the "political business cycle" as described in the preceding section? I think he should oppose it on two grounds: (i) that it does not assure lasting full employment; (ii) that government intervention is tied to public investment and does not embrace subsidizing consumption. What the masses now ask for is not the mitigation of slumps but their total abolition. Nor should the resulting fuller utilization of resources be applied to unwanted public investment merely in order to provide work. The government spending program should be devoted to public investment only to the extent to which such investment is *actually needed*. The rest of government spending necessary to maintain full employment should be used to subsidize consumption (through family allowances, old-age pensions, reduction in indirect taxation, and subsidizing necessities). Opponents of such government spending say that the government will then have nothing to show for their money. The reply is that the counterpart of this spending will be the higher standard of living of the masses. Is not this the purpose of all economic activity?

2. "Full employment capitalism" will, of course, have to develop new social and political institutions which will reflect the increased power of the working class. If capitalism can adjust itself to full employment, a fundamental reform will have been incorporated in it. If not, it will show itself an outmoded system which must be scrapped.

But perhaps the fight for full employment may lead to Fascism? Perhaps capitalism will adjust itself to full employment in *this* way? This seems extremely unlikely. Fascism sprang up in Germany against a background of tremendous unemployment and maintained itself in power through securing full employment while capitalist democracy failed to do so. The fight of the progressive forces for full employment is at the same time a way of *preventing* the recurrence of Fascism.

QUESTIONS

1. Why does Kalecki support government expenditure financed by borrowing in order to achieve full employment?

2. Why does Kalecki argue in favor of "the economic doctrine of full employment"? (273)

3. Under what conditions does Kalecki believe inflation can be avoided as a result of public investment by the government?

4. According to Kalecki, why do industrial leaders oppose full employment achieved by government spending?

5. Why does Kalecki believe that measures to stimulate private investment do not "eliminate the forces which cause cyclical fluctuations in a capitalist economy?" (278) Does he believe that the economic doctrine of full employment can avoid cyclical fluctuations?

FOR FURTHER REFLECTION

1. What economic support, if any, should the government offer those who are unable to find work? How should this support be financed?

2. If you agree with Kalecki that a portion of government spending be devoted to "the higher standard of living of the masses," how should that spending be allocated and financed?

3. Is Kalecki correct in referring to the doctrine of "sound finance" as a myth?

MILTON FRIEDMAN

M ilton Friedman (1912–2006) was responsible, more than any other economist, for reorienting the postwar Keynesian consensus in the direction of free-market thinking. Through a combination of rigorous theoretical analysis and careful empirical research, Friedman demonstrated that the impact of government monetary policy on economic growth may be at least as great as that of fiscal policy. He was highly influential as the acknowledged leader of the "Chicago school" of free-market economists, as well as through his activities as a presidential adviser and as a public intellectual.

Friedman was born in Brooklyn and educated at Rutgers University, the University of Chicago, and Columbia University. In the late 1930s he was employed as a statistician for the National Bureau of Economic Research, and during the war he worked for the Treasury Department and then in war-related statistical analysis at Columbia. Joining the faculty of the University of Chicago in 1946, he taught economics there for some thirty years. During this period he rose to international prominence, writing a regular column for *Newsweek* magazine from 1966 until 1983 and serving as economic adviser to President Richard Nixon and other world leaders. In addition to a great number of technical books and articles, Friedman wrote the widely read *Capitalism and Freedom* (1962) and, with his wife, Rose, *Free to Choose* (1980). In 1976, he was awarded the Nobel Prize in Economics.

Friedman is probably best known for his conviction that "money matters"—that is, that the money supply as determined by government policy deeply affects economic performance and prices. He was able to convince the academic economics community of this thesis thanks to his massively documented study, *A Monetary History of the United States, 1867–1960* (1963), coauthored with Anna J. Schwartz. This work presented evidence that the Great Depression was caused, at least in part, by the Federal Reserve's tight-money policy in the wake of the 1929 stock market crash. The following selection first appeared in the *New York Times Magazine* in 1970. In it, Friedman provides a penetrating analysis of the notion of moral responsibility as it applies to individuals in their roles as private citizens, as corporate leaders, and as elected officials.

The Social Responsibility of Business

When I hear businessmen speak eloquently about the "social responsibilities of business in a free-enterprise system," I am reminded of the wonderful line about the Frenchman who discovered at the age of seventy that he had been speaking prose all his life. The businessmen believe that they are defending free enterprise when they declaim that business is not concerned "merely" with profit but also with promoting desirable "social" ends; that business has a "social conscience" and takes seriously its responsibilities for providing employment, eliminating discrimination, avoiding pollution, and whatever else may be the catchwords of the contemporary crop of reformers. In fact they are—or would be if they or anyone else took them seriously—preaching pure and unadulterated socialism. Businessmen who talk this way are unwitting puppets of the intellectual forces that have been undermining the basis of a free society these past decades.

The discussions of the "social responsibilities of business" are notable for their analytical looseness and lack of rigor. What does it mean to say that "business" has responsibilities? Only people can have responsibilities. A corporation is an artificial person and in this sense may have artificial responsibilities, but "business" as a whole cannot be said to have responsibilities, even in this vague sense. The first step toward clarity in examining the doctrine of the social responsibility of business is to ask precisely what it implies for whom.

Presumably, the individuals who are to be responsible are businessmen, which means individual proprietors or corporate executives. Most of the discussion of social responsibility is directed at corporations, so in what follows I shall mostly neglect the individual proprietor and speak of corporate executives.

In a free-enterprise, private-property system, a corporate executive is an employee of the owners of the business. He has direct responsibility to his employers. That responsibility is to conduct the business in accordance with their desires, which generally will be to make as much money as possible while conforming to the basic rules of the society, both those embodied in law and those embodied in ethical custom. Of course, in some cases his employers may have a different objective. A group of persons might establish a corporation for an eleemosynary purpose—for example, a hospital or a school. The manager of such a corporation will not have money profit as his objective but the rendering of certain services.

In either case, the key point is that, in his capacity as a corporate executive, the manager is the agent of the individuals who own the corporation or establish the eleemosynary institution, and his primary responsibility is to them.

Needless to say, this does not mean that it is easy to judge how well he is performing his task. But at least the criterion of performance is straightforward, and the persons among whom a voluntary contractual arrangement exists are clearly defined.

Of course, the corporate executive is also a person in his own right. As a person, he may have many other responsibilities that he recognizes or assumes voluntarily—to his family, his conscience, his feelings of charity, his church, his clubs, his city, his country. He may feel impelled by these responsibilities to devote part of his income to causes he regards as worthy, to refuse to work for particular corporations, even to leave his job, for example, to join his country's armed forces. If we wish, we may refer to some of these responsibilities as "social responsibilities." But in these respects he is acting as a principal, not an agent; he is spending his own money or time or energy, not the money of his employers or the time or energy he has contracted to devote to their purposes. If these are "social responsibilities," they are the social responsibilities of individuals, not of business.

What does it mean to say that the corporate executive has a "social responsibility" in his capacity as businessman? If this statement is not pure rhetoric, it must mean that he is to act in some way that is not in the interest of his employers. For example, that he is to refrain from increasing the price of the product in order to contribute to the social objective of preventing inflation, even though a price increase would be in the best interests of the corporation. Or that he is to make expenditures on reducing pollution beyond the amount that is in the best interests of the corporation or that is required by law in order to contribute to the social objective of improving the environment. Or that, at the expense of corporate profits, he is to hire "hard-core" unemployed instead of better qualified available workmen to contribute to the social objective of reducing poverty.

In each of these cases, the corporate executive would be spending someone else's money for a general social interest. Insofar as his actions in accord with his "social responsibility" reduce returns to stockholders, he is spending their money. Insofar as his actions raise the price to customers, he is spending the customers' money. Insofar as his actions lower the wages of some employees, he is spending their money.

The stockholders or the customers or the employees could separately spend their own money on the particular action if they wished to do so. The executive is exercising a distinct "social responsibility," rather than serving as an agent of the stockholders or the customers or the employees, only if he spends the money in a different way than they would have spent it.

But if he does this, he is in effect imposing taxes, on the one hand, and deciding how the tax proceeds shall be spent, on the other.

This process raises political questions on two levels: principle and consequences. On the level of political principle, the imposition of taxes and the expenditure of tax proceeds are governmental functions. We have established elaborate constitutional, parliamentary, and judicial provisions to control these functions, to assure that taxes are imposed so far as possible in accordance with the preferences and desires of the public—after all, "taxation without representation" was one of the battle cries of the American Revolution. We have a system of checks and balances to separate the legislative function of imposing taxes and enacting expenditures from the executive function of collecting taxes and administering expenditure programs and from the judicial function of mediating disputes and interpreting the law.

Here the businessman—self-selected or appointed directly or indirectly by stockholders—is to be simultaneously legislator, executive, and jurist. He is to decide whom to tax by how much and for what purpose, and he is to spend the proceeds—all this guided only by general exhortations from on high to restrain inflation, improve the environment, fight poverty, and so on and on.

The whole justification for permitting the corporate executive to be selected by the stockholders is that the executive is an agent serving the interests of his principal. This justification disappears when the corporate executive imposes taxes and spends the proceeds for "social" purposes. He becomes in effect a public employee, a civil servant, even though he remains in name an employee of a private enterprise. On grounds of political principle, it is intolerable that such civil servants—insofar as their actions in the name of social responsibility are real and not just window dressing—should be selected as they are now. If they are to be civil servants, then they must be selected through a political process. If they are to impose taxes and make expenditures to foster "social" objectives, then political machinery must be set up to guide the assessment of taxes and to determine through a political process the objectives to be served.

This is the basic reason why the doctrine of "social responsibility" involves the acceptance of the socialist view that political mechanisms, not market mechanisms, are the appropriate way to determine the allocation of scarce resources to alternative uses.

On the grounds of consequences, can the corporate executive in fact discharge his alleged "social responsibilities"? On the one hand, suppose he could get away with spending the stockholders' or customers' or employees' money. How is he to know how to spend it? He is told that he must contribute to fighting inflation. How is he to know what action of his will contribute to that end? He is presumably an expert in running his company—in producing a product or selling it or financing it. But nothing about his selection makes him an expert on inflation. Will his holding down the price of his product reduce inflationary pressure? Or, by leaving more spending power in the hands of his customers, simply divert it elsewhere? Or, by forcing him to produce less because of the lower price, will it simply contribute to shortages? Even if he could answer these questions, how much cost is he justified in imposing on his stockholders, customers, and employees for this social purpose? What is his appropriate share and what is the appropriate share of others?

And, whether he wants to or not, can he get away with spending his stockholders', customers', or employees' money? Will not the stockholders fire him? (Either the present ones or those who take over when his actions in the name of social responsibility have reduced the corporation's profits and the price of its stock.) His customers and his employees can desert him for other producers and employers less scrupulous in exercising their social responsibilities.

This facet of "social responsibility" doctrine is brought into sharp relief when the doctrine is used to justify wage restraint by trade unions. The conflict of interest is naked and clear when union officials are asked to subordinate the interest of their members to some more general purpose. If the union officials try to enforce wage restraint, the consequence is likely to be wildcat strikes, rank-and-file revolts, and the emergence of strong competitors for their jobs. We thus have the ironic phenomenon that union leaders—at least in the United States—have objected to government interference with the market far more consistently and courageously than have business leaders.

The difficulty of exercising "social responsibility" illustrates, of course, the great virtue of private competitive enterprise—it forces people to be responsible for their own actions and makes it difficult for them to "exploit" other people for either selfish or unselfish purposes. They can do good—but only at their own expense.

Many a reader who has followed the argument this far may be tempted to remonstrate that it is all well and good to speak of government's having the responsibility to impose taxes and determine expenditures for such "social" purposes as controlling pollution or training the hard-core unemployed, but that the problems are too urgent to wait on the slow course of political processes, that the exercise of social responsibility by businessmen is a quicker and surer way to solve pressing current problems.

Aside from the question of fact—I share Adam Smith's skepticism about the benefits that can be expected from "those who affected to trade for the public good"—this argument must be rejected on grounds of principle. What it amounts to is an assertion that those who favor the taxes and expenditures in question have failed to persuade a majority of their fellow citizens to be of like mind and that they are seeking to attain by undemocratic procedures what they cannot attain by democratic procedures. In a free society, it is hard for "good" people to do "good," but that is a small price to pay for making it hard for "evil" people to do "evil," especially since one man's good is another's evil.

I have, for simplicity, concentrated on the special case of the corporate executive, except only for the brief digression on trade unions. But precisely the same argument applies to the newer phenomenon of calling upon stockholders to require corporations to exercise social responsibility (the recent General Motors crusade, for example). In most of these cases, what is in effect involved is some stockholders trying to get other stockholders (or customers or employees) to contribute against their will to "social" causes favored by the activists. Insofar as they succeed, they are again imposing taxes and spending the proceeds.

The situation of the individual proprietor is somewhat different. If he acts to reduce the returns of his enterprise in order to exercise his "social responsibility," he is spending his own money, not someone else's. If he wishes to spend his money on such purposes, that is his right, and I cannot see that there is any objection to his doing so. In the process, he, too, may impose costs on employees and customers. However, because he is far less likely than a large corporation or union to have monopolistic power, any such side effects will tend to be minor.

Of course, in practice the doctrine of social responsibility is frequently a cloak for actions that are justified on other grounds rather than a reason for those actions.

To illustrate, it may well be in the long-run interest of a corporation that is a major employer in a small community to devote resources to providing amenities to that community or to improving its government. That may make it easier to attract desirable employees; it may reduce the wage bill or lessen losses from pilferage and sabotage or have other worthwhile effects. Or it may be that, given the laws about the deductibility of corporate charitable contributions, the stockholders can contribute more to charities they favor by having the corporation make the gift than by doing it themselves, since they can in that way contribute an amount that would otherwise have been paid as corporate taxes.

In each of these—and many similar—cases, there is a strong temptation to rationalize these actions as an exercise of "social responsibility." In the present climate of opinion, with its widespread aversion to "capitalism," "profits," the "soulless corporations," and so on, this is one way for a corporation to generate goodwill as a by-product of expenditures that are entirely justified in its own self-interest.

It would be inconsistent of me to call on corporate executives to refrain from this hypocritical window dressing because it harms the foundations of a free society. That would be to call on them to exercise a "social responsibility"! If our institutions, and the attitudes of the public make it in their self-interest to cloak their actions in this way, I cannot summon much indignation to denounce them. At the same time, I can express admiration for those individual proprietors or owners of closely held corporations or stockholders of more broadly held corporations who disdain such tactics as approaching fraud.

Whether blameworthy or not, the use of the cloak of social responsibility, and the nonsense spoken in its name by influential and prestigious businessmen, does clearly harm the foundations of a free society. I have been impressed time and again by the schizophrenic character of many businessmen. They are capable of being extremely farsighted and clearheaded in matters that are internal to their businesses. They are incredibly shortsighted and muddleheaded in matters that are outside their businesses but affect the possible survival of business in general. This shortsightedness is strikingly exemplified in the calls from many businessmen for wage and price guidelines or controls or income policies. There is nothing that could do more in a brief period to destroy a market system and replace it by a centrally controlled system than effective governmental control of prices and wages.

The shortsightedness is also exemplified in speeches by businessmen on social responsibility. This may gain them kudos in the short run. But it helps to strengthen the already too prevalent view that the pursuit of profits is wicked and immoral and must be curbed and controlled by external forces. Once this view is adopted, the external forces that curb the market will not be the social consciences, however highly developed, of the pontificating executives; it will be the iron fist of government bureaucrats. Here, as with price and wage controls, businessmen seem to me to reveal a suicidal impulse.

The political principle that underlies the market mechanism is unanimity. In an ideal free market resting on private property, no individual can coerce any other, all cooperation is voluntary, all parties to such cooperation benefit or they need not participate. There are no "social" values, no "social" responsibilities in any sense other than the shared values and responsibilities of individuals. Society is a collection of individuals and of the various groups they voluntarily form.

The political principle that underlies the political mechanism is conformity. The individual must serve a more general social interest—whether that be determined by a church or a dictator or a majority. The individual may have a vote and say in what is to be done, but if he is overruled, he must conform. It is appropriate for some to require others to contribute to a general social purpose whether they wish to or not.

Unfortunately, unanimity is not always feasible. There are some respects in which conformity appears unavoidable, so I do not see how one can avoid the use of the political mechanism altogether.

But the doctrine of "social responsibility" taken seriously would extend the scope of the political mechanism to every human activity. It does not differ in philosophy from the most explicitly collectivist doctrine. It differs only by professing to believe that collectivist ends can be attained without collectivist means. That is why, in my book *Capitalism and Freedom*, I have called it a "fundamentally subversive doctrine" in a free society, and have said that in such a society, "there is one and only one social responsibility of business—to use its resources and engage in activities designed to increase its profits so long as it stays within the rules of the game, which is to say, engages in open and free competition without deception or fraud."

QUESTIONS

1. Why does Friedman reject the idea that business has a social responsibility?

2. Why does Friedman equate the spending of corporate money for "a general social interest" with the imposition of a tax? (283)

3. Why does Friedman condemn corporate charitable contributions?

4. What does Friedman mean when he says, "The political principal that underlies the market mechanism is unanimity"? (288)

5. Why does Friedman argue that "the doctrine of 'social responsibility' taken seriously would extend the scope of the political mechanism to every human activity"? (288)

FOR FURTHER REFLECTION

1. Is it true that corporations have no social responsibility to the wider community, provided they act within the law?

2. Is Friedman correct in his assertion that the private competitive enterprise "makes it difficult . . . to 'exploit' other people for either selfish or unselfish purposes"?

3. Do you agree with Friedman that corporate gift giving is "hypocritical window dressing" almost akin to "fraud"?

HYMAN P. MINSKY

Hyman P. Minsky (1919–1996) was a relatively little-known economics professor who achieved posthumous fame when his "financial instability hypothesis" was seized upon during the subprime mortgage crisis and recession of the late 2000s to justify the return to an earlier, Keynesian principle of government intervention in the economy. The financial instability hypothesis claims that the neoclassical view of the market economy as spontaneously self-correcting has been rendered obsolete by the tendency among investors to accumulate unsustainable levels of debt. Minsky's view that the modern capitalist economy is essentially unstable was then widely cited as a rationale by those in favor of the U.S. government's "stimulative" policies, such as low interest rates and deficit spending, in the aftermath of the 2008 global financial crisis.

Minsky was born in Chicago into a family of Russian Jewish political émigrés. His mother was a trade-union activist and his father was a member of the Socialist Party. Minsky was educated at the University of Chicago and Harvard University where he studied under Joseph Schumpeter and Alvin Hansen, a leading American disciple of John Maynard Keynes. Minsky taught at Brown University and at the University of California, Berkeley, before moving to Washington University in St. Louis in 1965, where he remained until his retirement in 1990. He then became a distinguished scholar at the Levy Economics Institute at Bard College, in Annandale-on-Hudson, New York, where he remained until his death. His major works include *John Maynard Keynes* (1975) and *Stabilizing an Unstable Economy* (1986).

Minsky is perhaps best known for his multistage theory of the business cycle and for his taxonomy of "hedge borrowers," "speculative borrowers," and "Ponzi borrowers." As a boom progresses, hedge borrowers overextend themselves until a critical mass of Ponzi borrowers develops, eventually leading to a system-wide crisis, or what has been termed a "Minsky moment." Recently, some so-called post-Keynesian economists have built upon Minsky's work in the articulation of their own critiques of free-market economics. In the following selection, taken from *Stabilizing an Unstable Economy*, Minsky makes his argument for why the self-correcting concept of the market economy is no longer accurate.

Perspectives on Theory

n all disciplines theory plays a double role: it is both a lens and a blinder. As a lens, it focuses the mind upon specified problems, enabling conditional statements to be made about causal relations for a well-defined but limited set of phenomena. But as a blinder, theory narrows the field of vision. Questions that are meaningful in the world are often nonsense questions within a theory. If such nonsense questions are *often* posed by developments in the world, then the discipline is ripe for a revolution in theory. Such a revolution, however, requires the development of new instruments of thought. This is a difficult intellectual process.

Within today's standard economic theory, which is commonly called the *neoclassical synthesis*, the question "Why is our economy so unstable?" is just such a nonsense question. Standard economic theory not only does not lead to an explanation of instability as a system attribute, it really does not recognize that endogenous instability is a problem that a satisfactory theory must explain.

Economists who offer policy advice are neither fools nor knaves. Knowing instability exists, they nevertheless base their analysis and advice upon a theory that cannot explain instability, because this theory *does* provide answers to deep and serious questions and *has had* some success as a basis for policy. Before abandoning or radically revising neoclassical theory, therefore, it is necessary to understand the significance of the deep and serious questions that this theory does answer and why any alternative economic theory must come to grips with the questions that neoclassical theory addresses.

The Importance of Theory

Understanding the strengths and weaknesses of standard economic theory is particularly important now that active economic policy is the norm rather

This selection is taken from chapter 5 of Stabilizing an Unstable Economy.

than the exception. Indeed, in a world with active policy the content of economic theories and the significance of differences in theory for policy are of special interest. James Tobin, who was a member of the Council of Economic Advisers during President Kennedy's first two years in office and who received the Nobel Prize in 1982, noted that "the terms in which a problem is stated and in which the relevant information is organized can have a great influence on the solution." But the way "a problem" is stated and the identification of "relevant information" reflect the economic theory of the policy adviser. That is, the game of policymaking is rigged; the theory used determines the questions that are asked and the options that are presented. The prince is constrained by the theory of his intellectuals.

Today's standard economic theory is largely a creature of the years since World War II. It integrates some aspects of Keynes's theories with the older classical analysis that he believed he was replacing. This neoclassical synthesis now guides economic policy.

It is ironic that an economic theory that purports to be based on Keynes fails because it cannot explain instability. The essential aspect of Keynes's *General Theory* is a deep analysis of how financial forces—which we can characterize as Wall Street—interact with production and consumption to determine output, employment, and prices. One proposition that emerges from Keynes's theory is that, from time to time, a capitalist economy will be characterized by persistent unemployment. The neoclassical synthesis accepts this result, even though a deeper consequence of the theory, which is that a capitalist economy with sophisticated financial practices (i.e., the type of economy we live in) is inherently unstable, is ignored. Keynes's analysis that leads to this deeper result provides the foundation for an alternative economic theory that leads us to an understanding of instability.

Essentially, the neoclassical synthesis says that fiscal and monetary policy measures can eliminate persistent unemployment and that there are self-correcting forces within decentralized markets that set the economy at full employment. The neoclassical synthesis, however, speaks with a forked tongue: on the one hand, interventionist policy can eliminate persistent unemployment or chronic inflation, and on the other, if nothing is done, in time and of its own workings, the economy will sustain stable prices and full employment.

This neoclassical synthesis will no longer serve. It cannot explain the business cycles with regular incipient crises that we are now experiencing as a result of the internal operation of the economy. Unless we understand what it is that leads to economic and financial instability, we cannot prescribe—make policy—to modify or eliminate it. Identifying a phenomenon is not enough; we need a theory that makes instability a normal result in our economy and gives us handles to control it.

Thus, in the light of the behavior of the economy in the years since the mid-1960s, any economic analysis that claims to be relevant needs to address:

1. how the ruling market mechanism achieves coherence in particular outputs and prices;
2. how the path of incomes, outputs, and prices is determined; and
3. why coherence breaks down from time to time: that is, why is the economy susceptible to threats, if not the actuality, of deep depressions?

Furthermore, these questions need to be answered in the context of the institutions and financial usages that actually exist, not in terms of an abstract economy. It may be that what the neoclassical theory ignores, namely institutions, and in particular financial institutions, leads to the observations it cannot explain. A fundamental question that economic policy analysis must confront is whether, and over what domain, market processes can be relied upon to achieve a satisfactory economic performance. The general view sustained by the following analysis is that while the market mechanism is a good enough device for making social decisions about unimportant matters such as the mix of colors in the production of frocks, the length of skirts, or the flavors of ice cream, it cannot and should not be relied upon for important, big matters such as the distribution of income, the maintenance of economic stability, the capital development of the economy, and the education and training of the young. In what lies ahead, we will develop a theory explaining why our economy fluctuates, showing that the instability and incoherence exhibited from time to time is related to the development of fragile financial structures that occur normally within capitalist economies in the course of financing capital asset ownership and investment.

We thus start with a bias in favor of using the market mechanism to the fullest extent possible to achieve social goals, but with a recognition that market capitalism is both intrinsically unstable and can lead to distasteful distributions of wealth and power.

The Current Standard Theory: The Pre-Keynesian Legacy

During the 1970s American economists engaged in what might have been taken to be a serious controversy between Keynesians and monetarists. The participants and the press made it appear that a deep debate was taking place. In truth, the differences were minor—as the competing camps used the same economic theory. Furthermore, the public policy prescriptions do not really differ. The debate was largely academic nitpicking, and the public controversy was largely created by the press and by politicians. In this debate, monetarists emphasized that changes in the money supply destabilize the economy, and Keynesians argued that fiscal variables can be used to stabilize the economy. Until late in the 1970s, and even into the first years of the Reagan administration, both believed that with correct (that is, their) policy the economy could be fine-tuned so that full employment without inflation would be achieved and sustained. Both schools hold that the business cycle can be banished from the capitalist world; and neither school allows for any within-the-system disequilibrating forces that lead to business cycles. Neither Keynesians nor monetarists of the policy establishment are critical of capitalism as such; at most they are critical of some institutional or policy details.

Both monetarists and Keynesians are conservative in that they accept the validity and viability of capitalism. Neither are troubled by the possibility that there are serious flaws in a market economy that has private property and sophisticated financial usages. The view that the dynamics of capitalism lead to business cycles that may be thoroughly destructive is foreign to their economic theory.

The economic theory that is common to the Keynesians and the monetarists is the neoclassical synthesis. Keynes held that his new theory of 1936 marked a sharp break with the economic theory that then ruled; the neoclassical synthesis, however, integrates strands of thought derived from Leon Walras—a nineteenth-century economist—with insights and apparatus derived from Keynes. The dominant view among contemporary economists was expressed by Gardner Ackley—a member and then chairman of the Council of Economic Advisers in the Kennedy-Johnson era—when he held "that Keynes' work represents more an extension than a revolution of 'Classical' ideas."

The process of assimilating Keynes's *General Theory* to the previous tradition began with the early reviews and academic interpretations. In this process, important aspects of Keynes's theoretical structure, which lead to revolutionary insights into the functioning of capitalism and to a serious critique, were ignored. This is why Joan Robinson called standard Keynesianism "bastard Keynesianism." As far as an understanding of Keynes by policy-advising economists and their political patrons is concerned, the Keynesian revolution is still to come.

The elements of Keynes that are ignored in the neoclassical synthesis deal with the pricing of capital assets and the special properties of economies with capitalist financial institutions. These elements can serve as the foundation for an alternative economic theory that is a better guide to interpreting events and is more relevant for policymaking than current standard theory. Indeed, these forgotten parts lead to a theory that makes instability, which has been of increasing importance since the mid-1960s, a normal consequence of relations that reflect essential attributes of a capitalist economy.

The view that instability is the result of the internal processes of a capitalist economy stands in sharp contrast to neoclassical theory, whether Keynesian or monetarist, which holds that instability is due to events that are outside the workings of the economy. The neoclassical synthesis and the Keynes theories are different because the focus of the neoclassical synthesis is on how a decentralized market economy achieves coherence and coordination in production and distribution, whereas the focus of the Keynes theory is upon the capital development of an economy. The neoclassical synthesis emphasizes equilibrium and equilibrating tendencies, whereas Keynes's theory revolves around bankers and businessmen making deals on Wall Street. The neoclassical synthesis ignores the capitalist nature of the economy, a fact that the Keynes theory is always aware of.

The Walrasian input to the neoclassical synthesis starts with a discussion of an abstract exchange (barter) economy: the analogue may be a village fair. Results are obtained by analyzing a model that does not allow for capital-intensive production, capital assets as we know them, and capitalist finance. Using an artificial construction of trading relations, the theory demonstrates that a decentralized market economy achieves a coherent result.

Standard economic theory then goes on to show that the property of coherence also carries through for an economy that produces, but only under heroic assumptions about the nature of capital and time. In further extensions, the analytical apparatus of the neoclassical synthesis is applied to problems of aggregate income, money prices, and economic growth. In particular, supply and demand relations for labor are derived, and it is assumed that a price-level-deflated wage will adjust so that labor supply and demand are equal. The theory is set up in such a way that any deviation from the labor supply–labor demand equality will be removed by market interactions; that is, the theory holds that full employment is achieved by means of the internal operations of the economy. The theory does not explain, however, how any initial deviation is brought about: unemployment as the result of economic processes is unexplained. The emphasis is upon the interactions that make for equilibrium and not upon endogenous disequilibrating processes.

In the neoclassical synthesis, capital accumulation and the rate of growth of the labor force determine the rate of growth of output. The savings ratio yields the proportion of income that is accumulated. The neoclassical theory treats household savings propensities as the tune caller, determining investment and, in turn, investment is the determinant of growth. The theory has no room whatsoever for institutions that finance investment and, in so doing, force saving.

Neoclassical theorists do short-run analysis—where inflation and unemployment exist—on the basis of a theory that does not allow for inflation or unemployment except as the result of outside forces. The monetarists identify an outside force—inept changes in the money supply—as the cause of unemployment and inflation. Neoclassical Keynesians do not have a consistent explanation of how unemployment and inflation are brought about. Their short-run theory is a muddle: they believe that the economy will not sustain full employment, but they do not identify the mechanisms that lead to unemployment and inflation.

In addition to demonstrating that decentralized market processes lead to coherent results, the tools and techniques of the neoclassical synthesis are used to demonstrate that a decentralized competitive market mechanism achieves an optimal result. The optimum that is derived is of a very special character: it rules out interpersonal comparisons of well-being and ignores the equity of the initial distribution of resources (and thus of income). Inasmuch as our aim is to indicate how we can do better than we have, and as the best is often the enemy of the good, we can forget about the optimum. Even though a tendency toward coherence exists because of the processes that determine production and consumption in market economics, the processes of a market economy can set off interactions that disrupt coherence. Accordingly, the flaws that lead to instability make questions as to the optimality of the results of the market mechanism irrelevant.

Current theory makes an economy a lifeless arena in which depersonalized agents play abstract auctioning or recontracting games. In our world of imperfect knowledge and imprecise actions, standard theoretical analyses posit either perfect knowledge or a fantastic capacity to compute. Nevertheless, these models (which are now highly mathematical) are interesting because they show that coherence is possible. But what practical people need to know is the extent to which market processes can be used to achieve desired results. The practical problem of economic policy is to identify the sources of instability and to determine policy interventions that constrain the emergence of incoherence, even as policy abstains from intervening in those markets whose internal operations tend to yield coherent results.

Coherence and Policy

A system is coherent if the connections among variables are stable enough that the reactions of the system to external changes are predictable. In an economy, coherence implies that a close approximation to equality between quantities supplied and demanded of the various commodities and services (including labor) almost always rules, and that such virtual equality is achieved and sustained by minor adjustments within the economy. Planning, interventions, regulation, or controls are not required.

We know, however, that from time to time the coherence of the market system breaks down: the Great Depression of the 1930s is one example. Economic theory must, therefore, explain both the coherence of the pricing process and allow for the possibility of a breakdown. One way to do this is to build a theory that does not allow incoherence to be a result of the internal process of the economy, but that allows the pricing process to collapse when an unusual shock or some institutional aberration occurs. Occasional disorder is consistent with underlying coherence, if outside forces are responsible for the disorder.

For the neoclassical synthesis to be valid, apparent incoherence must be explained by external factors, such as imperfect institutions or errors of human judgment. Intervention in economic affairs by an outside party, such as a central bank (Federal Reserve System), is an obvious scapegoat for observed incoherence; other possible outside parties are trade unions, giant firms that have market power, foreign cartels, and government. Many of the explanations of the Great Depression, the inflation of the 1970s, and the depression of 1981–82 are in terms of just such outside influences.

For markets in which the future is important it is difficult to show that the reactions required for coherence will take place; the decentralized pricing process may sustain coherence in some markets, while in others, processes will be at work that will, in time, disrupt coherence. If this is the nature of the economy, then it is necessary to inquire if policies can be adopted or institutions created that are able to constrain or offset the processes that would lead to incoherence.

If the pricing mechanism of a decentralized capitalist economy can lead to coherent results *only if* proper policy or institutions rule, then intervention is necessary even though the market mechanism can be relied upon to take care of details. Once such conditional coherence is accepted as a characteristic of a capitalist economy, blind faith in and acceptance of the results of market processes can no longer be sustained. Moreover, in an economy that is conditionally coherent, legislated and evolutionary institutional changes affect the policy actions needed to sustain coherence. Policy cannot be a once-and-for-all proposition: as institutions and relations change so does the policy that is needed to sustain coherence.

Furthermore, for coherence to rule in a set of markets a substitution principle must apply. One facet of this principle is that if supply conditions change so that the price of a commodity (or service) used in consumption or production rises (or falls) relative to other prices, the quantity taken will decrease (or increase); this means that demand curves are usually negatively sloped. The second facet is that if the price of a commodity rises (falls), the quantities that will be taken of other commodities at a fixed price will tend to increase (decrease). That is, the quantities demanded of the commodities whose relative prices rise tends to decrease, whereas the quantities demanded of those commodities whose relative prices fall tends to increase. The principle states that higher relative prices tend to discourage and lower relative prices tend to encourage the use of a commodity or service.

If the principle of substitution is sufficiently strong, then decentralized markets are reliable tools for allocating output to households and input to businesses. However, in financial and capital-asset markets, in which speculative and conjectural elements are powerful, the principle of substitution does not always apply. A rise in the relative prices of some set of financial instruments or capital assets may very well increase the quantity demanded of such financial or capital assets. A rise in price may thus breed conditions conducive to another such rise.

Demonstrating that an exchange economy is coherent and stable does not demonstrate that the same is true of an economy with capitalist financial institutions; the wage and price changes brought about by unemployment do not always lead to the increase in investment needed to eliminate unemployment. External controls and coordinating mechanisms may be needed in a capitalist economy. Indeed, central banking and other financial control devices arose as a response to the embarrassing incoherence of financial markets, an incoherence that indicates that free markets will not do as a *universal policy prescription* for economies with capitalist financial institutions.

Roots of the Neoclassical Synthesis: Prices as Parameters

The basic constructs of the Walrasian or price-theoretic core of the neoclassical synthesis are preference systems of households and production functions for plants. The units of the theory are households and business firms. The behavioral assumptions are that households try to maximize their well-being as defined by their preference systems under a budget—or total spending—constraint and firms try to maximize profits with defined production possibilities.

The task of neoclassical theory is to demonstrate that profit-maximizing firms, which are characterized by production functions, and utility-maximizing households, which are characterized by preference systems, interact in markets so that coherence results. To this end, supply and demand curves are determined by entering underlying preference systems and production functions with given prices of commodities and productive inputs. In competitive markets, each individual decision maker is assumed to take the price of all he sells and buys as given. Thus, each and every participant is powerless; the market is a thoroughly imperial and majestic instrument of control.

This is an impressive and beautiful result. Each person is powerless before the impersonal market, yet the prices that control behavior in the market are market-determined transformations of individual behavior. If one set of prices leads to supplies not equaling demand in all markets, then prices will change: some prices, those of output with excess supply, will fall, and others, those with excess demand, will rise. Each new set of prices will affect demand, supplies, and incomes in such a way as to improve the coordination of the system, Excess supplies and demand therefore are transient phenomena, and the market mechanism is an efficient adjustment mechanism. In effect, the laws of supply and demand provide all the planning that a market economy requires.

If, with each unit behaving as if the prices that now rule have always ruled and will always rule, the system of markets is not fully coordinated, then prices will change. If units, in spite of price changes, continue to behave as if the new set of prices always ruled and will continue to rule—changes are never extrapolated—then the adjustments will be such that coordination of the system will improve. No one calls signals, no one runs drills, nevertheless each unit behaves as if it were a perfectly disciplined and extraordinarily well-trained member of a team. Any economy in which each individual unit has no option but to act in its own best interest, on the assumption that existing prices will always rule, will achieve a well-coordinated set of outcomes; units without power and units behaving with present prices as parameters guarantee coherence.

The analysis of firms with market power and markets in which units have power is foreign to the essential core of the neoclassical theory. Too much monopoly, and monopolies confronting one another, can lead to a breakdown of the ability of the market to achieve coherent results.

In addition, if units act as if today's prices need not be tomorrow's prices, and decisions take into account what may happen in the future, then the market can also break down as an effective coordinating device. By their very nature, capital-asset and financing decisions involve action over calendar time; yesterday, today, and tomorrow exist. Of necessity, capital-asset decisions need to take into account what can happen over the life of projects; present decisions must allow for the future, and what happens today is the future for some prior decisions. It is impossible to sustain a naive argument that all such decisions are made on the expectations that what is will rule forever or, alternatively, that rational agents make capital and financial decisions assuming they know the future.

Where monopoly power exists and when financing and investment are undertaken, present prices are not parameters for decisions. In these cases prices either vary with the unit's own decisions or the future enters in a significant way in determining behavior. Under these conditions markets can fail to be effective control and coordinating mechanisms.

We are left, then, with a split attitude toward the market. On one hand, the market is a very effective control and coordinating device if units are forced to take prices as parameters and to behave as if current prices will exist forever. On the other hand, the market can fail to achieve coherent results in situations in which units know either that their actions will have an appreciable effect upon prices or that current prices will not necessarily rule forever.

In market economies prices distribute outputs among households, and they allocate productive resources, which have alternative uses, to the production of various outputs. The price system therefore has distributional and allocational functions in the world of the neoclassical price theorists. In a world with capitalist institutions, however, prices will or will not validate past financing and capital-investment decisions as well as distribute income to workers and to owners of capital assets. But the relation between capital-asset compensation and the allocation of capital-asset services to various outputs is not as direct and simpleminded as the relation between labor compensation and the allocation of labor services to various productions. Time, investment, and finance are phenomena that embarrass neoclassical theory; once the problems associated with capital accumulation in a capitalist environment are introduced, the theory breaks down.

In essence, then, the valid part of neoclassical theory boils down to visualizing the economy as an interrelated set of supply and demand curves. For each commodity a supply and demand curve is defined. These curves link the quantity of the commodity to the price of the commodity and to other prices; price in the neoclassical theory is the signal that determines quantities offered or taken. This way of looking at the economy is good enough for consumer spending out of income where the purchase is not only a repetitive act but also is not an overwhelming part of the total budget, but it breaks down where the purchase is a unique act, has consequences over a period of time, and involves large-scale financing that carries future commitments, that is, where the budget constraint on spending is not independent of financial-market decisions.

The interdependent supply and demand curves combined with the dynamic assumption that the system will move around until it reaches the sets of prices that simultaneously has supply equal demand for *all* markets is *the* Law of Supply and Demand that is so beloved of writers of editorials and conventional textbooks. But the validity of this law is restricted to a domain of markets in which the ability to spend is governed by some predetermined budget. Once the budget equations, which enter into the determination of demand curves, are affected by financing conditions and ruling expectations about the future, then the assumption that the interrelated supply and demand curves wiggle around until equilibrium is achieved is no longer valid. Markets involving finance and investments can achieve prices, quantities, and payment commitments that may not be sustained by future demand or profits.

The visions, constructs, and results of neoclassical price theory are all pre-Keynesian in the sense that the problems and the insights that Keynes introduced into theory are nowhere evident. The neoclassical synthesis is, however, an amalgam of the pre-Keynesian theory with ideas and constructs derived from Keynes's great work. The amalgamation does not take place in price theory; it takes place when the domain of economic analysis is extended to include the determination of employment, money wages, and prices in money terms. Accordingly, although today's aggregate theory is different from the pre-Keynesian aggregate theory, much of the aggregate theory of the neoclassical synthesis exists in a form that ignores Keynes's contributions.

Neoclassical Aggregate Theory: The Pre-Keynesian Basis

Neoclassical aggregate theory is an extension of the constructs and methods of analysis of neoclassical price theory to the determination of employment, output, accumulation, and the price level. It rests upon the heroic assumption that once relative prices and quantities are determined by the relations and processes examined in neoclassical price theory, then output and employment are also determined. The only problem that neo-classical aggregate theory has to address is the determination of prices measured in terms of money.

Aggregate production functions and collective-preference systems are the key construct of neoclassical aggregate theory. From the aggregate production function a relation between employment and output, the demand curve for labor, and a demand curve for increments to the stock of capital assets (a demand curve for investment) are derived. The collective-preference system yields the supply curve for labor and a supply curve for savings. Both the demand and the supply curves of labor are functions of a price-level-deflated money wage—what is called the *real wage*. The intersection of the supply and demand curves for labor determines this real wage and employment. Thus, the economy is placed at full employment, for that is what the situation determined by the intersection of labor demand and supply curves signifies. Once employment is determined, the production function yields output.

Neoclassical price theory, when used as a basis for aggregate analysis, leads to the labor market dominating in the determination of aggregate output. As some of Keynes's ideas were assimilated in the neoclassical synthesis, the real wages and employment of the intersection of the demand

and supply curves for labor became the goal or objective that market processes achieved. In neoclassical theory, if labor demand is less than labor supplied (i.e., if unemployment exists), then an external barrier is preventing the attainment of the real wages and employment of the intersection, or some time-consuming process is under way that will, eventually, lead to full employment. If unemployment persists, it must be because the real wage of labor is too high and barriers in the form of union pressures or legislation prevent the real wage from falling, or because the equilibrating process is at work but takes a long time to achieve the equilibrium.

Supply and demand analysis is also used to derive savings, investment, and interest rates. The supply curve of savings reflects an assumption that consumption will be forgone only if there is a promise that future consumption will be larger. The increment to future consumption is discounted back to today at a discount rate, which makes that which is forgone now equal to that which is attained in the future. The preference system is assumed to be such that increasing doses of future consumption are needed to compensate for incremental sacrifices of current consumption. In this way the savings out of current income are a rising function of the interest rate.

Investment is much like savings in that it involves a present sacrifice for a future benefit. Investors exchange the present costs of the investment output for a future income that will accrue as the investment output is used as a capital asset in production. If the present cost and future incomes are known, a discount of interest rate can be calculated for each investment project.

The amount of savings investment that takes place and the interest rate are determined by assuming that savings are a function of the interest rate, that investment is a function of the interest rate, and that the interest rate varies so that saving equals investment. Savings, investment, and interest rate determination are thus no different from that of any other price.

The rate of accumulation that rules depends upon thrift, as a characteristic of preference systems, and productivity, as revealed by production functions. Money, bonds, and other financial instruments—and financial markets—do not enter into the determination of interest rates. In neoclassical theory, the connection between the fluctuating interest rates as observed in bond and stock markets and the obviously slowly moving—if it moves at all—productivity of capital assets as revealed by production functions is not explored. In neoclassical theory, if investment decreases rapidly—as it did between 1929 and 1933—it must be because of a sudden exhaustion of the technical ability of increments to the stock of capital assets to aid production or of a sudden increase in the future payoff required to compensate for forgone consumption. *In the neoclassical view, speculation, financing conditions, inherited financial obligations, and the fluctuating behavior of aggregate demand have nothing whatsoever to do with savings, investment, and interest rate determination.*

In neoclassical theory, the only way a present demand for future consumption can be realized is by storing some of current output, either in the form of the commodities to be consumed or as productive capacity. The supply of savings must become a demand for inventories and additional capital assets. Nowhere do money and finance affect the real variables—output, employment, and the division of output between current consumption and investment. The interest rate, also, is independent of money, reflecting thriftiness and productivity.

But money exists and is an economic phenomenon; furthermore, the prices we pay are money prices. Economics must come to grips with money, even though the subject is foreign to the village-market perspective and distasteful to the pure theorist because when money is recognized institutional detail intrudes upon the purity of generalized abstract reasoning.

The Quantity Theory of Money

Money enters into neoclassical theory because of the need to transform real wages and the relative prices of commodities into the wages and prices we observe, that is, wages and prices denominated in money. In neoclassical theory, money does not have any significant relation to finance and the financing of activity. Even though money becomes the fixed point, and other prices, as well as index numbers of prices, move relative to the value of the money unit, money in the neoclassical theory is, by definition, sterile. Money yields no income, and in the neoclassical view it only yields benefits in terms of facilitating transactions involving goods and services. Inasmuch as there is no uncertainty in the neoclassical world, the possession of money does not yield a subjective benefit in the form of protection against uncertainty.

Money is sometimes called a store of value because it is a way of carrying command over goods and services from one time to another. However, in neoclassical arguments that equate saving and investment, capital assets are the way in which consumption is carried from today into the future. Money as a store of value is inconsistent with interest rates adjusting to assure that investment equals full-employment savings.

In an economy in which money is used, the value of money paid equals the value of money received; the value of commodities and services bought equals the value of those sold. These identities state that the two sides of an exchange are equal in dollar terms: the money turned over equals the value of goods, services, or assets bought and therefore sold.

In order to utilize an identity in the construction of a theory, behavioral relations have to be established for the variables in the identity. The identity is the equation of exchange which, following Irving Fisher, is conveniently written as $MV = PT$, where M is the money supply, V is the velocity or turnover of money, P is the price level, and T are the transactions. The relations that are assumed in transforming the identity into the quantity theory are:

1. M is assumed given from outside by the "authorities."
2. V is institutionally determined by the existing integration of production, payment conventions, and so on.
3. P is the price level, which is to be determined by the quantity theory.
4. T is the output as determined by the supply and demand for labor and the production function (when so defined, O for Output replaces T for transactions in the equation).

When the quantity theory of money is added to (1) the labor market determination of income, (2) the saving-investment determination of the interest rate, and (3) the consumption-investment division of output, a precise theory emerges that determines the price level and its change over time. "Money is neutral" is the conventional phrase: it is an assertion that money does not matter, except for the determination of the price level.

As a result, in the quantity theory of money, the general level of wages and prices are made a function of an exogenously determined money supply, but the institutional arrangements by which money is created are not considered to be important. In a world in which money is mainly demand deposits at commercial banks, much of the financing of business involves the creation of money—as debts are entered upon the books of banks—and the destruction of money—as debts are repaid. The effect of money upon the behavior of the economy has some connection with the processes by which it is created and destroyed. But in the quantity theory of money, what follows after an increase in the money supply is independent of whether the money enters the economy by means of loot from the Incas, a pirate's raid, the financing of business activity, or the purchase of government bonds by banks from prior holders. Such considerations are irrelevant: how money is created and the complex nature of money in a sophisticated capitalist economy are ignored.

Neoclassical Aggregate Theory: A Summing Up

Neoclassical aggregate theory is a hierarchical system: labor demand and supply determine employment, the real wage, and, by entering employment into the production function, output. The consumption and investment allocation of this output reflects the reconciliation of productivity and thriftiness by means of the interest rate, which is determined in the saving and investment process, The quantity theory of money determines prices, but the determination of the real variables—production, employment, techniques of production, investment, and so forth—is independent of monetary influences.

Neoclassical aggregate theory is an extension of the model that is used to explain relative prices and output. Each commodity and its market can be treated as a separate entity, and the system can be required to satisfy *simultaneously* the clearing conditions for each commodity market as well as for money. In this formulation, money enters as a substitute or a complement with other specific commodities; however, in the aggregate an excess supply of money needs to generate an excess demand for commodities. But an excess demand for commodities leads to a rise in the market-clearing money price of commodities. Higher prices, in general, reduce real or price-deflated wages for a given money wage. In this way a general model of interdependence can be set up in which a quantity theory of money is added to the relative price-determining system.

The neoclassical model is a full employment model; all who want to work at the prevailing price-deflated wage are employed. The dynamics of the aggregate model are predominantly particular market dynamics. Disequilibrium in a particular market—be it for underarm deodorants, labor, or savings investment—is presumed to be resolved mainly by its own market dynamics. How an equilibrium is attained if the initial condition is not an equilibrium is discussed, but how the economy through its own processes would get to such an initial condition is foreign to the analysis.

In neoclassical theory, markets absorb disturbances from outside and transform them into displacements from equilibrium and determinants of a new equilibrium. Perhaps the fundamental difference between that viewpoint and the financial instability hypothesis—the theoretical core of what follows—centers on the notion of disequilibria and how they are generated. To the neoclassical synthesis, deviations from a full employment-stable price level equilibrium have to be explained by shocks; strong deviations, such as the Great Depression of the 1930s, the chronic and accelerated inflation of the mid-1960s through the 1970s, and the serious recession of 1974–1975 and 1981–1982, have to be explained by strong shocks. Thus, in the neoclassical view "outside" disturbances are responsible whenever the performance of the economy is unsatisfactory. The usual villains are the monetary system and the government. Depressions and inflations are due to some combination of the structure of monetary institutions, the operations of monetary policy, and government policies that affect institutions or change the level of government activity. In particular, any inquiry into what goes wrong in the monetary system need look no further than the behavior of the quantity of money. No differential effects of monetary changes depending upon the behavior and evolution of money institutions and markets is allowed—in particular the causation always runs from money to economic disturbances rather than from changing economic circumstances to monetary changes.

The neoclassical model is a weak intellectual and logical reed to lean on in explaining the behavior of and in formulating policy for our economy. Too much is either ignored or posited out of consideration. The neoclassical theory—as well as the neoclassical synthesis that is built upon it—does have one important and valid contribution to make to economic policy. The demonstration, albeit under strict conditions, that a competitive market mechanism can do the job of guiding production to conform to consumer's demands means that, for those subsystems of the economy where conditions are apt, the market can be relied upon, particularly if the market is *not* relied upon for (1) the overall stability of the economy, (2) the determination of the pace and even the direction of investment, (3) income distribution, and (4) the determination of prices and outputs in those sectors that use large amounts of capital assets per unit of output or per worker. The last point follows from the peculiar way in which the pricing of capital assets and their returns enters into the neoclassical theory when compared with the actual way returns to capital assets are determined in our economy.

Thus, a major theorem—the proof of the possibility of coherence—of the classical theory remains valuable. The demand curves of the economy reflect consumer preferences—once income distribution is taken for granted and allowance is made for the cultural determination of preference systems. Coherence will be sustained even as excise taxes and subsidies are used to both constrain and expand various outputs. Laissez-faire is not resurrected, however, by the realization that coherence can rule; what is valid is that intervention into the details of the game might be unnecessary once the aggregate outcome of the game is rigged.

QUESTIONS

1. Why does Minsky say that "The game of [economic] policymaking is rigged"? (293)

2. According to Minsky, why is "neoclassical synthesis" unable to explain economic instability? (293)

3. What does Minsky believe is responsible for economic and financial instability in the capitalist system?

4. According to Minsky, what do Keynesian, monetarist, and neoclassical synthesis economics have in common? How are they different? What are the implications of each for economic policymaking?

5. Why does Minsky question "*the* Law of Supply and Demand"? (301)

FOR FURTHER REFLECTION

1. Is Minsky correct in saying that "market capitalism is both intrinsically unstable and can lead to distasteful distributions of wealth and power"?

2. What do you think is most responsible for U.S. economic instability in recent years—flawed economic policies or factors beyond the control of any policymaker?

3. Is periodic economic upheaval an inevitable part of the capitalist system? Can anything be done during periods of economic instability to minimize large-scale unemployment?

The following books offer thoughtful background material on many of the writers included in *Consuming Interests*. While not intended as substitutes for the works of the writers themselves, these books will help you understand the complex issues and concepts they addressed, as well as the historical context in which they worked.

Buchholz, Todd G. *New Ideas From Dead Economists: An Introduction to Modern Economic Thought*. New York: Plume, 2007.

Heilbroner, Robert. *Teachings from the Worldly Philosophy*. New York: W. W. Norton & Company, 1996.

Heilbroner, Robert. *The Worldly Philosophers: The Lives, Times, and Ideas of the Great Economic Thinkers*. 7th ed. New York: Touchstone, 1999.

Nasar, Sylvia. *Grand Pursuit: The Story of Economic Genius*. New York: Simon & Schuster, 2011.

Skousen, Mark. *The Making of Modern Economics: The Lives and Ideas of the Great Thinkers*. 2nd ed. New York: M. E. Sharpe, 2009.

All possible care has been taken to trace ownership and secure permission for each selection in this anthology. The Great Books Foundation wishes to thank the following authors, publishers, and representatives for permission to reprint copyrighted material:

Ethics and the Economic Interpretation, from SELECTED ESSAYS BY FRANK H. KNIGHT, by Frank H. Knight. Copyright © 1922 by Frank H. Knight. Reprinted by permission of Oxford University Press.

Transactions, from THE ECONOMICS OF COLLECTIVE ACTION, by John R. Commons. Copyright © 1986 by the Board of Regents of the University of Wisconsin System. Reprinted by permission of the University of Wisconsin Press.

The Civilization of Capitalism, from CAPITALISM, SOCIALISM, AND DEMOCRACY, 3rd ed., by Joseph A. Schumpeter Copyright © 1942, 1947 by Joseph A. Schumpeter. Reprinted by permission of HarperCollins Publishers.

The General Theory of Employment, by John Maynard Keynes, from the *Quarterly Journal of Economics*, vol. 51, no. 2. Copyright © 1937 by John Maynard Keynes. Reprinted by permission of Oxford University Press.

Who, Whom? from THE ROAD TO SERFDOM, by Friedrich Hayek. Copyright © 1944 by the University of Chicago Press. Reprinted by permission of University of Chicago Press.

Political Aspects of Full Employment, by Michał Kalecki, from the *Political Quarterly*, vol. 14, no. 4. Copyright © 1943 by Michał Kalecki. Reprinted by permission of John Wiley and Sons.

The Social Responsibility of Business, by Milton Friedman, from THE ESSENCE OF FRIEDMAN, edited by Kurt R. Leube. First published as "The Social Responsibility of Business Is to Increase its Profits," from the *New York Times Magazine*, Sept. 13, 1970. Copyright © 1970 by Milton Friedman. Reprinted by permission of the *New York Times*.

Perspectives on Theory, from STABILIZING AN UNSTABLE ECONOMY," by Hyman P. Minsky. Copyright © 2008 by Hyman P. Minsky. Reprinted by permission of McGraw-Hill Companies, Inc.